94/50

D0518347

The A-Z of House Plants

Hamlyn
LONDON · NEW YORK · SYDNEY · TORONTO
in association with Phoebus

Editor   Susan Joiner
Assistant Editors   Pamela Hunter
                        Sarie Forster
Design   Mary Cooper
                        Roger Hammond
Picture Research   Diane Rich

We are indebted to Hugh Young for
his translation and to Mary Everett
for her expert advice.

Published 1977 by
The Hamlyn Publishing Group Limited
London · New York · Sydney · Toronto
Astronaut House, Feltham, Middlesex,
England

ISBN 0 600 34529 7

© 1977 Phoebus Publishing Company
BPC Publishing Limited
169 Wardour Street
London W1A 2JX
© 1972/76 Amsterdam Boek B.V.

Made and printed in Great Britain by
Purnell and Sons Ltd, Paulton (Avon)

G. E. Hyde

ABOUT THIS BOOK

No one has 'green fingers' – it's just a matter of knowing how to handle plants the right way.

This complete A–Z guide to more than 100 popular house plants, compiled by an international team of experts, will tell you all you need to know to make your plants thrive.

It contains a wealth of information on the basics of cultivation for each plant – its soil, light, heat, and water requirements, when to cut back, and how to propagate.

In addition there is a section on plant care that answers the questions indoor gardeners ask most frequently:

> Where is the best place to grow ferns?
>
> How can I make my hippeastrum flower?
>
> When should I cut back the begonias?
>
> What should I do with my plants when I go on holiday?
>
> Why does that rubber tree look so bare?

And – more important – it gives you enough 'dos and don'ts' so that you never need to ask, 'What did I do wrong?'

Lavishly illustrated throughout with beautiful full-colour photographs of every plant and its variations, as well as clear step-by-step pictures of plant care, *The A–Z of House Plants* is an indispensable, authoritative addition to any gardener's bookshelf.

Passiflora caerulea

CONTENTS

CARE OF HOUSE PLANTS

A-Z OF HOUSE PLANTS

indoor plants arranged under
their botanical names

PLACES FOR PLANTS

GLOSSARY OF TERMS

DICTIONARY OF POPULAR NAMES

CARE OF HOUSE PLANTS

NATURE INDOORS

When the Indian rubber tree sheds its leaves, when the African violets wilt, when the Easter cactus refuses to flower, inexperienced indoor gardeners often give up and declare, 'I haven't got green fingers.'

This myth of 'green fingers' goes back a long time, but it is still only a myth. No one has 'green fingers' —it's just a matter of handling the plants in the right or wrong way.

We must always bear in mind that every plant is a fragment of nature—that in the hall, in the living room, on the windowsill, even in the greenhouse with all its technical equipment, plants are being kept alive in surroundings that are foreign to them. They will flourish only if the indoor gardener can manage to reproduce the actual conditions in which they lived in the open air.

So anyone who supposes he can come back from a holiday in the Canary Islands smuggling a dragon tree past customs officials and into his home and get it to grow on the sunny balcony right away has simply overlooked the fact that the dragon tree has not had time to adapt itself to another climate. Unless the climatic conditions of the Canary Islands can be reproduced fairly exactly in the conservatory, it will die.

It is possible to imitate nature indoors only when you are quite clear how many different factors have to be combined and adapted. Plants—either flowering or simple foliage plants—depend on many different environmental conditions, each one of which must be satisfied. There is, first, the warmth of their natural habitat, then the amount and intensity of light that reaches them there, the moisture of the air and of the ground and the general constitution of the soil. If any one of these demands is not met, the plants will react; they wilt and shed their leaves, run to seed or die completely.

WARMTH

If you are to give an indoor plant the right amount of warmth, you have to know where it comes from. Plants from the tropical rain forests naturally need more warmth than plants that are at home in the Alpine highlands. Indoor gardeners have agreed on three different categories of plants.

Cold-house plants in our houses must, in winter, have a temperature of not more than 12°C (54°F) and not less than 3°C (37°F). You can put them outdoors altogether in the summer, either on a balcony or terrace or, if you like, actually planted in the open.

Temperate-house plants are the plants typically found in living rooms. They can stand the temperatures of rooms with no heating as well as those in well-heated rooms. The normal temperature range for them in winter is 12-20°C (54-68°F). In summer quite a few of these plants can be put out in the open, but some of them must only go in light and airy places.

Hot-house plants are the ones you see in the conservatories at botanical gardens. In the house you must take special care to keep them warm. In the winter they need temperatures of over 18°C (64°F); in summer they want humidity and temperatures of 20-25°C (68-77°F).

These three categories are not inflexible. After all, we must not forget that even in their natural habitat plants sometimes have to cope with exceptionally warm winters or cool summers. There is really no point in constantly hovering over them with a thermometer. The three categories—cold-house plants, temperate-house plants and hot-house plants—are useful as guides that can always be varied for limited periods. There is no harm in keeping cold-house plants and temperate-house plants together. They will do very well. But if you ask a hot-house plant to pass the winter in temperatures of 5°C (41°F), it will freeze.

Plants' need for warmth is not constant. That is because in their natural surroundings all plants pass through periods of rest and periods of growth. Since they need water and warmth to make them grow, they take their rest periods in the cool, dry season.

The countless house plants that originally lived in the tropical regions of Africa, Asia and South America illustrate the adaptability of nature. In the tropical heat they grow to really enormous size—*Dracaena draco*, the dragon tree, reaches a height of nearly 20 m (65 ft) in its native habitat—while in our houses they are satisfied with a normal room size. This more limited growth is a direct result of the lack of warmth. If you transfer these plants to the hothouse of a botanical garden they will reach heights that would make them unsuitable as house plants.

You should, however, be warned against trying to acclimatize tropical plants yourself, even if you are allowed to bring them into the country. To begin with, such experiments call for expert knowledge and the equipment of a nursery. Secondly, the plants do not really like reducing their growth; if they are not warm enough they simply die. Thirdly, you must remember that as a rule younger plants need more warmth than older. Actually this is an advantage. Older palm trees, for example, can be left out on the balcony in summer, whereas for the younger plants it is not advisable.

LIGHT

Light, like warmth, is vital for plants. Without light plants cannot live. They need sunlight to manufacture their food from the carbon dioxide in the atmosphere and from water. But essential as sunlight is to plants, it can also be deadly. Too much light —direct sunshine, or the sun shining straight on to a window so that it works like a magnifying glass—will burn the plants.

As with warmth, plants are divided into three groups according to their light requirements: plants that need sunny, half-shady and shady positions. Unfortunately the human eye is not an adequate measure of light or dark, sunny or shady. Many an indoor gardener wonders why his favourite fuchsia, although it is standing on the windowsill, presumably in full light, suddenly sheds its flowers and leaves. The reason may be that a great pot with a sansevieria (mother-in-law's tongue) is standing next to it and taking so much light from the fuchsia that it finds its position permanently shady, and protests.

The need for light varies greatly, not only between different families and species of house plants but also at different times of the year. In their periods of growth and flowering, plants need a great deal of light. The smaller amount of light that most plants need in their rest period fits with the short days of winter. But the rest period of cultivated plants does not necessarily correspond with the seasons. During the winter, Northern Hemisphere gardeners must reserve a favoured place by the window for plants that come from the Southern Hemisphere.

Instructions for the care of plants often specify a light position. Do not make the mistake of confusing light and sunny. Plants that need bright light but cannot tolerate direct sunlight must be properly protected. You can use curtains for that, drawing them at the time of day when the sun is shining directly on the window. Venetian blinds are especially useful as they can be adjusted to control the amount of light coming in as required. It is not advisable to keep moving the plants about simply to keep them out of the direct sunlight.

In considering how much light house plants need, we can look back again at the conditions in which the plant grows in nature. Even a pure

shade plant like saintpaulia (African violet), which comes from the rain forest of East Africa, can never in its natural habitat find a position that is free from the sun all the year round. So you can put your African violet permanently in a north window, where it will still be reached by the first rays of the morning sun. The same is true of cyclamens and rhododendrons (azaleas). On the other hand you need not worry that the most sun-hungry cacti and echeverias will suddenly cease to flourish because they are no longer in full sunlight. These are adaptable plants.

As a general rule, flowering plants need more light than foliage plants, and plants with brightly coloured leaves more than dark green-leaved plants.

The best source of light for house plants is the sun. Sometimes you cannot rely on it, however, and then artificial light will work quite well. Not ordinary electric light bulbs, though; the least you will need are fluorescent tubes giving a warm-toned light. But once again, as always with house plants, too much is harmful. The plants cannot really stand it if you leave the light on all the time. You are actually stimulating their growth night and day, which is what gardeners do in the forcing

Prevent climbing plants from overshadowing light-loving varieties.

house to make flowers blossom before the natural season.

Whether the plants are standing in sunlight or artificial light, it is not good to move them too often. Experienced indoor gardeners, especially when working with particularly delicate plants—the rhododendron, or even rhipsalidopsis (Easter cactus) or zygocactus (Christmas cactus) —use what are called light marks. They make marks on the flowerpots and on the window ledge or wherever the plants are standing, and then if they have to move them they can always put them back in exactly the same place.

To get enough light, plants, both outdoors and indoors, will always grow towards the source of light. The phenomenon is called phototropism. If their position is changed, or even if the pots are turned around, the plants will no longer get the accustomed amount of light. In some cases they react very markedly; for example, Christmas and Easter cacti shed their buds. As a rule, foliage plants are less sensitive than flowering plants. But even they should really be allotted a place of their own in the house and not moved.

WATER

It has been only a hundred years or so since scientists abandoned the notion that plants 'ate' soil. They then discovered that plants consume nothing but liquid food—apart, that is, from such curiosities as carnivorous plants. This is because plant foods are dissolved in water. So you do not have to water your plants because they are so thirsty. It is true that plants do suffer if they are not watered enough. But what they suffer from primarily is not thirst, but hunger.

Water also maintains the plant's 'circulation'. A steady stream of water is sucked up by the roots, rises through the plant's vascular system and evaporates through the leaves. In the reverse direction, the product of assimilation (that is, of the conversion of carbon dioxide into starch with the aid of sunlight) is carried out of the plant into the storage cells. If the supply of water is interrupted the plant breaks down in the truest sense of the word. First it does not extract enough food from the earth, secondly the supply system does not work any more, and finally the circulation itself breaks down: the plant withers.

The water that plants need can be supplied in various ways. Watering lets them suck up water through the roots. Spraying raises the humidity of the surrounding air and so reduces evaporation. So in high

No wonder that the watering can is smiling! It is only in the last hundred years that scientists have realized plants absorb food from water.

humidity plants need less water because they have to lose less, though actually they can absorb only very little of the water sprayed on them.

Occasionally the earth around a plant dries out so much that it no longer gets properly moist again with ordinary watering. Soil that has dried into dust does not absorb water well, and the water simply runs through it so that the roots can absorb only a very small amount. If this happens you should put the flowerpot or tub into a bucket of water until the soil is completely damp.

Everyone in a hard-water area knows that from time to time the kitchen kettle or saucepans have to be 'scaled'. The 'scale' consists of lime, which is dissolved in drinking water and is precipitated when the water is boiled. So if you water your plants with water out of the mains, in the course of time they acquire a substantial, unwanted deposit of lime. The lime settles into the soil and there follows a slow process of leaching, chemically known as alkalization, which acts as a poison to many plants.

Lime shows its presence by 'lime flowers' on the russet brown of the flowerpot. Flowerpots that leave whitish or brownish rings on glass-topped tables or china plates also indicate an excess of lime in the water used for watering.

To be able to water plants properly you should understand a little about chemistry. Scientists have developed a scale of pH values to measure acidity and alkalinity (lime content). At one end, at pH 0, is hydrochloric acid, and at the other, at pH 14, a normal solution of caustic soda. Pure water has a pH value of 7. Water with a pH value of less than 7 is chemically acid; if the pH value is greater than 7, it is alkaline.

If you make a regular practice of using water that has a pH value of

more than 7, then soil that started by being slightly acid will slowly but surely be given a greater concentration of lime and will gradually begin to be chemically too alkaline. Eventually the plants find themselves standing in the wrong sort of soil and begin to droop. They have been poisoned, quite slowly, by the water they were watered with.

What can you do about it? The safest method is always to work with distilled or previously boiled water, which is chemically completely neutral and does not change the composition of the watered soil. This, however, is quite a nuisance, and it is usually enough to repot your plants when necessary in fresh soil. It is not necessary to throw the old pots away. Soak them in vinegar overnight and the lime will be dissolved.

In unpolluted areas the best thing for watering is rain water, unless it is collected from the roof by way of gutters and drainpipes, because then it will be teeming with bacteria and dirt. Rain water has a pH value of exactly 7, so that it is soft, and it also comes at a temperature that the plants like.

You can also damage your house plants (and garden plants, for that matter) by watering them with cold water. The plants suffer a severe cold shock and temporarily stop absorbing as much water as they need. You can often see the plants begin to wilt when this happens. As a general rule always use water just at or below room temperature.

Insufficient water will cause the plant's circulatory supply system to break down.

Cold water can send plants into such a state of shock that they will not take in the water they need.

FRESH AIR

Plants, like most living things, cannot live without air. Plants of course need a different gas in the air; while it is the oxygen that is vital to men and animals, plants need carbon dioxide. The plants absorb it almost exclusively through tiny pores in their leaves. We are therefore not far wrong if we describe the leaves as the lungs of the plant.

And just as men can be poisoned by foul air, so can plants. Both need fresh air. If the carbon dioxide in the air is almost exhausted, then plants react just as men do when they have to live in a room that is short of oxygen—they begin to droop.

This magnified section of a leaf shows the stomata, or tiny openings in the epidermis or outer layer, through which the leaf breathes in carbon dioxide and exhales oxygen.

The supply of fresh air to house plants does however have its problems. Plants can easily 'catch cold' and if placed in a draught will before long begin to drop their leaves. Next to draughts, what house plants like least is dry air from the heating, which forces the plants to exude moisture continuously. Unless they are watered all the time, they dry up. But even a continual supply of new water does not really help. It overloads the plants' circulation. However often you water them, the plants will eventually begin to wilt. Instead use humidifiers or put a bowl of water on the radiator to keep the air sufficiently moist. It also helps to spray plants regularly with a fine mist, using a hand pressure sprayer.

SOIL

Coming up with the perfect soil for house plants is something of an art. Only this much is certain: ordinary garden earth is no good at all for indoor plants. It will contain weed seeds, pests and maybe diseases, though it can be sterilized. And unless you get professional help you will not know if it has the necessary nutrients and trace elements.

This need for special soil is also logical when you consider the origin of most of our house plants. Only a tiny proportion come from northern latitudes; the others almost all come from the forests of the tropical and subtropical regions. The soil in those forests consists largely of rotted leaves and only to a small extent of mineral materials like sand and clay, so it is easy to understand why we most commonly use a soil consisting of three parts leaf mould, two parts old cow dung and one part sand.

Nowadays it has become more and more difficult for the ordinary townsman to get cow dung, so industry has taken up the problem and produced composts consisting mainly of peat, animal manure and the necessary trace elements. What is true about pH values of water applies equally to soils. The pH value of soils consequently should lie between 4.5 and 7.5. Unfortunately there is still no control over the composts marketed by the trade, and it is only too easy to get composts that are far too acid or too alkaline.

Most house plants that originated in the tropical rain forests need humus-rich soils with an acid reaction of 4.5 to 5.5 pH. You need not be too meticulous: variations of 1 or 2 in pH values are normal and plants can tolerate them. But it is important not to put acid-loving plants like coleus in alkaline soil, or the lime-loving campanula (bellflower) in acid soil.

In case of doubt, you can avoid mistakes by seeking information from a professional about the right soils for your flowers or foliage plants. There is, however, one mistake that you should never make, though it is quite common. Never store compost in an open container or where it can get damp. Nothing is so susceptible to animal and plant parasites as unused, slightly rotting soil, and any fertilizers it contains become inactive after a while.

No less important than the composition of the soil and its chemical reaction is its warmth. Pot plants, especially if they are standing on window ledges, often suffer from 'cold feet'. Sometimes this is because the window lets in a draught. In addition they suffer from 'evaporation chill' through evaporation of water from the soil.

It may be that you are keeping a hot-house plant in a soil temperature which would be more suitable for a cold-house plant. That can cause serious damage to the root system. In the worst cases the plants die. As a general rule, soil should never be at less than room temperature.

House plants from tropical countries are simply not at home in common garden soil.

Even if you pot the immigrants in special compost they will not thrive if temperatures are low.

9

WHERE TO PUT PLANTS

Light and air, water and warmth and the right kind of soil are the factors that have to be satisfied if plants are to grow and flower properly. Too much or too little light, widely fluctuating air or soil temperature, too little or too much water, even a type of soil that does not meet the plant's requirements—any of these can seriously impair the plant's growth.

Since you can influence and adjust all these factors, you can in theory—and also, very nearly, in practice—construct the ideal site for house plants. Of course, if you live in an apartment you may find you have certain imposed limitations. But, if you keep the structural conditions of your apartment or house in mind, you can always choose for your indoor garden those plants that will do best in the conditions available.

It should be obvious, but must be stressed because so many shocking examples make it necessary: plants are not furniture, not pictures, not simply ornaments. Plants are living creatures and must be treated as such. So if you want to keep plants in your apartment or your house, the first thing to decide is where they are to stand even before you make up your mind what sort of plants you want to stand there.

PLANTS FOR THE SHELF

If you want to keep plants on a bookshelf, on a stool in a corner of the room or in a niche in the wall, you must remember that only the most robust will flourish there. The fluctuations in temperature are generally too great, and not enough sunlight will reach the plants. You will do best to stick to foliage plants.

For heated rooms, a good choice will be from tillandsia, *Dracaena draco* (dragon tree), and aspidistra.

For rooms that are not continuously heated, or for the hall, there are chlorophytum (spider plant), sansevieria (mother-in-law's tongue or snake plant), fatsia (fig leaf palm or castor oil plant), and asparagus fern.

In cool rooms you can keep the typical cold-house plants such as phoenix (date palm), monstera (Swiss cheese plant), and araucaria (Norfolk Island pine).

All these plants are suitable for what indoor gardeners call shelf positions. This means that the plant shares the general climate of the room, which you can do nothing to improve. At best it is possible to improve the lighting conditions by fitting lights over the shelves where the plants stand. If the source of heat in the room is near the shelf, you must take that into account in your choice of plants. As a rule humidity will be lower in a room where the temperature is higher. As far as possible, avoid hanging plants in such positions; the rising warm air is bad for them.

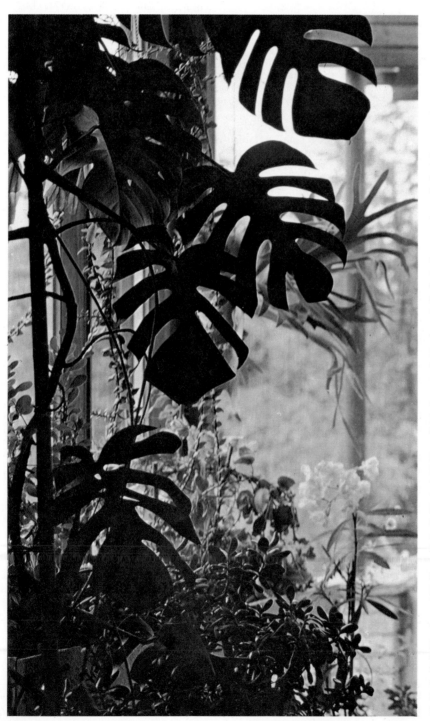

The Swiss cheese plant or shingle plant (monstera), a robust climbing shrub, does well in the shady corners of cool, airy rooms. Mature specimens, as on the left, will easily reach 4 m (13 ft) high, but younger plants will thrive in a flowerpot.

PLANTS AT THE WINDOW

Conditions for plants kept on the window ledge are very similar to those on shelves. In most centrally heated houses the radiator is fitted under the window so even in winter the house plants kept there have a good, warm spot. But they are exposed to very dry air and above all to draughts. If you want to keep plants on the window ledge, you really must fit the window with draught-proof strips.

Plants standing by a window get a great deal of light, which suits many of them but does make some special precautions necessary. Venetian blinds are a good way to keep out the fierce sunlight of a south window, and as a rule the circulating air keeps the room cool and prevents spots on the leaves and curled-up foliage. If this does occur in plants on the window ledge it will generally be those standing in the corners that are affected. It is often due to curtains hanging down at the sides of the window and preventing the air from circulating in the corners, so damaging the plants.

PLANTS ON THE MOVE

One answer to the question of the plants' position—one that is actually contrary to nature—is the use of flower benches or flower tables. Contrary to nature, because plants are static and anchored to their positions, whereas the plant benches or tables are specifically intended to be pushed from one part of the room to another.

A plant bench does make the work of caring for plants easier: you simply put the plants in a loose row on top of the bench, which should be at least 20-25 cm (10 in) wide.

A plant table, on the other hand, is better from the plants' point of view, because of the foundation put in the tray on which the plants stand. A damp foundation will prevent the evaporation of water through the pots and the consequent cooling off of the root system. It is a good idea to cover the bottom of the tray with a layer of medium coarse pebbles—

about 1 cm ($\frac{1}{2}$ in) deep—and then spread wet peat over it. The tray itself must be watertight and not susceptible to damage by humus acids and fertilizers. Glazed upper surfaces are not only resistant but are easy to look after.

If you were thinking of making a flower table yourself with a tray made of tinplate, remember that the tray will need a protective coating which must be renewed twice a year. Not only does this cause extra work but some plants can be harmed if you take them out too often.

PLANTS IN A TERRARIUM OR BOTTLE GARDEN

Giving your plants the care they need sounds a good deal easier than it is. You may intend to do your best by them, but what if your home is suitable for humans yet difficult for plants? Your family may be used to central heating, draughts, cigarette smoke and drastic changes in temperature, and no plant will thrive in these conditions. The answer may be plant cases, properly called terraria, and bottle gardens.

It all started with a Victorian, Doctor Ward. He discovered, quite by accident, that some very delicate ferns which had previously died when he tried to grow them in the open air thrived in a completely closed glass container where they were protected from dust, fumes and dry air. What is more, he was able to leave the container for years without attention. The ferns had been able to create a perfect microclimate in the container. His discovery led to a tremendous interest in this kind of gardening, and elaborate plant cases took pride of place in many homes.

Modern terraria are not so elaborate as the Victorian originals, but you can heat them and provide artificial lighting. You can grow almost any plants in them depending on size.

For those with little time, foliage plants are probably the best as they need less attention than flowering ones. Obviously do not include any plants that are going to grow rapidly and spoil the whole effect. The main thing to remember is that all the plants in a case or bottle must be compatible. Do not mix moisture lovers with cacti, for example. If you want to put the case on a sunny windowsill, be sure that all the plants will be happy in such a situation. If the only place for it is a dark corner, fill it with shade-loving woodland ferns. And if the case is placed so that the plants receive only artificial light, change them at intervals. They could not survive long without sun.

You can have fun with these cases, too, by creating a miniature landscape with soil to resemble hills, or studding them with rocks. Make a desert with sandy soil and cacti. Or just fill a terrarium with exotic foliage plants and light it from behind for tropical drama.

Bottle gardens work on the same principle as plant cases, and most plants, safe from outside hazards, will thrive—except, of course, for those which need a dry atmosphere. Inside a bottle garden the humidity is always fairly high. Clear glass is best, although it is possible to get healthy growth in tinted glass.

Planting a case is easy because you have plenty of room to manoeuvre. Bottle gardens need more dexterity, as you will discover. Both types of container must be scrupulously clean before you start, and good drainage is essential for success. Washed shingle or pea gravel is a suitable foundation, and over this you must have a layer of horticultural charcoal, which filters out impurities and keeps the soil 'sweet'. The charcoal is especially important to the more enclosed conditions of a bottle. The growing medium goes on top of the charcoal. This can be a soil-based compost or one of the soilless mixtures.

Take your time arranging plants in a terrarium so that each is shown to advantage. Make sure each individual plant looks well next to its neighbour. You can either plant them all on the same level, or by building up the compost, have them at different heights. Finally, firm the compost lightly round the roots and

water. Be careful with the watering —you want neither to flood the case nor to splash compost up against the glass you have cleaned. A case full of moisture-loving plants needs a lid, just a little bigger than the case for easy handling. Plants that like drier air should be uncovered.

Filling a bottle needs more patience and the plants you use should be small enough to pass through the neck undamaged. Drainage material, charcoal and moist compost can be poured in through a funnel of stiff paper or a long cardboard tube, then spread out evenly with a teaspoon lashed or wired onto a long stick. It is very important not to dirty the sides of the bottle while you are doing this as it can be so difficult to get the glass spotless again. You can see where the dexterity comes in. Next drop in the little plants and when they are in position make small holes for their roots in the compost. Manoeuvre the plants into the holes (use two sticks if it helps) and work some compost over the roots. Firm it lightly. The roots will soon take hold.

Finally, watering. It is all too easy to wash the compost away from the plants or make muddy splashes against the glass sides, so tilt the bottle slightly and let the water run gently down the sides—it will soon soak through to the middle of the bottle. Do not pour in too much at first for it takes a long time for the moisture to evaporate from a bottle.

To cover or not to cover the bottle is arguable. Certainly it is a good idea to keep it closed while the plants are settling in. Use the bottle's own cork if it has one, or cover with something like plastic wrap if not. But if the glass is running with condensation then the top must come off until the compost has dried a little. Aim to have the top half or so of the bottle covered inside with light condensation and use this as a guide to watering, too. It may take a little time before you can judge how much water is needed to keep a healthy balance of moisture, but it will come with experience. The main thing is that eventually you will be able to leave the bottle alone for months.

Even the healthiest terrarium or bottle garden will need grooming now and then. Caring for a terrarium is easy, but you will need a long bamboo cane with a razor blade stuck into the end to remove dying leaves or to prune away too vigorous growth from a bottle garden. Remove the debris with two sticks, using them like tongs or chopsticks.

A MODERN CONSERVATORY

Years ago most large houses had a conservatory. These were deliciously romantic places with cool tiled floors, wicker chaise-longues, or lacy wrought-iron tables and chairs tucked away under giant palms or among green ferns. Bougainvillaeas climbed up to the vaulted glass roof, the air was filled with the sweet scent of jasmine, there were tubs of tender camellias, immaculate in flower and leaf, perhaps an exotic bird tethered to a pillar, and to lull the senses even more, the gentle splash of a fountain. Just the setting for gentle courtship.

It was all very grand and rather delightful. But the really exciting thing about these conservatories was that they were marvellous places for growing plants. They had space, all the light a plant could need, a certain amount of humidity, and enough heat to encourage growth.

Life is not so lavish now. Few of us have room for such spacious structures, or could afford to heat and maintain them. Courtship would be a teeth-chattering affair and most of the plants would turn up their toes in the cold winter months. The next best thing is a home extension.

Usually these are built on to the sunny side of a house to provide extra living space for the family, but with a little planning you can turn them into a jungle of happy, healthy plants. Buy the largest extension you can afford and have room for. You can buy components in many sizes and materials to suit your site and house. Then, when you have made sure the family have enough room to sit and move around without knocking things over, start furnishing the remaining space with plants. If you have chosen an extension with a glass or clear plastic roof, so much the better. You will have more light, though you will lose more heat. You can, of course, buy models with double roofs or double glazing to overcome this problem, but be sure that there are enough windows to ensure good ventilation.

Unless you are sure you can provide lots of heat, which you probably would not want anyway in a living area, choose only those plants which will tolerate cold, provided that they are protected from frost at night. A small heater will prevent night frosts, and during the day the extension will be quite warm if the sun is shining,

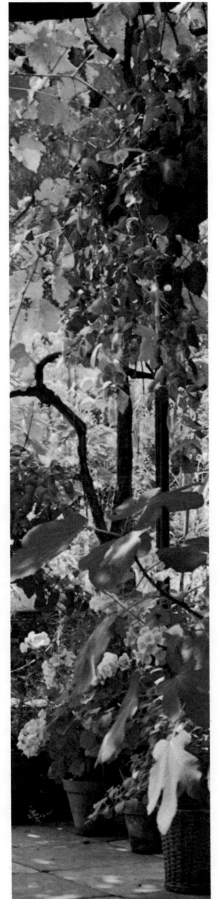

even in winter. Some of the warmth from the house wall will be trapped inside the extension too.

If you grow tender plants in pots outside during the warm weather, bring them into the extension during the winter. Then have a look at the plants already in the house. Many of them, however much you pamper them, can never look their best in living rooms. That monstera, for instance, will become quite exuberant in a light and airy extension. If you give it something like a moss-wrapped branch to cling to, you will get some idea of what it should really look like.

For scent, grow stephanotis on trellis or wires. Have hanging baskets full of the heavenly *Campanula isophylla*, the plants our grandmothers were so fond of, or ivy-leaved geraniums, ferns, and, of course, as many varieties of fuchsias as you have room for.

Nor is there any reason why you cannot have a small pool and fountain. The pool need only be a large plant container, fitted with a small submersible pump. Decorate it with plants like cyperus and let a few fish slip among the stems. If you cannot have a fountain, choose plants that are at home around still water, like zantedeschia (arum lily). Many of the plants we call marginals—that is, those which grow on the boggy edges of ponds—will grow in a shallow, water-filled container with perhaps a layer of colourful pebbles lining the bottom. They will be magnified by the water.

Unlike a greenhouse, where some plants can be grown in an earth border, you will want to keep extension plants in pots, and some will eventually need quite large ones. This will keep the more vigorous kinds under control and means that you can change them or move out any that are not doing too well, or simply resting.

In a room which is really intended for living you will probably have to prune back growth that threatens to interfere with the family's activities. Climbers particularly will need trimming, to prevent them from covering the windows and blocking out all light.

If you really have no room for an extension but feel you must have a good home for your plants, alternatives include small hexagonal greenhouses that stand on a balcony or patio, or even in a sunny room, or greenhouses which you fit with a few screws and plugs over a window on the outside of the house.

FLOWERPOTS

Once the clay flowerpot was virtually the only kind ever used, but more recently a number of other kinds of plant containers have been introduced. Clay pots have given way to plastic, papier mâché, metal, even concrete, as gardeners learn more about the behaviour of plants. People used to think that flowerpots had to be porous, permeable by both air and water; they used to lay a clay shard over the drainage hole to make sure that the water could get out. Now we know that what matters is not the porosity of the pot walls but the soil with which it is filled.

If you do use clay pots, new ones must be thoroughly washed and plunged in water. This washes away all traces of the firing, and the pot soaks up water until it is saturated. If you were to put a plant into a new clay pot without soaking it, the porous material of the pot would suck water out of the soil and so out of the plant, and the plant would wither. It is amazing what a lot of water a clay pot can swallow.

Plant composts used to be finely sieved, so that they were very compact and admitted very little air. Modern composts are much looser and admit more air and water, so that the porosity of the container is unimportant. Fertilizers also move through these light, spongy mixtures more easily and are readily available to the roots.

The root system of a plant is even more important than what grows above ground. If stalks, leaves or flower buds are damaged, they just stop growing, but damaged roots affect the entire well-being of the plant.

Roots have three functions. First, they anchor the plant firmly to the ground; secondly, they absorb the water and food that the plant needs; and thirdly plants—to some extent, —store food in their roots. The roots of plants may take a variety of forms, according to the conditions in the plant's natural habitat. We divide them into tap roots and plate roots.

Tap roots extend deep into the ground, with a strong main stem. Plate roots spread out equally in all directions, at no great depth. You must choose the shape of flowerpot that is suited to the roots of your plant.

Clay pots are graded according to size and, like plastic pots, come in different shapes. Conventional plant containers taper towards the bottom. The only object of that is to make it easier to get the plant out when you are repotting, for the root system of a plant would fill a wide-bellied pot just as well since the fine rootlets of the plant make for the wall of the pot. Most commonly the top diameter is equal to the height. You can also get pots of special shapes for special purposes—flatter pots for plants with plate roots, for example. The additional outer pots often used nowadays (correctly called cache pots) are purely decorative and have no effect on the plants.

Which is better for the plants, clay or plastic, is the subject of much vain discussion. The good old clay pot has served its purpose for hundreds of years and has done the plants no apparent harm. On the other hand, plastic pots are lighter, easier to clean and less likely to break, though cheaper qualities become brittle and crack quite quickly.

The only important difference is that a plastic pot is not porous and water cannot evaporate through the sides, so water less frequently.

There is one more thing about pots that causes controversy among indoor gardeners: the drainage hole. While it is not essential, a drainage hole at least does no harm. Even experienced gardeners overwater sometimes, and a drainage hole will let the excess escape so that it does not collect in the bottom and rot the plant's roots. And, of course, if you see roots growing out of the drainage hole, this is a sure sign that your plant needs a new pot.

REPOTTING

If something like two-thirds of the amount of soil—which also, of course, means the amount of food—in a pot has been displaced by roots, the time has come to give your plant a new and larger pot.

The job needs a bit of preparation. To start with, if you use new clay pots you must begin by washing and soaking them 24 hours in advance. If you are reusing old pots, scour off any lime deposits and clean them thoroughly to reduce the risk of infection to your new plants. Any old soil left in them may harbour pests.

As a general rule, never repot in the rest period of a plant or when it is in flower—except for plants that flower continuously, like the pelargonium (geranium). During the rest period the plant's roots will not grow into the soil, which will go sour. When a plant is in flower repotting interferes so seriously with its growth that the flowers will be destroyed. Even if the plant tells you unmistakably that its pot is too small by raising its root ball, you should never disregard this rule—never in flowering and never in the rest period. A few weeks will not make that much difference. The only exception is if you drop the pot and damage it.

To repot, take the plant carefully out of the old pot simply by turning it upside down and either giving the bottom one sharp tap or bringing the rim down sharply on a table. With very delicate plants, break the old pot to be sure of avoiding damage to the roots or shoots.

The old soil at the top of the root ball, where the plant breaks the surface, is generally just thrown away. To clean the bottom part of the ball, just shake gently. Cut out diseased roots or any parts affected by pests, and snip off dead roots. If you have delayed repotting too long, so that the root ball is thickly matted, you can carefully cut out a part of the roots from below. That will be especially necessary with young plants, which always tend to form too many roots.

The root ball should be put into the new pot right away and packed in with new soil. Only beginners leave root balls lying about while they look for a knife or the soil they need. Then replace the upper layer of soil on the root ball, pressing the new soil down lightly. Finally, water the plant, but do not drown it.

Dislodge hardy plants by upending the pot and bringing its rim down sharply on a hard surface.

Extract the plant and discard old surface soil, taking care to keep the root ball intact.

Sink the plant with root ball in a larger pot and fill it with new soil until the soil level reaches the same height on the plant as before.

Firm the plant in gently, pressing the soil down with both hands. Keep the repotted plant out of direct sun for a few days and water well.

You can tell by looking at the root ball whether a plant is healthy or diseased. Healthy plants have light brown roots, and the tips are almost white. Diseased roots are dark brown to black or quite rotten. They must be cut out and so must roots that are broken or have been damaged in repotting. If you leave the damaged part on the root ball it will soon begin to rot and cause the plant to become diseased.

Avoid using a pot more than two sizes bigger than the old one. If you use too large a pot, unless the plant is very vigorous, it will not send roots into all the new soil, or it will spend all its strength at first in forming new roots at the expense of top growth.

But for very large plants it is not always possible to find a bigger pot, so all you can do with them is reduce the root ball. Do not make the mistake of just cutting underneath and all round the root ball. That would be fatal—you would be killing all the most vital roots. Instead cut out a small section from the middle and then press the reduced root ball together again.

Make sure when you repot that the plant reaches the same height above the rim in the new pot as it did in the old. Since larger pots are normally also taller, you should put the old, possibly cut-down, root ball on a correspondingly higher layer of soil in the new pot.

As a final measure, keep repotted plants out of direct sunlight as much as possible for the next two weeks. Repotting will have interfered with the absorption of water through the fine roots, and if the plants stand too much in the sun you cannot be certain that the water will be replaced. If a plant is not too big—you cannot do this of course with a large indoor shrub—you can increase the humidity of the air around the plant by putting a plastic bag over it. That will ease the shock of repotting. Or you can spray it with a fine mist of tepid water twice a day for a week or two.

FEEDING PLANTS

Plants require more than the proper position. Not only must they be given enough light and air, warmth and water and the right soil; they must also have all the food they need, regularly and at the right times. Watering and feeding are inseparable in plant care, unless you want to stand in front of plants that grow more and more unattractive, complaining, '. . . but I've always given them plenty of water!' Good watering by itself is not enough.

Besides light, water and the carbon dioxide they draw from the atmosphere, plants live on nitrogen, phosphorus and potassium. These are the three principal foodstuffs that fertilizers can supply, plus small amounts of other necessary elements, primarily boron, iron, calcium, magnesium and manganese. These substances occur naturally in soil, if not always in adequate amounts.

The foodstuffs in a small flowerpot are consumed quite quickly and must be replaced. And since the plants can only absorb food in water, fertilizers must be given in a liquid form. Modern inorganic fertilizers are made up in such a way that they do not dissolve all at once—if they did the plants would get a severe shock from overfertilization. The foods are absorbed gradually as the plants are watered.

It is vital for plant development to give nitrogen and potassium at the

Lack of nitrogen inhibits growth.

right time and in the right quantities. Nitrogen promotes growth and is important in the formation of chlorophyll, the substance that makes the leaves green. A plant that gets too little nitrogen stops growing; its leaves turn yellow and the flowers are small and of poor quality. Too much nitrogen, on the other hand, means that the leaves turn an unnaturally pale green and grow large and sappy. Flowers that get too much nitrogenous fertilizer also become particularly susceptible to diseases and lose their resistance to parasitic fungi.

Too much potassium has much the same effect on plants as too little nitrogen. Too little potassium causes discoloration of the leaves: what was originally green will show yellow and red at the edges. But plants that get enough potassium grow very strong and have brilliantly coloured flowers and fruits.

The main importance of phosphorus, the third of the principal foodstuffs, is in the growth of roots and the formation of buds and flowers. A plant that gets too little phosphorus becomes stunted, and its leaves become discoloured.

There are excellent balanced fertilizers on the market for house plants, containing essential trace elements as well as the three main foodstuffs. If you buy prepared soil from the nursery you can take it for granted that it will contain adequate amounts of the basic necessities, but you will have to start fertilizing eventually, depending on the type of soil you use.

In addition to fertilizers, it is a good idea to give plants some organic manures if you can get them.

You should always combine the operations of manuring and watering, for again it is only through water that the plant receives a sufficiently diluted supply of food. If you manure without watering you may inadvertently damage the roots when they absorb the food.

There are five rules for manuring.
- Feed in the evening, preferably on an overcast day.
- If you manure by day, you must give the plants extra protection from the sunlight so that they do not lose too much water.
- After manuring, plants must be well watered and sprayed.
- Never manure plants if the soil has dried up; the plant must first be well watered so that the fine roots become capable of absorption again.

- Do not get any on the leaves! If you do, spray it off at once with clear, tepid water.

Nothing is more important in plant cultivation than understanding the 'life rhythm' of the plants. That applies to every aspect of cultivation. Plants orient themselves in their growth to the rhythm of light and darkness. Some start to form flower buds when the days are growing shorter and so are called short-day plants. Others flower when the days grow longer. These are called long-day plants. Between the two extremes are the plants that can flower and grow regardless of the length of day or time of year.

Only during the growth period do plants need a lot of watering and feeding. For the remainder of the year, when growth and flowering are over, the plants rest. To feed them then is not only superfluous but actually dangerous; it can cause damage to the roots.

After the growth and flowering period, which differs from family to family, from species to species, even from one plant to another, you must stop feeding. But do not stop watering. Although plants need less water in their rest period, hardly any of them can tolerate completely dry soil. Only quite robust plants like the sansevieria (mother-in-law's tongue) and other succulents can survive a dry root system, but it is not good gardening to let them get that dry. It is impossible to give precise instructions; this is where you have to learn by trial and error.

Feeding resting plants is harmful.

PRUNING

Pruning does more than make plants look nice and neat. Faded flowers and withered leaves are a permanent source of danger. Points of infection can quickly form on them which in a short time will endanger the whole plant. Remove fallen flowers and leaves before watering. If there are faded flowers hanging on to stems in which the sap is still flowing, you must take off the dead head and the stem with it. The withered flowers of the cyclamen are pulled off; withered blooms of the saintpaulia (African violet) or begonia, for instance, are broken off; with primulas the stalk must be cut off. What remains of the stems will dry and can easily be plucked off shortly afterwards.

Withered foliage and faded or spotted leaves must always be removed with the stalk. If a leaf is difficult to remove, then it must still be in contact with the sap circulation and the plant has not yet extracted all the reserves of food out of it. If you have to make an effort to tear off the leaf you may damage the plant tissue. That is dangerous, not so much because it harms the plant as because parasitic pests can infect it.

Often it is hard to remove leaves that clasp the stem or stalk as soon as they wither. This problem arises with the monstera and dieffenbachia. You have to cut off the leaves or their stems along the stalk with a sharp knife. What remains of the leaves is not picked off until later, when it has dried up completely.

Pruning also controls growth and can make the difference between a weak spindly plant and one that is bushy and flourishing. When shoots are removed from a young plant, it immediately tries to develop new shoots, often two or more, just below the cut. *Ficus elastica* (the rubber tree), for example, must be pruned as soon as it reaches a height of about 45 cm (18 in) above the rim of the pot. Prune at the end of the rest period, before the plant starts to put out new shoots. The pruning point (and this is true also of cutting back) should be no more than 1 cm ($\frac{1}{2}$ in) above the base of a leaf or side shoot. Botanists call this a node. If the stump left above the shoot is too long there is a danger that it will become infected and so a source of disease to the plant.

Pruning to alter the appearance of a plant is especially necessary with hanging or bushy plants. But you

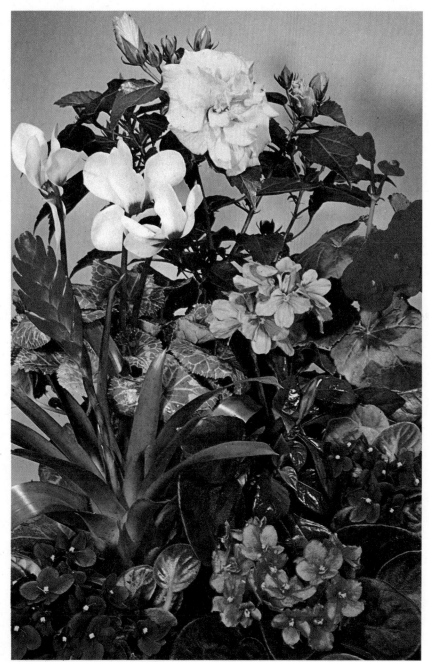

must prune with care. Hard pruning can so check the growth, especially of flowering plants like fuchsia, peperomia, and pelargonium, that it damages their blossoming.

Cutting back older plants restores their youthful shape and encourages them to form new, more productive shoots. On the rubber tree, for instance, you can cut back as far as the woody parts. The plant will look desperately bare for a time, but it will recover and form new shoots.

If a bushy plant grows too quickly and begins to crowd the plants around it, then you must cut it back, simply to make room. Do this before and during the growth period

Breaking dead blooms from the begonia, seen here with other house plants, will ensure fine, healthy growth.

(younger specimens will generally stand more cutting back) and aim for a balanced shape.

One more job in caring for indoor plants is the occasional cleaning of leaves. Wipe off dust and remove any chalky residue from watering using a cloth dampened with lukewarm, previously boiled water. You do not have to use detergents or soap, milk, olive oil, or beeswax. They clog the pores in the leaves and the plants cannot breathe.

17

PROPAGATION

It is always a thrill to raise new plants from ones you already have. You may not always have much luck with tropical plants like orchids and cacti, but even trying is fun.

Unlike those grown outdoors, house plants are hardly ever grown from their own seed, because they seldom set ripe seeds from the flowers. Also, hybrids and some varieties will not come 'true' from seed, that is the seedlings will not be like the parent. And some species simply take too long to propagate by seed.

Usually you will have to rely on vegetative propagation for the second growth of house plants. The most important of all forms of vegetative propagation is propagation by **cuttings,** which are parts of a plant separated from the main plant. They may be cuttings of side shoots and the tips of leading shoots, or stem cuttings, for which the stem of the plant is cut into a number of finger-length pieces. Then there are leaf

Propagating cuttings in bottles or jars of water will allow you to see how the roots progress. Transfer the cuttings to pots when they are 10-15 cm (4-6 in) long.

bud cuttings (a leaf plus a bud) and finally leaf cuttings, which are particularly easy to work with.

Shoot cuttings generally need a very warm soil to make them root. The shoots are cut from the old plant and put into sandy soil immediately after separation. Always work with a sharp knife. If you do, the stem below the cut will not be damaged, but if you use secateurs the stem gets crushed before the cutting is separated.

At the base of the cutting the cells form a growth of harder tissue called a callus. If you insert the newly separated cutting into slightly damp, sandy compost before the callus begins to dry, new roots are formed from the callus which will support the life of the cutting, or from which new young plants develop. When the callus dries on the parent plant, corky cells form and the wound heals over.

Basically, the procedure with stem, leaf bud and leaf cuttings is the same as for shoot cuttings. Propagation by stem or leaf bud cuttings is very rare, but leaf cuttings are frequently used. Choose fully grown leaves and cut them off with their stems. Leaf and stem are inserted in the compost and new plants form at the base of the leaf blade. Propagation by leaf cut-

ting is particularly simple with the pelargonium (geranium), saintpaulia (African violet) and related plants, and most succulents.

You must take cuttings only from healthy plants or shoots. The best time is when the plant is beginning to awake from its rest period and sending out new shoots. Do not take cuttings if the plant is already in flower; the formation of roots then is very slow and hesitant. Flower buds at the tip of shoots taken as cuttings should be carefully removed, for they will develop even on cuttings and deprive the young plant of the strength to form roots. Whether or not to prune shrubby cuttings that have plenty of leaves depends on the species, but remember that even a cutting needs leaves to breathe. On the other hand transpiration from a big leaf area may be so great that the tiny new roots cannot supply enough water.

You can, of course, root cuttings under glass. In a glass frame—or even a plastic bag—you get high humidity, so that the plants do not lose so much water by transpiration. But do not try to create humidity by overwatering the soil or the cutting will rot.

A cutting must always be kept in a warm, light position well sheltered

From left to right: slice the shoot almost through, plug the cut with moss to prevent healing, cover with moss and seal in a polythene strip, secure with string or adhesive tape. Roots will soon form in the bag.

Stem, shoot and leaf cuttings can all be used in vegetative propagation. Do not take a cutting from a plant in full flower and remove even the tiniest bud or it will develop at the roots' expense.

Shrubby ferns are easily propagated. Upend the pot, tap the base to dislodge the plant, then work the root ball loose until you can see where the roots will easily divide. Cut through here. Repot.

from the wind. As soon as you see that it is forming roots, the young plant must be gradually acclimatized to room temperature.

Certain house plants—like tradescantia, pilea (aluminium plant), African violet, or geranium—root incredibly quickly and easily. But woody plants—like *Ficus elastica* (rubber tree)—give a good deal more trouble. If you are not successful at first, put the cuttings on to a warm foundation so that the temperature in the rooting medium stays at about 25°C (77°F). The other way is to stand the cuttings in bottles filled with water. In full sunlight, when you occasionally have to spray the outside parts of the cuttings with water, the submerged parts will begin to form roots. When these are 10-15 cm (4-6 in) long, gently take the cuttings out of their bath and pot them carefully.

A method of vegetative propagation that has proved very effective especially in the cultivation of the rubber tree is called **air layering**. Here you can do two jobs at once. When the rubber tree has grown so tall that it must be pruned anyway, you cut the shoot nearly half way through, preferably just below a leaf node. To stop the plant closing the wound at once, put a small piece of wood or a little moss into the cut, then cover it with a thick layer of damp moss, and wrap some polythene around this, securing it with string or adhesive.

Within three months, roots will have formed at the point where you cut the stem, under the moss covering. Then cut the head off just below the roots, remove the covering, and

set the new plant in loose soil. If this seems too complicated, you can, of course, simply cut the top off the rubber tree and root it in warm sand or water.

Layering is also one of the best methods of propagating creepers. Lay a shoot along the ground and fasten it down carefully with wire at intervals of 8-10 cm (3-4 in), covering these points with soil. If the soil is kept moist the plant will form roots at the points where it is buried. Sever them from the parent and pot up.

The simplest of all forms of vegetative propagation is **division**. Shrubby plants like ferns, which have grown so luxuriant that they threaten to burst their pots, can be cut apart

vertically with a sharp knife. There are still so many roots on each part that it will grow in a new pot with no trouble. It is not always necessary to divide the plants with a knife; sometimes it is enough to tease the roots apart and then carefully divide them. But tuberous plants like begonias must be divided with a sharp knife and each piece must contain at least one eye. This form of propagation is also particularly suitable for zantedeschias (arum lilies) with their fleshy rootstock.

Cuttings need special care. Create a sheltered environment with a tank where they will have ample warmth, light, humidity and air.

PESTS AND DISEASES

There is no doubt that house plants are more delicate than anything that grows outdoors—more susceptible to errors in cultivation and pests and disease. This is not only because nearly all our house plants come from regions with very warm climates and have difficulty with the climatic conditions far from their native habitat. They also have to live in places that are designed primarily for men, and men make different demands on their environment.

Plants which sicken as a result of cultivation errors are a sad sight. Drooping leaves, shrivelled flowers, weak growth or rotting or damaged foliage can result, damage that is difficult to remedy.

One of the commonest mistakes is standing the plant in the wrong position, with too much or too little light, too much or too little warmth, too much or too little water. And not enough care is taken to provide for plants' urgent need of humidity in the atmosphere, especially in winter when indoor heating makes the air extremely dry.

If you do not look after your house plants properly, it may not only cause damage to them directly but may also make them more susceptible to pests of all kinds, animal parasites, bacteria, fungi or viruses.

Sometimes it is hard to tell where all the aphids and red spiders, mildew and cutworm, mites, even snails, come from. You may have carefully sealed the terrarium, meticulously disinfected all the soil and inspected all the tools you use. But the pests arrive just the same. Even professional gardeners shrug their shoulders resignedly when you ask them where the pests come from. 'Out of the air!' they will often tell you. It sounds unlikely, but it can be true enough. The air actually contains countless bacteria, viruses and fungus spores, most of which are harmless, but which can suddenly discover suitable food on a plant that has been damaged by inadequate care and attention, descend on it all at once and do serious harm.

Many diseases—particularly white fly—are introduced through other plant material, or they may be present on your plants already and, in the right conditions, thrive. And you should not be too surprised to find even earthworms or eelworms, espe-

cially on plants that have been outdoors in summer, as the eggs of these creatures can for short periods withstand temperatures up to boiling point. Even steam has sometimes proved inadequate for disinfecting garden soil.

Remember when you use pesticides that you are not only exterminating the harmful parasites but you may also be harming human beings and pets (especially fish, birds and cats) in the house. Never use them in closed rooms. If you cannot work on the balcony or in the garden, at least you should have a window open, and keep children away. Check labels for warnings, follow all instructions and wear gloves. Always use the prescribed amount —too much can be harmful.

If in doubt seek professional advice before beginning any treatment. Garden shops or centres are glad to help, too, provided you do not walk in with a pot plant covered with disease germs which could infect all the healthy plants there.

Even without professional advice, you must always take a plant that shows symptoms of disease away from the others. Plants with bacterial or virus infections must be destroyed at once. Never use them for composting; the source of infection can remain active for years.

Here is a list of some common plant diseases and their sources, possible ways of tackling them, and the appearance of the disease symptoms.

Plants affected by **bacteria** begin to wilt. They stop growing, and growths appear on the plant tissue—on the roots, the stems, the leaves or the flowers. The plant develops soft patches, generally yellowish or grey. Drooping leaves and yellowing foliage are also signs of bacteriosis, as are galls on roots or stems. The begonia, pelargonium (geranium) and various cacti are often affected this way.

Bactericides are only effective against bacterial infection as a prevention. To avoid infection, keep the plant in an airy and dry position. Diseased plants must be destroyed, and no seeds or cuttings from them may be used, since they are almost certain to be affected.

Fungus diseases have much the same effect on plants as bacterial infection. They are caused by little thread-like parasites on the plant. They enter through wounds in the plant, but they can also enter through the natural pores in the tis-

sue. After a short time they become visible on the plant in mouldy patches. Fungi can affect both the roots of a plant and the parts that grow above the ground. As with bacteria, prevention is the only way to deal with fungi. Spray with fungicides and destroy infected plants immediately.

Among the commonest fungus infections are powdery mildew and downy mildew. Even experts cannot easily distinguish between the two—in both, the plants are covered with a silvery, floury powder. With powdery mildew the leaves shrivel; with downy mildew they fall. Powdery mildew is caused by too dark a position and too much nitrogen in the fertilizer. Downy mildew may be brought on by too much moisture in the air and in the soil.

Plants with bulbs, corms or rhizomes are prone to fusarium foot rot. Dark, almost black spots appear, mostly at the neck of the roots, which later become moist and rotten. The plants wilt and cannot be saved.

Botrytis, often confused with mildew, arises from excessive humidity, generally only on dead parts of the plant. Healthy plants are seldom attacked by it. It causes brown spots on leaves and flowers. If the plant is only mildly infected you can remove the spotted leaves and spray with preparations of copper. That will save most plants. You may get this disease in the cyclamen, pelargonium (geranium), and saintpaulia (African violet).

You will quite often find spots on the leaves of house plants, but you need not always suspect the worst. Often they are burns caused by strong sunshine or spots of water. But they can also be due to fungus infections that even experts find hard to diagnose. Rust causes spots of an almost orange colour on the underside of the leaves, from which patches of mildew later develop. Red spots on the underside, and also on bulbs and on flower stalks, are a sign of red burn. But if the leaves have rust-red spots, later turning black, on their upper sides, then the plant has septoria. In all three cases you can use preparations of copper and sulphur, and take the plants out of the room or window. With injuries only to the stalk or stem you can occasionally hope for recovery.

Virus diseases, carried mostly by animal pests, are especially dangerous for all plants. They are indicated by serious interference with the growth and extreme colour changes

There is no hope of saving plants once they are diseased but, to avoid more serious harm, take the affected plants out and burn them at once.

Among virus diseases are leaf roll, which makes the leaves roll up like paper bags, leaf curl and mosaic disease, in which light and dark patches of discoloration appear on the leaves. Another virus disease may cause chlorosis.

The only thing you can do about virus diseases is to control the animal pests that carry them, either with insecticides or by removing the pests by hand—in practice not generally very effective.

There are many **animal pests** that can trouble an indoor gardener. Among the most common are scale insects, woolly aphids, root lice and, especially, white fly, a scourge to house plant growers and very difficult to control. These all feed by sucking sap from plants, not only depriving them of essential nourishment but also causing the leaves to curl up and eventually drop. They also spread every kind of virus disease, and fungus infections settle in their secretions and damage the plants still further.

Infection is a sign that the plant is not standing in the right conditions. Generally it is too warm, and the air too dry. You can prevent infection by increasing the humidity and by thorough watering.

If the plants are already infested, wash them with a mild solution of soft soap, or simply use a spray. Some insecticides work entirely on contact, so that they have to be directed on the pests. Others are systemic—that is, they are absorbed by the plant which itself then becomes toxic to the pest. These are more effective and longer lasting than contact poisons, and you do not have to cover the whole plant. With

any product, read the manufacturer's instructions to make sure it is safe.

Other common pests found on plants are the dangerous mites, who also suck the green parts of the plants. Wherever they occur light spots will appear on the leaves, which soon fade to a pale green, shrivel and fall. This kind of damage is caused most of all by the red spider, a tiny mite which is not always as red as its name suggests. The little creatures can sometimes be white, yellow, green or orange-brown. You can spot them when you see infected leaves covered with a fine, glittering web. Red spiders are a sign that the plant is standing in too dry air. Spray the plants with water and then with an insecticide.

In contrast to the red spider, both root mites and soft-skin mites are signs of too high humidity. You can control them by spraying and by giving the plants plenty of air. The soft-skin mite in particular is responsible for many ugly changes in plants—twisted, corky patches on

the leaves and stems, leaves turning brown on the underside, shrivelled buds and spotted flowers.

More a nuisance than a menace are ants and woodlice. Both feed on all parts of the plant. Woodlice eat only at night, and their presence is a sign that the plant is not being kept clean. The best way to deal with ants is to block the way from their nest, usually outdoors. With woodlice, hunt them out of their hiding places —under fallen leaves or in any unused flowerpots that are lying around—and make sure there are no places where they can lurk. Only when these measures fail should you consider using various poisons.

The pelargonium (begonia), cyclamens, and ferns are infested by a particularly harmful insect, the vine weevil. It is as dangerous as a larva as it is as a mature beetle. The larvae, white with a brown head and growing to nearly 1 cm ($\frac{1}{2}$ in) long, feed from late summer until winter on roots, corms and bulbs. If a cyclamen suddenly falls sick, you should turn it out of the pot at once and look to see whether the corms are being eaten by one of these larvae. If the damage is not too great you can generally rescue the plant by cutting out the part that has been eaten and dusting with charcoal. The mature beetle, nearly 1 cm ($\frac{1}{2}$ in) long with a broad snout, avoids daylight and hides under flowerpots. Leaves eaten from the edges are a warning signal that the vine weevil is about. Control this pest by reducing its hiding places and using insecticides.

Finally, beware of the minute, transparent eelworm. They live in plants, sucking the sap from the cells and causing growths and distortions. You find them in the leaves as well as in the roots. Chemical control is difficult; it is safest to destroy infested plants.

Greenfly or aphis.

The black ant (*Lasius niger*).

Black leaf spot.

HYDROPONICS-PLANTS WITHOUT SOIL

When botanists discovered that plants did not live on soil but got their food solely by absorbing inorganic substances dissolved in water, they had the theoretical basis of hydroponics. The botanists asked, quite logically, why plants should have to stand in soil at all. From there, as a complement to geoponics (soil cultivation), grew the concept of hydroponics (water cultivation), a revolutionary idea first brought to public attention in the United States in 1929 in a work by Professor W. F. Gericke.

As with so many scientific discoveries, the full significance of this one became evident only as a result of wartime conditions. During World War II the Americans found difficulty in supplying their troops in the barren Pacific islands with fresh vegetables, and then they remembered Gericke's discoveries. They began to grow vegetables in huge troughs full of a nutrient solution, arranging the plants on wire netting above the troughs so that their roots grew down into the fluid they fed on. The vegetables grew marvellously well without soil, and what is more they were absolutely free from infection by the fungi and bacteria found in the soil of the islands. Hydroponics had passed its first practical test.

But of course plants need soil not only as a source of food but also as a support to hold them upright. The Americans' lettuces had all the support they needed on the wire netting over the hydroponic troughs, but a house plant would just not be able to stand up once it had grown tall. Unless its roots are anchored in the soil, it simply falls over. So now a number of artificial cultivation bases have been developed, or natural substances have been pressed into service as bases for hydroponics.

A cultivation base must provide more than support for the plants; it must contain air so that the roots can breathe. (This is also true for ordinary house plant soil, and it is a good idea to break up the soil in pots occasionally.)

It really does not matter whether the cultivation base or aggregate is quartz or gravel or coal slack, basalt chips or crushed granite, pumice or cinders, broken bricks or the popular

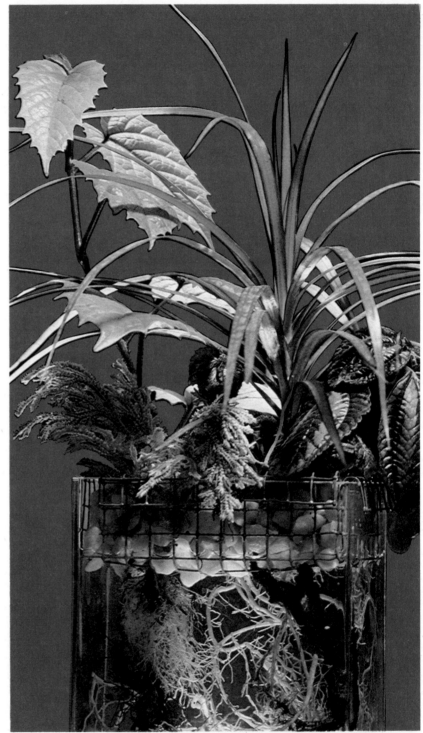

vermiculite. What does matter with all these aggregates is that they should be inert, that is they should not react chemically with the nutrient solution, because only then can the substances in the solution be extracted to meet the plants' needs. Secondly, the aggregate must be absorbent, so that it can absorb the nutrient fluid quickly and yield it up slowly. Finally, whatever this artificial soil is made of, it must be something

Loose absorbent aggregate supports the plants while the roots feed on the nutrient solution.

that has no sharp corners that can hurt the delicate root system.

In geoponics a plant needs a container full of soil. In hydroponics it needs two containers. The lower container holds the nutrient solution, while the plant supported in the aggregate stands above it in the inset container. This upper container has holes in the bottom of it so that the roots can grow down into the nutrient solution. Roots cannot tolerate bright light, so use only containers with a protective tint for the fluid. This not only shields the roots from the rays of the sun but also prevents the sunlight from encouraging algae formations in the solution. Be sure also to use containers of the right shape. Bulb plants are best kept in cylindrical containers, because they form long roots. For all other plants, round solution containers and tapering inset containers have proved best.

The nutrient fluid must contain the right ingredients in the right concentration and the right proportions. You need not worry too much about the ingredients and the proportions, for the various fluids on the market contain all the necessary ingredients for the nourishment of the plants. All you need to know is what pH value your plant requires.

The concentration of the fluid is more of a problem. Since the dissolved inorganic substances do not evaporate with the solvent, the concentration of the fluid gradually grows stronger, and the roots can get seriously burnt. And finally you must always keep the level of the nutrient fluid constant. If there is too little the roots will not reach their food; if there is too much, the roots will not be able to breathe and will start to rot. The hydroponic containers commercially available have either a little window in the fluid container through which you can observe the level, or a little tube that shows you how much nutrient fluid there is in the container.

If you have plants grown in soil that you want to transfer to hydroponics, you must realize that this involves a certain risk. Transplant plants only at their most active, just after the rest period. First rinse the root ball thoroughly in lukewarm water, then put the plant for ten to twelve hours in a pot of boiled water cooled to room temperature. Remove only those roots that are diseased or damaged. As you fill the inset pot with aggregate, hold the plant loosely until the aggregate is supporting it. Never press the artificial cultivation base down as you would ordinary house plant soil or you will crush the roots.

As with ordinary repotting, be careful that when the plant has been placed in its 'hydro-pot' the aggregate comes no higher than the old soil mark on the stem. It is best to use a height mark and a light mark.

To give the plant time to get used to its new conditions, go on feeding it with liquid fertilizer for ten to fourteen days and keep it in water with the right pH value. During this period of acclimatization make sure that the plant has a light, warm position, but protect it from direct sunlight. Remember that its whole circulation has been reorganized and supplies to it have been interrupted.

HOLIDAY CARE

Every year it's the same problem: what to do with your plants when you go away on holiday. If you have a lot of plants you can hardly hire a removal van to take them to relatives or friends. And even then you can never be sure they know enough about plants to look after yours properly.

So here are a few tips to help your plants last out the holidays, so long as you are not going to be away for six or eight weeks. Remember, though, that these are emergency measures—things might still go wrong. A plant-loving neighbour is always better.

Before leaving for your holiday, stand the plants in a bath and give them a long drink; then put them in transparent plastic bags loosely tied at the top. In this sealed enclosure the moisture will last for a long time, and if you put some liquid manure in the water the plants will not suffer from hunger. Although you cannot treat indoor shrubs quite the same, it will be enough to put the pot and the base of the stem in a large plastic bag and tie it up around the stem.

More robust house plants can be put into a bath on the balcony in a position sheltered from wind and sun. Put a layer of clay crocks or aggregate 5-8 cm (2-3 in) deep on the bottom of the bath and saturate them with water and nutrient. Clay flowerpots put into this material will absorb water and nutrient fluid through their porous walls, and both clay and plastic pots can take up nutrients through the drainage holes.

Another well-tried method is to put the pot over a bowl so that the bottom of the pot stands immediately above the nutrient fluid. Push a wad of absorbent material through the drainage hole to act as a wick, through which water and nutrient are sucked up. A similar method uses one or two woollen strands laid on the soil and then led into a container of water; if you put the water container at least as high as the flowerpot the water will be slowly and steadily transferred to the soil in the pot. This is no substitute for real watering, but at any rate it will keep the plants from drying out completely, which could be fatal.

Plants that have to be looked after during the winter holidays require extra precautions. A simple but adequate protection for all cold-house and temperate-house plants against draughts from the windows is to wrap pots and plants together in several sheets of newspaper so that only the tops of the plants show.

Plants often suffer more from the dry air of central heating than from the cold, so it is important to turn off the heating unless you can somehow arrange to keep up sufficient humidity. Dry cold is not so dangerous for

Feed plants by sinking absorbent pots in a liquid feed or by 'piping' water along woollen strands.

plants as dry warmth.

Hot-house plants must of course be kept in their special cases with a high air temperature.

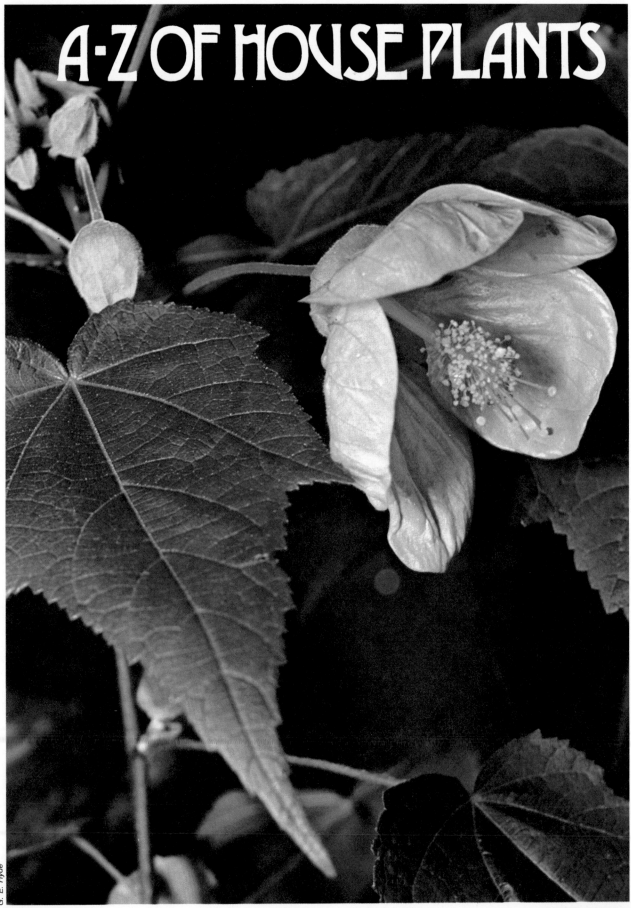

G. E. Hyde

Abutilon hybrid

ABUTILON

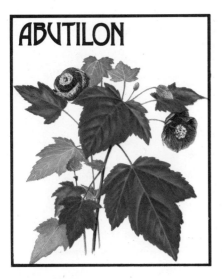

Indian Mallow

Small tropical flowering shrub with colourful hybrids, a few suitable for house plants.

Position light, warmish, airy room, otherwise outside.
Height up to 1 m (3 ft).
Flowering summer.
Propagation by cuttings or seeds.

The wild species which grow in Mediterranean countries and in South America are not so colourful as the hybrids developed by crossbreeding. They can be made to grow more than 1 m (3 ft) high and have hanging and climbing species.

Species
Beside the hybrids, two true species should be mentioned. *Abutilon*

striatum is a climber with orange, dark-veined, bell-like flowers growing singly in the leaf axils. The variety 'Thompsonii' has yellow-mottled leaves.

Abutilon megapotamicum is a hanging plant with narrow wedge-shaped leaves. Its beautiful flowers grow singly almost all year round.

Cultivation
Abutilons are fresh-air fiends. They do well by an open window, but are sensitive to draughts. Put them outdoors in summer, but with the first cool days bring them back into the house. There they like a light, cool place with a minimum temperature of 12°C (54°F). Water the plants freely while in flower and feed them once a fortnight. When flowering is over, keep them dry and do not feed them. Repot in spring and later clip back the foliage to encourage bushy growth.

Propagation
Leaf tips of about 5-10 cm (2-4 in) can be taken as cuttings. They need warmth and moisture to root in spring. Plant them 2 cm (1 in) deep in a pot of sandy soil with a glass cover to protect the topsoil from drying. The young plants will begin to grow when they have put out roots. Water them freely and pot on when necessary. They develop best in a room temperature of 18°C (64°F), or out in the warm sunshine. Keep them from draughts, or aphids will easily attack them.

Acalypha hispida

ACALYPHA

Copper Leaf, Red-Hot Cat's Tail

Indoor shrub with ornamental leaves and in one species attractive flowers.

Position essentially sunny and warm, with high humidity, in loamy soil.
Height up to 3 m (10 ft).
Flowering winter through autumn according to species.
Propagation by cuttings.

Acalyphas belong to the spurge family of which about 400 species are known in tropical and subtropical countries in all parts of the world.

Species
Only one of the commonly seen species, *Acalypha hispida,* has attractive flowers. It has bright red tassels of blossom up to 50 cm (20 in) long from which the nickname 'red-hot cat's tail' is derived.

We value *Acalypha wilkesiana* only for its marvellously coloured foliage. The flowers are so small and dull that they are almost invisible against the dazzling leaves. Most commonly we see the many hybrids of this South Seas species. Among the most attractive are the varieties 'Marginata' (olive green leaves edged with pink), 'Musaica' (greenish brown, dark red and orange-speckled leaves), and 'Obovata' (dark green iridescent leaves bordered with orange).

Cultivation
For the leaves to retain their lovely colours the plants must stand in a light place, but not in full sunlight. *Acalypha hispida* does well in half-shade. The air must not be too dry, the temperature not below 16°C (61°F).

The loamy soil must be kept good

25

and moist. Feed twice a month from spring through summer. Older plants bush out if you cut them back from time to time. Remove dead flowers regularly.

Propagation
Insert cuttings in sandy soil under glass. With *Acalypha hispida* plant shrubby cuttings from summer to winter and do not prune them during the growth period. *Acalypha wilkesiana* hybrids can be propagated all year round. To encourage growth, cut off the tips of cuttings from time to time.

Below: *Acalypha wilkesiana*
Middle: *Achimenes*
Bottom: *Adiantum*

ACHIMENES

Perennial flowering house plant.

Position warm and light in ordinary garden soil, but not in direct sun.
Height 20-50 cm (8-20 in).
Flowering summer and autumn.
Propagation by tubers.

Most species of achimenes are relatively modest, but numerous splendidly flowering hybrids have been developed by crossbreeding. The rather flat flowers grow in the axils of the transverse growing leaves. The petals, of various colours, unfold at the top of a narrow tube.

Species
Achimenes grandiflora grows to 50 cm (20 in). The big, elongated leaves are slightly hairy and reddish underneath. The red flowers are violet inside the tubes.

Achimenes longiflora grows to no more than 20 cm (8 in) and has small, pointed leaves, with big, bluish red flowers with yellow centres.

Cultivation
Achimenes do best in a light but not too sunny position with steady temperatures of about 18°C (64°F). Water well until near the end of flowering. When flowering is over and the leaves wilt, cut the stem off just above the ground, but leave the yellowish rhizomes, with their scaly surface, in the pots.

Propagation
Cut off 5 cm (2 in) lengths of rhizome in spring or summer and insert eight to ten pieces in a medium-sized pot of sandy soil. Cover the shoots with soil at most 2 cm (1 in) deep and at first do not water them much. Later give them more—and only softened —water, and after a month feed them once a fortnight.

ADIANTUM

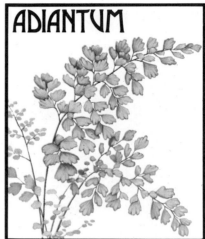

Maidenhair Fern

Evergreen house plant.

Position shady positions and slightly acid humus-rich soil.
Height 30 to 60 cm (12-24 in).
Propagation by division.

The maidenhair fern is a citizen of the world. You can find hardy species near the polar circle, while others are at home in the tropical rain forests of South America. This wide distribution has naturally brought about considerable variation in the appearance of the different species, but all have shiny generally dark brown leaf stems.

Species
Adiantum macrophyllum is a delicate species with large leafy fronds which are red to start with but later turn green.

Adiantum raddianum, a species of many varieties, forms magnificent bushes. Long pinnate leaves with many leaflets, mostly light green to yellowish green, grow on long stems. Famous varieties are 'Brillantelse' with leaves that start red-brown, 'Fragrantissimum' with long, narrow, dark green leaves, and 'Gracillimum' with little ornamental leaflets.

Cultivation
Indoors, adiantums need watering with lime-free water early spring to autumn and also plenty of food. The plants like a warm position with high humidity. They lose their foliage in dry soil, and in insufficiently moist air the tips of the leaves dry up.

Propagation
Older plants are propagated most easily by division. Propagation by spores is possible but difficult.

AECHMEA

Urn Plant

Popular perennial house plant with exotic inflorescence.

Position warm, light place with no direct sun and a constant temperature.
Height up to 18 cm (7 in).
Flowering spring through autumn.
Propagation by suckers.

As a house plant, aechmeas need what they were used to on branches of trees in the Brazilian forests—constant warmth, light and humidity.

It is undoubtedly one of our most beautiful house plants. Extraordinary, pink bracts grow in a thick cluster on a long stem with, between them, short-lived little yellow, red or violet flowers. Even though flowering time is quite short, the attractive bracts last for months.

Species
Its pretty flowers make the *Aechmea chantinii* particularly impressive. Fiery red with yellow-mottled points, they grow close together on branching stems. Beneath the spikes hang long, narrow spathes, like a ruff round the neck of the flowers. The leaves of the cup-shaped rosette, up to 50 cm (20 in) long, have a pattern of transverse dark green stripes and silver scales.

The leaves of *Aechmea caudata* have toothed edges and a slightly curved spike at the point. Brilliant flowers grow between green bracts.

Aechmea fasciata (often sold as *Billbergia rhodocyanea*) makes a powerful impression, due to the little grey scales on the leaves, which are toothed and have stripes on the underside. It has prickly bracts on the inflorescence of small blue-violet flowers.

Aechmea fulgens is one of the giants of the genus. The leaves of the spreading cup rosette can grow up to 5 cm (2 in) wide and 40 cm (16 in) long. They are dotted with grey up to the middle and have blue-green tips. The variety *Aechmea fulgens* 'Discolor' is particularly colourful, with olive green leaves whose violet-red undersides have a greyish sheen. The coral flowers have blue tips.

Aechmea miniata will take up less room on your windowsill. It is lower growing and has narrower, less spreading leaves.

Cultivation
Aechmea must be kept warm, and at a steady temperature. It does not need a tropical climate, but requires a minimum temperature of 15°C (59°F). While in flower it does best at temperatures around 18°C (64°F).

Aechmea is undemanding. Not even the dry air from central heating distresses it. Its place on the windowsill should be light, but sheltered from the midday glare of the sun. Water with water at room temperature, but give it less in winter. Keep the soil in the pot moist, but not wet, and until the plant stops flowering. Top up the cup formed by the leaf rosette with softened water.

Propagation
As a rule one leaf rosette will produce only one inflorescence, and when it dies off, the whole plant dies. But in the meantime new rosettes will have formed at the foot of the old. You cannot always manage to get these suckers to develop, but it is worth trying. Leave them to grow on where they are, or when they are half the size of the parent detach, allow to dry for a day or two and then plant in an open, lime-free compost.

Aechmea chantinii

AESCHYNANTHUS

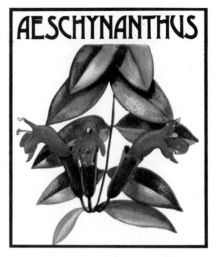

Evergreen, flowering hanging plant, very decorative, but rather delicate and difficult to grow.

Position in a hanging pot or basket, very warm, shady, high humidity.
Length up to 50 cm (20 in).
Flowering summer and autumn.
Propagation by cuttings.

In their homeland, the tropical regions of Asia, the various species of aeschynanthus display bright red and often also yellow and orange flowers. The flowers are at the tip of thickish, overhanging tubes with long projecting stamens. They grow in clusters or singly, nearly always at the end of drooping stems with fleshy, leathery leaves. Unfortunately most are difficult to grow. They will flower only at temperatures above 22°C (72°F), and lose their flowers if the temperature fluctuates below this level.

Species
Among the most famous species is *Aeschynanthus pulcher,* with its clusters of red flowers. The closely growing, oval leaves can reach a

length of 5 cm (2 in).

Aeschynanthus marmoratus decks itself with greenish flowers. The lanceolate leaves, up to 10 cm (4 in) long, are light green on top and reddish underneath.

The species *Aeschynanthus speciosus* has clusters of up to twelve flowers. You cannot fail to notice their yellow-red petals with black-spotted borders and protruding stamens.

Cultivation

The species of aeschynanthus do best in peat or sphagnum moss with high humidity. In summer the temperature must not be less than 22-25°C (72-77°F); at other times keep them at 16-18°C (61-64°F). If the plants are kept at the same temperature for the whole year, they will not flower. Water the plants only moderately with lukewarm water, but spray them quite frequently. During the winter it is important to keep the soil almost completely dry.

Propagation

Take shrubby cuttings about 5 cm (2 in) long in spring, and plant them in a loose mixture of peat and sand. At temperatures between 25-30°C (77-86°F) they will form roots within two or three weeks. Plant the young plants in coarse, open soil or peg trailers from spring onwards.

ALLAMANDA

Bushy, climbing evergreen house plant with magnificent flowers.

Position light and sunny with high humidity, away from draughts.
Height with support, up to 2 m (6 ft).
Flowering spring through autumn.
Propagation by cuttings or seeds.

The allamanda comes from Brazil and has a preference for warm positions with high humidity, such as you only find in a hothouse. The allamanda flowers almost without ceasing from spring to autumn.

Almost the only species we find as a house plant is *Allamanda cathartica*, a climbing shrub with leaves like those of the laurel. The golden flowers have a diameter of 5 cm (2 in) and form cymes, generally growing three or four together. The yellow flowers of the variety 'Grandiflora' grow up to 10 cm (4 in) across. Even bigger —some 12 cm (5 in) across—are the flowers of the variety 'Hendersonii', which gleam reddish yellow with light spots over the rather leathery foliage.

Cultivation

While the allamanda tolerates sunlight well in summer when it is in flower, you should shelter it during the resting period in winter. Even then the plant needs plenty of warmth, though less humidity. It is a good idea to support the strong-growing plant with wire or canes so that the flower stems can find room to hang down.

Cut back long stems on weak plants after flowering. It will make the plants bushier and encourage later flowering. Feed the plants every week during the spring and summer.

Propagation

Propagation by seeds is possible, but difficult. Propagation by shrubby cuttings in spring is generally more successful. Keep them under glass at a temperature of about 25°C (82°F).

Allamanda cathartica

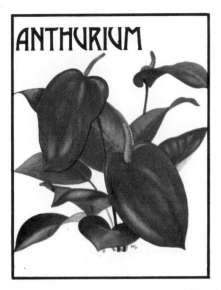

ANTHURIUM

Flamingo Flower, Painter's Palette, Tail flower

Perennial house plant with beautiful spathes.

Position light but not sunny.
Height up to 45 cm (18 in).
Flowering at all seasons.
Propagation by division or seeds.

The first specimens of this decorative plant came to Europe from the tropical rain forests of Central and South America in the middle of the last century.

Species
Of the many tropical anthuriums, we have only two of importance: the great flamingo flower *(Anthurium andreanum)* and the little flamingo flower or painter's palette *(Anthurium scherzerianum).*

The great flamingo flower has heart-shaped leaves up to 20 cm (8 in) long and leaf stalks that grow as much as 1 m (3 ft) long. Its striking inflorescence, with a spathe some 10-15 cm (4-6 in) long and a brilliant white to yellowish green spadix with the tiny flowerets growing on it, looks most exotic. The spathe is generally red, but can be orange, white or spotted.

The little flamingo flower has smaller spathes and spirally twisted or curved spadices, usually red.

Cultivation
The anthurium must stand in the light but not in the sun; a north or east window is best. The room temperature should not fluctuate or go below 15° C (59° F). The plant grows best in coarse standard compost or in a mixture of friable leaf mould or coarse peat, with a deep layer of pebbles in the bottom of the pot. Whatever medium is used must be porous and provide good drainage. Anthuriums also do very well in hydroponics.

Water the plants only with tepid, previously boiled water. Since the flamingo flower can produce flowers all the year round, virtually without a break, it must be fed with liquid manure or general fertilizer every 12 or 14 days for the whole year except during winter. The great flamingo flower needs repotting every few years; plant it in its new pot so that the lowest leaves are just above the soil. This is because the species gradually forms little stems. In this way you can completely shake out the soil from the old pot and cut off rotten roots.

Propagation
Old plants can be propagated by division or by separation of rooted side shoots. Propagation by seeds is also possible but very difficult—an operation reserved for the specialist. You need pedicels of different ages, because the flower is bisexual and the stigma ripens before the pollen. The seeds ripen in nine months and are immediately laid on leaf mould, but not covered.

Below: *Anthurium scherzerianum*

APHELANDRA

Zebra plant

Evergreen house plant with strikingly beautiful leaves and flowers.

Position shady, humid, warm place.
Height 20-60 cm (9-24 in).
Flowering summer to winter.
Propagation by cuttings.

Of the many species of aphelandra in the primeval forests of Central and South America we grow only one, *Aphelandra squarrosa,* which is a very popular house plant. Its leaves are oval, pointed and up to 25 cm (10 in) long, and green with silver-white patterns. Little yellow flowers form between the bracts.

Cultivation
The aphelandra is very demanding. It needs a warm, humid atmosphere and a light position, but at the same time it must be kept out of the full glare of the sun. The soil must be porous and rich in humus and must be fed every two weeks until the plant flowers. It does best at temperatures between 18-25°C (59-82°F). It is a good idea to spray it every day. While in flower it must be watered regularly, but not sprayed.

Four to six weeks after flowering the plant needs a somewhat cooler position, less water and no feeding.

After this rest period cut the aphelandra back to about 10 cm (4 in) and repot in new soil after reducing the root ball. Water sparingly at first, then more freely. Begin feeding again four weeks after repotting.

Propagation
The aphelandra is propagated by top cuttings 10-15 cm (4-6 in) long and also by leaf cuttings with a 'latent' bud. Root in a sand-peat mixture, preferably at the beginning of spring. A warm position is essential. To maintain temperature and humidity, enclose young plants in glass.

ARAUCARIA

Norfolk Island Pine

Evergreen house plant with needle-shaped leaves.

Position airy, cool and shady, in sandy soil.
Height in a room, 2 m (6 ft).
Propagation by seed or cuttings.

The ancestors of our Norfolk Island pine were discovered by Captain Cook in the Norfolk Islands in the Pacific Ocean and are magnificent pine trees, growing to a height of 60 m (200 ft). The miniature version became a popular house plant.

The lower part of the upright stem, up to 2 m (6 ft) tall, becomes almost bare after a time unless it is cut back to stimulate new growth. But at the top the needle-shaped leaves, often bluish in colour and growing on horizontal branches, form elegant fronds.

Cultivation
What the araucaria needs chiefly is plenty of air and not too much warmth.

In summer give it a light but not sunny position. Water moderately from spring to the end of summer; feed fortnightly.

From winter on you hardly need water the araucaria at all, though the soil must not be allowed to dry out. In cold weather, keep the temperature between 7-10° C (45-50° F), and keep the room aired.

Normally the araucaria has to be repotted only every few years. Be particularly careful that the soil comes up just to the base of the root.

Propagation
The araucaria can be grown from seed, but it is easier to take young shoots—8 cm (3 in) long—and root them in sand or peat.

ASPARAGUS

Asparagus Fern

Evergreen house plant, sometimes climbing, sometimes hanging. Certain species grow berries.

Position sunny to half-shady, in porous humus-rich soil always kept moist.
Height up to 2 m (6 ft), both climbing and hanging.
Propagation by division or seeds.

Asparagus is known chiefly as a vegetable, but it has a number of related species that make very popular house plants because they are so little trouble. All these bushes and subshrubs have scaly, quite dull leaves, but grow what are called phylloclades on their branches. These spurious leaves are needle-shaped or leaf-shaped and grow singly or in bunches on the upright or hanging, branching stems. Only a few species will flower as house plants. Pretty red berries develop from the flowers; they are not edible.

Species
Asparagus crispus is a twining or hanging plant. It has very small phylloclades and from winter to early spring bears isolated, strongly scented flowers from which decorative red berries develop. It is a good plant for a basket.

Asparagus densiflorus is a widespread house plant, often still known by its old botanical name of *Asparagus sprengeri*. This species comes from South Africa and has elegant, drooping stems with pointed, needle-shaped phylloclades. A very robust and undemanding species, it can be kept on the balcony in summer.

Another species that can be kept on the balcony in summertime is

Asparagus scandens var. 'Deflexus', a robust house plant, often confused with *Asparagus crispus* on account of its small phylloclades.

Asparagus setaceus, sometimes called asparagus fern, is sold as *Asparagus plumosus.* It is a climbing subshrub which does best in the greenhouse. There it will grow shoots up to 2 m (6 ft) or more long, covered with fine phylloclades.

Cultivation

Asparagus is an ideal basket plant and prefers a light position, though it should not be put in direct sunlight. *Asparagus setaceus* is particularly intolerant of the sun. No species can tolerate a dry root ball, so they must be regularly watered and sprayed, especially in centrally heated rooms.

All species including *Asparagus densiflorus* should be kept at temperatures of 20°C (68°F) in winter.

The plants grow quickly and should be repotted every year, when you can reduce the root ball a little. Plant in good humus-rich soil, and do not use too big a pot or the growth and flowering will be poor.

Propagation

The propagation of asparagus is no problem. Divide the bushes and sub-shrubs at the beginning of spring, when you are repotting. You can grow the plants from seed, sown in autumn in moist humus at 20°C (68°F).

**Below: *Asparagus sprengeri*
Below left and right: *Aspidistra* and *Aspidistra elatior* 'Variegata'**

ASPIDISTRA

Cast Iron Plant

Resistant, trouble-free, evergreen foliage plant with insignificant brownish purple flowers.

Position half-shady to shady, cool or warm, in good potting compost.
Height 30 cm (12 in).
Propagation by division.

Nothing can upset the aspidistra. It does just as well in a dark corner as it does on the balcony. It can stand fluctuating temperatures, draughts and dust. Consequently you often see it in entrance halls and corridors and on the counters of shops. This strong constitution has given it the popular name of cast iron plant.

Of the few species that grow wild in the mountains of the Far East, we cultivate only one. *Aspidistra elatior* has lanceolate, leathery leaves that can grow up to 70 cm (28 in) long and 10 cm (4 in) wide. The flowers sprout from an underground pedicel at the lower end of the leaves; they are a brownish purple with a curiously shaped stigma.

More decorative, but more trouble, is the variety 'Variegata', with leaves striped white and yellow.

Cultivation

Do not worry about finding a favourable position for the aspidistra: the cast iron plant is equally content with any kind of light and temperature over 10°C (50°F). 'Variegata', however, needs bright light and temperatures between 10-12°C (50-54°F), or the white and yellow pattern on the leaves will fade.

Propagation

You can divide the rootstock during late winter or early spring into parts each having two or three leaves, and transplant these in new pots.

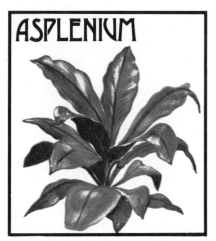

ASPLENIUM

Bird's Nest Fern, Spleenwort

Decorative pot fern for the hothouse or conservatory.

Position shade or half-shade, in moist soil, with high humidity.
Height up to 80 cm (32 in).
Propagation by division or spores.

The immense genus *Asplenium* —botanists give it over 700 species—occurs all over the world. Among its species are our wall rue as well as huge leaf ferns, epiphytes found in tropical countries on the tops of trees.

Some have been cultivated as house plants for a long time. But generally you can keep them only in a conservatory, as they require a lot of warmth and high humidity.

Species
The bird's nest fern *(Asplenium nidus)* is by far our most popular species. It has a short, erect rhizome and as a young plant has tongue-shaped fronds which grow broader as it matures. In its homeland, the tropical forests of Africa, Asia and

Asplenium nidus

northern Australia, it lives on the branches of tall trees. It needs only a small pot, even when the roots are completely matted. It prefers light humus-rich soil but can get along with an ordinary garden variety.

Less delicate is *Asplenium dimorphum.* Its leaves, up to 90 cm (35 in) long and almost 50 cm (20 in) wide, are triangular and slightly drooping. On the upper side of its leaves it grows adventitious buds—young plants that drop off and grow in the ground.

Adventitious plantlets up to 60 cm (24 in) long grow also on the finely divided, drooping fronds of *Asplenium bulbiferum.* This species occurs naturally in all tropical countries bordering the Indian Ocean. It thrives only in the hothouse.

Cultivation
The spleenworts, which include all the ferns mentioned above, need a shady or half-shady position. Unlike the species *Asplenium dimorphum,* which comes from the Norfolk Islands in the South Seas and is content with normal room temperatures, the bird's nest fern needs temperatures of around 20°C (68°F) and above, as well as high humidity. Water the spleenworts with lime-free warm water and spray them frequently. Put some liquid fertilizer in the water once a month. Repot the plants every two or three years, but do not use larger pots than necessary.

Propagation
The species with adventitious buds can easily be propagated by the indoor gardener simply by keeping the plantlets at air temperature with a bottom heat of 20°C (68°F). Propagate *Asplenium nidus* by spores, sown in the earth at temperatures of about 30°C (86°F).

Aucuba japonica **'Variegata'**

AUCUBA

Hardy evergreen shrub with ornamental foliage, kept outdoors in tubs when warm, but indoors when cold.

Position cool and shady place in loamy soil.
Height 1-2 m (3-6 ft).
Propagation by cuttings.

In Japan, its original homeland, the aucuba grows in the open air to make a magnificent evergreen shrub. It is one of our most sturdy house plants, used especially in entrance halls and on landings, as well as for decoration in unheated display windows. The aucuba grows to 1-2 m (3-6 ft) high and has toothed leaves, some yellow striped, some spotted.

A particularly popular variety is *Aucuba japonica*, 'Variegata', whose green leaves have golden-yellow spots. They produce insignificant flowers in spring. Only if you have male and female plants standing near to one another can you expect the red berries after flowering.

Cultivation
The tub plants can overwinter in rooms in which it is no warmer than 6°C (43°F) provided they are not too dark. If you put your aucuba outside in summer, put it in half-shade to start with or the tender leaves will scorch. Later the shrub will even stand the midday sun. The plant needs very little attention: regular watering, and weekly feeding in spring and summer. Repot smaller aucubas every two years. To encourage bushy growth, occasionally cut back selected shoots almost to the ground.

Propagation
Cuttings taken in late winter or late summer will root at temperatures of 12–20°C (54-68°F). The cooler they are kept, the longer they take to root.

BEGONIA

Begonia
Large genus of beautiful flowering outdoor and house plants, which includes herbaceous and sub-shrubby annuals and biennials.

Position with few exceptions, semishade and high humidity in humus-rich, porous soil.
Height 15-20 cm (6-9 in); some species up to 2 m (6 ft).
Flowering at all seasons.
Propagation by leaf or stem cuttings, tubers and seeds.

All begonias are by origin shade plants, for they come from the tropical rain forests or subtropical regions of America, Asia and Africa, where even to this day new species or unknown natural hybrids are still being discovered. There are even some species that flourish in mountain forests.

In the tropical forests begonias live either as ground plants or as epiphytes on trees. In the course of

Begonia **hybrids and others**

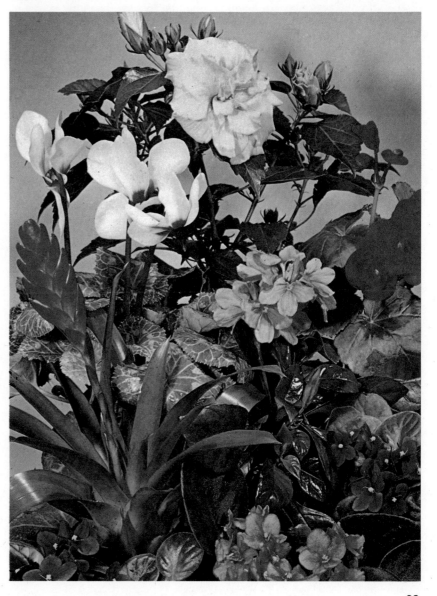

the last two centuries the form of the plants, the shapes and colours of the flowers, have been greatly modified by cultivation. New hybrids and a vast number of varieties have been developed. Consequently even experts have difficulty in finding their way about the genus *Begonia*.

Ornamental-leaved species

These begonias are grown chiefly for their beautifully shaped and coloured foliage, though in certain species you do also get some fine colour from the flowers. The best known species of leaf begonia—its crosses and varieties are almost countless—is *Begonia rex*. It can have either large-toothed leaves of red or violet, often with a green border, or much smaller leaves, often lobed and coloured red, grey or green and generally also speckled with silver-grey.

The shrubby begonias are among the ornamental-leaved species. These subshrubby, upright species come mostly from tropical parts of Central and South America. Many grow as much as 1 m (3 ft) in height. The *Begonia coralina* hybrids can reach a height of 2 m (6 ft) and keep their abundant flowers all year.

All shrub begonias have branching stems, but they do not form wood. The flowers, hanging down in clusters, are very big, generally red or pink, with wonderful leaf shapes and colours. The *Begonia albo-picta* grows really tall. Its green, asymmetrical heart-shaped leaves have a great number of silver-white spots; its flowers are greenish white.

Begonia credneri, a hybrid, produces its pale pink flowers almost all the year round. It too has branching stems, and the leaves are heart-shaped, dark green on top and red and hairy underneath. A good plant for indoor cultivation, it grows 40-50 cm (16-20 in) high.

The fuchsia begonia *(Begonia fuchsioides),* of shrubby habit, has slightly drooping stems and small leaves of an asymmetrical rounded egg shape. It grows up to 1 m (3 ft) or more high. Its red or pink flowers, rather like those of the fuchsia, appear in the winter months.

The easily grown *Begonia maculata* is a favourite house plant. It is rather like *Begonia albo-picta*, but its leaves are speckled with white, and reddish below. The flowers are white or pink.

Begonia metallica gets its name from the beautiful metallic sheen of the green upper side of its leaves.

The underside is red and the entire surface is wrinkled. The plant can reach a height of 80 cm (32 in), and flowers in thick pinky white clusters. In winter it needs a room with a temperature of between 12-15°C (54-59°F).

The less branching *Begonia scharffiana* is covered with bristly red hairs. Its asymmetrical heart-shaped leaves come to a long point, dark green on top, deep red underneath. Big white-pink flowers grow on long stems.

One of the loveliest of the shrubby begonias is *Begonia serratipetala*. Its leaves are pinnate, each segment double-toothed, bright green with blood-red spots.

Lastly, the ornamental-leaved begonias include those that are particularly suited to growing in hanging pots or baskets. The most attractive of them—the fern begonia, *Begonia foliosa*—has little leaves no more than 1 cm ($\frac{1}{2}$ in) long. Its fern-like shoots are strong and branching, the flowers small and whitish. It needs more warmth and humidity than other species and so is ideal for a conservatory.

The leaves of *Begonia limmingheiana* are a good 10 cm (4 in) long, with deckled edges. The shoots are pendulous; the flowers are light red or orange and white inside.

Cultivation of ornamental-leaved species

Begonias do best in warm rooms, particularly in a north-facing window, for they cannot bear direct sun-

Begonia rex

light. After their strong growth period, they lose some of their flowers in winter but quickly regain their former beauty after repotting the next year.

Water with tepid water and keep the root ball constantly damp. Feed from spring to summer. It is very important to cut back older plants, preferably during vigorous growth.

You need flat pots for all begonias, whose roots spread outwards rather than down. The soil must be rich in humus, porous and nutritious. A mixture of old leaf mould with a generous addition of compost and farmyard manure, peat and sand has proved very successful, but begonias also grow well in standard compost. As the plants grow older you will not need to repot them so often; instead, give them extra manure. Try not to turn the pot or change its position more than necessary. Begonias hate to be disturbed.

Propagation of ornamental-leaved species

Begonia rex particularly, but the basket begonias too, are best propagated by leaf cuttings. Take the fully ripe leaf during the summer and carefully nick the stronger veins on the underside where they branch. Immediately lay the leaves in a bowl one-third to two-thirds full of sterile sand and weight them down with a few pebbles or small pieces of glass so that the ribs or veins of the leaf lie at least partly on the wet sand. After four to six weeks young plants form at the spots where the leaf was nicked, and these you plant in little pots filled with a mixture of sand and soil.

If the leaves are big you can cut a triangular piece out of them, but it must include a vein at the bottom corner. Young plants will develop in the same way within four to six weeks in a mixture of soil and sand.

If there are old plants available, propagation by stem cuttings is also possible. Cut the section of stem into short pieces and powder with charcoal. Then immediately lay the cuttings in the propagation bed, once more with a mixture of sand and peat. Strong plants will develop comparatively quickly.

Shrub begonias can be propagated from top cuttings and similarly planted in a peat-sand mixture. Keep the air moist and the temperature between 20-25°C (68-77°F).

Flowering species

The most beautiful of the indoor

begonias are those grown for their flowers. Flowering begonias have been divided into four groups.

Lorraine begonias
These are available in late autumn and winter. In light rooms—but not in sunny windows—at temperatures of about 18°C (64°F), they are easy to keep. The thick bright pink clusters of flowers complement the light green foliage. Water only moderately, and never on the leaves and flowers, or spots and rot will appear.

Begonia semperflorens

Elatior begonias
Elatior begonias are the breeders' favourites, because their magnificent flowers last so long. They flower white, yellow, pink and light and dark

red. Their natural flowering period is autumn, even winter. Elatior begonias are short-day plants: they produce their flowers when the days are shortest. The many different varieties of Elatior begonias vary in size. The pointed leaves grow up to 20 cm (9 in) long, the flowers may grow up to 8 cm (3 in).

Their flowering period may last as long as six months if they stand in a shady but light position and are not watered too much. Remove dead heads immediately and do not let seeds form.

Semperflorens begonias
Unlike other begonias, semperflorens begonias can readily be planted in outdoor beds and are tolerant of the sun. You can also of course keep them as pot plants.

The individual varieties have fleshy leaves and stems, flower very abundantly, and grow from 15-35 cm (6-14 in) high. The leaves are mostly green, quite often dark brown.

They flower until the first frosts, white and pink and sometimes bicoloured. Propagation is by tiny seeds, and is very difficult; it is really best to get your semperflorens from suppliers.

Tuberous begonias
Tuberous begonias are equally well suited for the garden, the balcony and the living room. In the garden they cannot be planted out until after all danger of frost is past. They are best grown in half-shady positions.

Tuberous begonias are divided into various groups: the large-flowered tuberous begonias have flowers that measure 12-16 cm (5-7 in) across, in red, pink, orange and white. The various forms include single, double, deckle-edged, camellia-flowered and bicoloured.

The small-flowered tuberous begonias grow no higher than 25 cm (10 in) and their flowers are from 2-4 cm ($\frac{3}{4}$-$1\frac{1}{2}$ in) across. They are particularly attractive both in bowls and beds.

The size of their flowers puts the 'Bertini' hybrids also into this group. They have small, scarlet or orange flowers with reddish leaves. Unlike the general run of tuberous begonias, they are tolerant of sunlight.

The medium-flowered begonias come from crossing large-flowered and small-flowered varieties. Their flowers may measure 5-7 cm (2-3 in) across.

Basket begonias are branching,

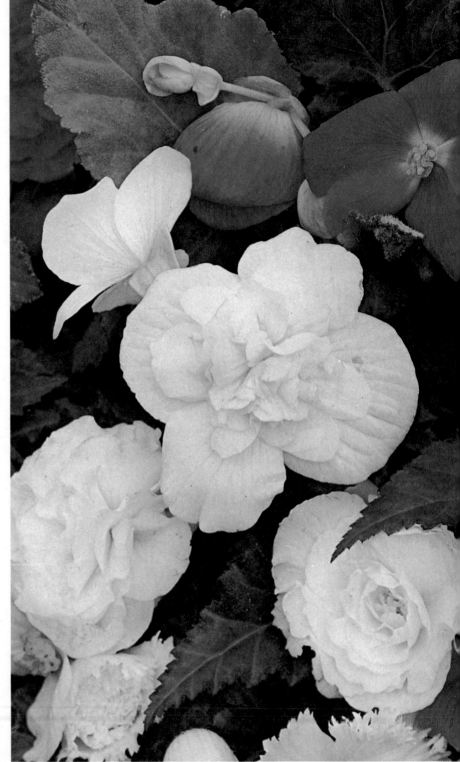

pendulous plants with pointed leaves and flowers averaging 3-6 cm (1-2 in). They do well in baskets by the window or on the balcony.

Propagation of tuberous begonias
Breeding can be successfully carried out from seeds or tubers. Set the tubers out close together in the propagation bed of a greenhouse or in a bowl in a warm room, from midwinter. The depression above each tuber tells you where the shoots will appear. The soil—a humus-rich, nutritious mixture of soil with added peat and sand—must always be kept

BELOPERONE

Shrimp Plant

Abundantly blooming evergreen sub-shrub.

Position in sun and half-shade in moist humus-rich soil.
Height up to 1 m (3 ft).
Flowering at all seasons.
Propagation by cuttings.

The shrimp plant seems to be in flower almost all the year round. Even though the white, tubular flowers with their violet spots fall prematurely, the green to reddish brown bracts can still be admired.

The only commonly found species, *Beloperone guttata*, is grown primarily for its bracts, which really do look like shrimps.

Cultivation

Young shrimp plants should be repeatedly pruned to bring them to a bushy growth. Experts recommend putting the young plants in a half-shady position and pinching off the first flowers to stimulate growth. Later you can put the shrimp plant in a light, sunny window.

Keep these subshrubs moist from spring to autumn and feed regularly. Give the plant less water in the other months, but the root ball must never be allowed to dry completely. If it does, the plant will go for a whole year before producing any more flowers. Repot every year.

Propagation

The shrimp plant is propagated by stem cuttings of half-ripe shoots, which you can take at any time in the year except during the winter, putting them under glass at a soil temperature of about 20°C (68°F). They generally root after two to three weeks, when it is advisable to plant the rooted cuttings in a pot to grow.

moist. Temperatures should range from 18-20°C (64-68°F). When the shoots appear, plant them out in the nursery bed and leave them there until they grow accustomed to the outdoor air. All hybrids must be sheltered from the sun.

In late autumn, shelter those plants

Hybrid tuberous begonias

still in the open from early frosts. After the first real frost, lift the tubers out of the ground, cut off the shoots and lay the tubers out to dry indoors. Clean off the soil and store them in dry peat at 10-12°C (50-54°F).

Beloperone guttata

BILLBERGIA

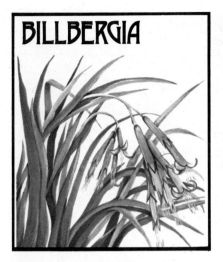

Angel's Tears, Queen's Tears

Very robust, fine flowering perennial house and greenhouse plant.

Position light, but not in full sunlight, with high humidity and plenty of warmth.
Height 50 cm (20 in).
Flowering spring or summer, according to cultivation and age.
Propagation by suckers or seeds.

The billbergias come from the tropical forests of Central and South America, where they generally live as epiphytes on trees, like orchids. They are hardy plants, popular not only for their flowers but also for their decorative, beautifully coloured elongated bracts. The inflorescence generally droops or hangs down from the stem.

Species
Billbergia nutans, sometimes known as angel's tears or queen's tears, is the species most often seen in Europe. Its narrow, dark green leaves, slightly scaly on the underside, grow from 30-50 cm (12-20 in) long and form rosettes. The nodding inflorescences have finger-long light pink or red bracts. The flowers are green, light red, and tipped with blue. The petals reflex to show golden-yellow stamens.

Billbergia pyramidalis has an upright inflorescence with pink blue-tipped flowers. The long, light green leaves form a deep tube in which to catch moisture. The woolly flower stem is enclosed by pink bracts from which the closely packed globular flower cluster extends.

Billbergia saundersii is notable chiefly for its leaves, the upper sides

Billbergia pyramidalis

of which are bright green, the undersides brownish red and covered with white spots. The lighter the position in which the plant stands, the brighter becomes the pattern on the leaves. There are two popular and pretty varieties of *Billbergia saundersii* obtainable from nurseries: 'Fascinator' and 'Fantasia'.

Cultivation
Once they have reached a certain age, billbergias will flower at any time of the year. If you keep them warm in winter, they will bloom in spring. If kept in a cool place they will not produce their flowers until the summer. They do not like glaring sunlight, but develop especially well in high humidity. Make sure when watering them that some water remains in the funnel formed by the leaves, and that the soil in the pot does not get too moist. Water minimally to prevent rotting. Repotting is best done after the flowering period. Feed about twice a week from spring well into autumn. Provide a humid atmosphere throughout the year.

Propagation
Propagation is by suckers for the hybrids, but billbergias in the greenhouse can also be propagated by seeds. This is a complicated task much better left to professionals.

BOUGAINVILLEA

Decorative shrub with big, colourful bracts.

Position in a sunny room with loam soil.
Height climbs to 6 m (20 ft).
Flowering spring.
Propagation by cuttings.

Bougainvillea is certainly one of the most beautiful plants in the Southern Hemisphere, distinguished not so much for its flowers as for its big, brightly coloured bracts. They are not easy to keep indoors, or to propagate. They need a lot of room and temperatures which vary at different seasons of the year. Climbing varieties need a framework of wires or bamboo.

Species
The branches of *Bougainvillea glabra* have thorns and oval leaves that come to a point at the tip. The little flowers, tubular and yellow, are overshadowed by striking, brilliant rose-coloured, heart-shaped bracts. This is the best species for growing in a pot as it will flower when quite small. The variety 'Sanderiana' has darker leaves and bracts. 'Alexandra' is lower growing, with purple-violet bracts.

The hairy bougainvillea, *Bougainvillea spectabilis,* has larger bracts in many colours. It climbs to 6 m (20 ft) and looks very well in a big conservatory.

Cultivation
If bougainvillea is really going to flourish, it must have plenty of air, sun and food, and in winter a position with temperatures between 8-12°C (46-54°F). During this time it needs only a little water. Many of the leaves fall in these months.

In spring the plant must be moved to a warmer place, transplanted if necessary, and sprayed in sunny weather. Later the best position is in front of the window in full sunlight, on the balcony, or in a warm spot in the garden. Water the plants once a week with a complete fertilizer solution from spring to autumn. Proper care will usually ensure flowering —but not in cold, wet, sunless years. Rich compost is the most suitable soil.

Propagation
Bougainvillea is propagated by 15 cm (6 in) cuttings of half-ripe, not yet woody, shoots. Winter is the best time, but it must be done under glass and with a bottom heat of 18°C (64°F). They will take about three weeks to root. Or take 8 cm (3 in) cuttings in summer and set them in sandy soil with a bottom heat of 20-25°C (68-77°F).

Browallia speciosa

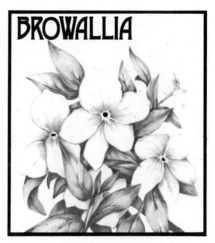

BROWALLIA

Annual garden and pot plants with pretty flowers or flowering subshrubs for living room and balcony.

Position sunny but as well sheltered as possible from the wind.
Height up to 50 cm (20 in).
Flowering all year, depending on variety.
Propagation by seeds.

Browallia is a botanical curiosity from tropical America. Three of the four species are annuals which will grow equally well in a pot or sheltered place in the garden. The fourth is a subshrub which can flower at any season of the year.

Species
The subshrub *Browallia speciosa* grows to 50 cm (20 in) high. Above its dark green leaves grow its great mauve, white-centred flowers. When grown as a house plant, this species generally bears its flowers in winter. They last until the following autumn.

Browallia viscosa flowers in late summer. Its abundant small flowers are light blue with a white eye. It has a sticky calyx.

Browallia grandiflora, a species we do not often see, grows 50 cm (20 in) high. It forms thick bushes and bears soft blue or white flowers in summer.

Cultivation
Browallia does well in standard compost and needs only moderate watering—rather less in the winter. During its growth period it likes a weekly application of fertilizer.

Propagation
To get flowers in summer, sow the very fine seed in spring at a temperature of 18°C (64°F). Prick out the seedlings later in 12 cm (5 in) pots and grow on. For winter indoor flowering, sow in autumn.

CALADIUM

Beautiful perennial tuberous plant with variegated foliage that does best in a conservatory.

Position light to half-shady in loose humus-rich soil.
Height up to 1 m (3 ft).
Propagation by division or offsets.

Caladium comprises magnificent foliaged plants of striking colour combinations. Of some 15 species that grow in the Brazilian forests, we have kept only a few. In their place we have developed sturdier decorative crosses. But even these will only disclose the full glory of their long-stemmed ornamental leaves in a warm environment. In an ordinary room the speckled or marbled patterns can seldom be retained. The darker the plant's position, the more the pattern on the leaves disappears.

Species
Caladium humboldtii is one of the few original species. The little, white-speckled, sagittate leaves grow on slender stems up to 10 cm (4 in) long. This small bushy species is relatively hardy and suited for keeping at normal room temperatures.
Most beautiful of all are the varied green, red, white and yellowish coloured leaves of the *Caladium bicolor.* These hybrids have big leaves and bear insignificant little flowers.

Cultivation
During its growth period caladium needs high humidity and a constant temperature of 20-22°C (68-72°F). The plants cannot tolerate full sunlight or draughts. For the hybrids a warm conservatory or greenhouse is essential. Keep the plants good and moist during growth and give them less water after that. When in autumn the caladium has lost its leaves, store

the dry tubers in their pots at 16-18°C (61-64°F). In late winter throw away the old soil, clean the tubers and plant them afresh in rich peat-based compost. Water them sparingly at first and only with lime-free water. As the leaves develop, gradually increase the amount of water.

Propagation
Young shoots about 10 cm (4 in) long can be carefully separated from the tubers and planted in a new pot —preferably in sandy soil. You can also propagate the plants by cutting the tubers or separating offsets. The best time is late winter. Wait till the offsets have formed their own leaflets. If you are dividing the tuber, dust the cuts carefully with finely powdered charcoal to prevent rotting. The divided parts of the tuber will root in a mixture of peat mould and sand. After rooting, plant up.

CALCEOLARIA

Slipper Flower

Annual abundantly flowering pot plant for living room or balcony.

Position half-shady, but light and cool with high humidity, in compost.
Height 20-40 cm (9-16 in).
Flowering spring to mid-autumn.
Propagation by seeds.

The calceolaria originally came from the upper regions of the Chilean and Peruvian Andes, a climate dominated by fog and heavy rainfall. To do well indoors, it must stand in similar conditions.
Of the many species of this genus of the figwort family—some are herbaceous, some subshrubs or shrubs —only the slipper flower has survived as a house plant. It is cultivated only as an annual and thrown away as soon as the abundant, long-lasting flowers are over.

Left: *Caladium*
Below: *Calceolaria* **hybrid**

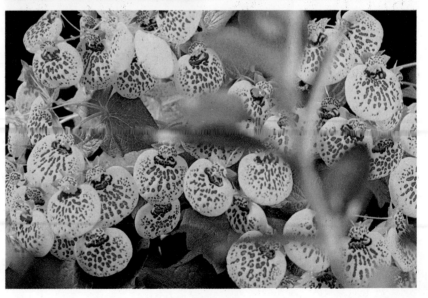

Species

Of the many varieties of calceolaria hybrids—which are called slipper flowers because the rather inflated flowers are said to look like shoes or slippers—we can distinguish four groups.

The flowers of the 'Grandiflora' hybrids are up to 5 cm (2 in) across. The plants grow to about 40 cm (16 in) with very little branching.

The 'Grandiflora Pumila Compacta' is described as a dwarf calceolaria. They too have flowers 5 cm (2 in) in diameter, but they grow no more than 20 cm (9 in) high.

Among the commonest are the 'Multiflora' hybrids, freely branching plants 30 cm (12 in) high, with flowers 3 cm (1 in) across growing out of their medium-green, velvety leaves.

Finally there is the group 'Multiflora Nana'. They are fully 5 cm (2 in) shorter than the 'Multiflora' hybrids, and their flowers are somewhat smaller. All slipper flowers have yellow or orange flowers with remarkable red-brown to red spots on the 'slippers'.

Cultivation

The calceolaria is a flower for the north window, as it dislikes direct sunlight. You can keep it best at temperatures of 10-12°C (50-54°F). Water freely if the room temperature rises, so that the evaporation chill will keep the plant cool enough. Do not let the soil dry out completely.

Propagation

Indoor gardeners are advised not to try to propagate calceolarias. You can try with seeds, which are simply laid on standard compost in summer and will—perhaps—begin to germinate at room temperatures around 15°C (59°F). But it is only a slim chance.

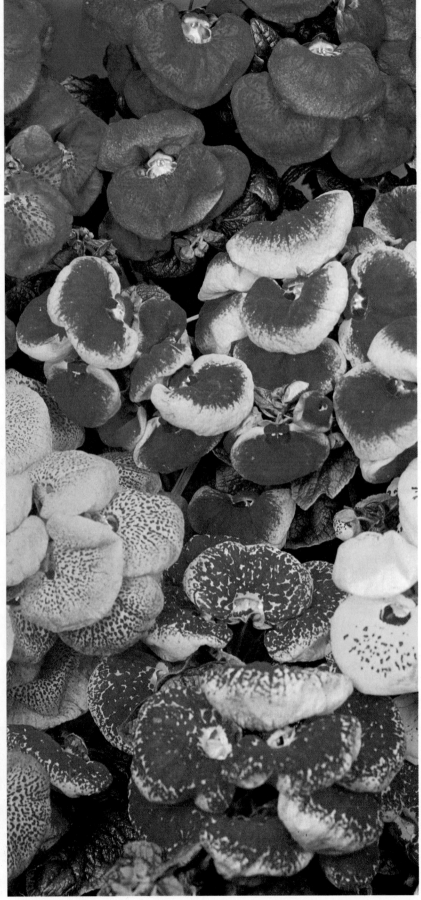

Above: *Calceolaria*
Right: *Calceolaria multiflora*

CALLISTEMON

Bottle Brush

Evergreen house plant with ornamental flowers.

Position sunny and airy in standard compost.
Height up to 1 m (3 ft).
Flowering summer.
Propagation by cuttings.

The red flowers of this decorative pot plant are unmistakable. They really do look exactly like the little brushes used to clean the inside of small bottles.

At home in Australia, some species of this genus grow as trees some 3 m (10 ft) high, but elsewhere they are kept as pot plants or in tubs. The erect stems have hard, lanceolate leaves up to 5 cm (2 in) long. The bristly inflorescence, some 10 cm (4 in) high, grows at the top of the stem. The fine, purple-red stamens grow close together, almost horizontally, from the middle of the stem. The red flowers with their yellow stamens cluster thickly.

Cultivation
Try to put your bottle brushes outdoors during the summer. They need a lot of light and air. Water them plentifully and feed them once a week. In winter give the plants a light place at a temperature of 6-8°C (45-46°F).

Propagation
You can take cuttings at any time in autumn or winter. Plant them in sand under glass at 18°C (64°F). After about four weeks, when roots have formed, put the young plants in lime-free soil and in the first period prune them fairly often.

Callistemon

CAMELLIA

Evergreen shrub with particularly lovely flowers.

Position half-shady and cool, in well-drained, lime-free soil.
Height up to 60 cm (24 in).
Flowering winter to spring.
Propagation by cuttings.

The transitory beauty of the camellia is almost proverbial. But unfortunately it almost always gives the indoor gardener endless trouble. Many species of the shrub grow wild in South Asia, where some are trees of over 15 m (50 ft) high. The most famous member of the camellia family, the tea plant, is now grown commercially.

Species
The most common domestic species are *Camellia japonica* and *Camellia williamsii,* which after some three years can grow up to 60 cm (24 in) high. The dark green of the shiny, leathery leaves makes an attractive

Camellia japonica **hybrid**

Camellia japonica 'Apollo'

contrast with the delicate, rose-like flowers. This decorative appearance has encouraged breeders over the years to produce endless new varieties, so that now we can get camellia flowers in white, pink, and bright and deep red. They include single, semidouble and double varieties, some of which are as much as 6 cm (2 in) across. The most famous is 'Chandleri Elegans', a speckled pink and white variety.

One thing is common to all varieties of every colour and shape: camellias are very sensitive to any change in their position, temperature, humidity and moisture. They drop their buds easily, especially if they do not get enough water when they are forming flower and leaf buds.

Cultivation

Camellias are at their best in the garden in warm weather. Bury the flowerpot in soil in a half-shady and airy but not too draughty corner of the garden. A place on the balcony will do as well, but do not keep them indoors.

Until late summer the root ball should be kept reasonably moist with lukewarm water in porous, limefree soil which is mixed with peat and sand. After that, you should water more sparingly so that the buds develop well, and five weeks later normal watering can be resumed. During the late winter and spring, feed the plant once every two or three weeks.

Camellias cannot stand the dry warmth of central heating. They must be kept relatively cool, at 10-12°C (50-54°F), or the flowers will not open and the buds will fall. After flowering, the plants should be kept even cooler until they are planted out in the open.

Propagation

Camellias are propagated by cuttings. But the procedure poses many problems and is rarely successful. For this reason it is best left to the professional gardener who would possess the necessary specialized equipment.

Camellia japonica 'Donation'

CAMPANULA

Bellflower

Very beautiful, mostly blue perennial or annual. Good basket plant. Only a few species are suitable for growing as house plants.

Position a sunny place out of draughts, in porous soil.
Height indoors 30 cm (12 in).
Flowering summer and early autumn.

Propagation by seeds, division or cuttings.

More than 300 different species of bellflower—which gets its name from the shape of its delicate flowers —bloom in the meadows of Europe, tall annuals and low-growing carpet plants, wood plants and mountain plants, and also annual and biennial summer flowers. Most species are grown out of doors and can be planted out in the garden as soon as warm weather arrives. Two species predominate as house plants, and both originally grew wild in the Mediterranean countries.

Species

Campanula fragilis, which can be trained as an espalier or used as a basket flower, produces its blue flowers with a white centre at the end of the shoot. It flowers in early summer, grows up to 30 cm (12 in) high, and is propagated by seeds.

Quite different from it is *Campanula isophylla,* with its pendulous stems and light blue flowers. The variety 'Alba' has white flowers and grows 30 cm (12 in) high. This variety, and this species, go equally well as climbers and in baskets. In cold weather they must be kept cool and given plenty of air. Both species have very fragile, prostrate stems, which exude a milky juice if damaged.

Cultivation

Bellflowers like a light, warm position in summer, but must not be put in direct sunlight. After the last frosts are past, towards the middle of spring, you can also put them out on the balcony or the terrace. But they will scarcely flower at all if they are in a draught. Remove old shoots carefully in early spring to stimulate a strong new growth.

It is advisable to repot them every two or three years. Clean off the old soil, but do not put the plant into too large a pot or it will use all its strength to develop its roots.

The plants cannot tolerate dry soil, so you must water them regularly. During their winter rest period, cut down the watering a little. Give a little liquid fertilizer twice a month during the growth period.

Propagation

Just before or after the growth period, sow seeds, take cuttings of nonflowering basal shoots to insert in peat or sand, or divide plants with more than a single crown. When roots form, transplant to compost.

CAPSICUM

Chillies, Red Pepper

Annual decorative plant with beautiful, brightly coloured pods.

Position half-shady and cool.
Height 20-50 cm (9-20 in).
Flowering summer.
Propagation by seeds.

Most people probably think of the pepper as a spice or a vegetable, but they can be cultivated as ornamental pot plants with small, brightly coloured fruits. There are more than twenty species in Central and South America, where pepper comes from, but we cultivate only one species for ornamental purposes, *Capsicum annuum.*

This annual plant grows as a small bush to a height of 50 cm (20 in). Insignificant, circular flowers, white or reddish in colour, grow between the little, ovate leaves, but you will see them only if you grow the plants yourself. Larger ornamental pepper plants are generally offered for sale in late autumn or winter with the brilliant fruits already ripe. You can now also get cut and dried branches which will last a long time in a vase.

There is a very small-growing variety, 'Wolbeck Gnom', which grows no higher than 20 cm (9 in), but which fruits as luxuriantly as the full-size variety.

Cultivation

You cannot go far wrong with capsicums. With regular watering and a cool, half-shady position, the fruits will retain their splendid appearance for a long time. They shrivel a little earlier in a warm room than they would outside, but even then they do not look unsightly.

Propagation

If you want to grow ornamental peppers yourself, you can buy seeds. Sow them in seed compost in spring, cover with glass and keep them in a warm place. Prick out the developing plantlets, pinch out the growing tip to make plants bush out, and plant in pots. It is best to put them in an airy position outdoors while they are in flower.

Capsicum annuum

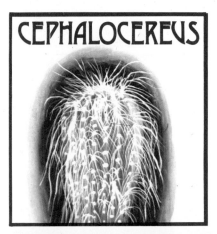

CEPHALOCEREUS

Old Man Cactus

An immense columnar cactus, which never flowers when it is kept as a house plant but is immensely popular for its truly extraordinary appearance.

Position in full sun, very warm, in poor, porous soil.
Height up to 4 m (12 ft).
Propagation by seeds.

It is not their great age that gives the old man cacti their name, but the white, fluffy down, up to 12 cm (5 in) long, that grows at the top of their stem and, allegedly, resembles the sparse and snowy hair of an extremely old man. This head of hair protects the slow-growing, many-ribbed, green plants from the fierce sun of their native Mexican mountains.

Species

Not until the old man cactus *(Cephalocereus senilis)* reaches a height of 6 m (19 ft) does it begin to flower. It then develops a sort of

Cephalocereus senilis

peruke on the top and upper sides of its stem, out of which grow pink flowers about 5 cm (2 in) long. In this form it is hardly suitable as a house plant, but even if the plants are not able to flower in the house, they still look very decorative.

Another uncommon species is *Cephalocereus chrysacanthus*, which differs from *Cephalocereus senilis* in having wavy yellow hair and, in addition, it has yellow thorns, which grow sideways and downwards. This species has reddish-coloured flowers that open up only at night. It grows up to a height of 4 m (13 ft).

Cultivation

The old man cactus does well on a sunny windowsill in poor and porous soil mixed with small limestone chippings. Do not water too often or the plant begins to rot, but spray the plants now and again. The 'old man' should be kept at temperatures of about 15°C (59°F) in winter. Like real old men, it is rather sensitive to draughts, so never put it by an open window.

Younger specimens should be repotted every spring. Be careful not to damage the root system. The repotted plant is sometimes glad of some support, but do not stick the canes into the soil or you may easily damage the roots and the plant will begin to wilt.

Propagation

Propagation is for the enthusiast. Seeds can be sown in slightly sandy soil, but the results are fairly unpredictable and may prove a disappointment for the amateur gardener.

Chamaedorea elegans

CHAMAEDOREA

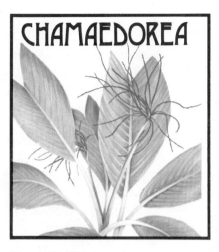

Mountain Palm

Evergreen, flowering miniature tree.

Position light places, but must be protected from direct sunlight from early spring to autumn.
Height up to 2 m (6 ft).
Flowering the whole year.
Propagation by seeds.

The attractive, evergreen mountain palm has become increasingly popular as a house plant over the past decade. Originally it came from the mountains of South and Central America.

Species

The most common is *Chamaedorea elegans*, sometimes sold as *Neanthe bella*. Its leaves grow to 1 m (3 ft) in length and are pinnate, with 14 leaflets. It begins to flower as a very small plant, male and female flowers appearing on different plants. Less common is *Chamaedorea metallica*, which has large, incised leaves.

Cultivation

The mountain palm needs a fairly light position, but dislikes direct sunlight. It needs plenty of water in summer, so water it complete with the pot once a week. Spray the leaves now and then, or leave it out in the warm rain.

In winter, its rest period, it needs only a little water and no feeding at all. Sponge the leaves every week with soft warm water, and if the air in the room is dry, spray the leaves regularly or the tips of the leaves will turn light yellow.

Propagation

To propagate, sow some seeds in a mixture of sand and peat. They will germinate comparatively easily in a moist heat, and grow quickly.

CHLOROPHYTUM

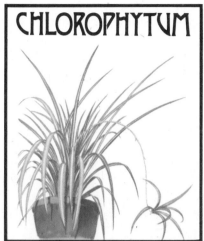

Spider Plant

Trouble-free house plant with tiny insignificant flowers and striking pendulous scapes. Good basket plant.

Position light, but not in direct sunlight, in ordinary potting compost. Should not stand in water.
Height up to 20 cm (9 in). Hanging scapes up to 1 m (3 ft).
Propagation by side shoots or division.

The spider plant is a rewarding house plant. It will tolerate the dry air in offices as well as the steam of the kitchen, it comes to no harm if you sometimes forget to water it, and it is so helpful in producing side shoots for propagation that even a complete beginner at gardening will have absolutely no trouble with this South African member of the lily family. It will survive in poorly lit positions but will not produce side shoots.

Species

The most common spider plants are almost without exception the variety 'Variegatum' of the species *Chlorophytum comosum*. The narrow lanceolate leaves, growing up to 40 cm (16 in) long, are light green with creamy white stripes and white edges. The true species, often referred to as *Chlorophytum capense*, has only green leaves. The insignificant little flowers develop in early summer on long scapes, on which young rooting plants also appear and can be potted up.

The spider plant has a short earth stem and thick, fleshy, tuberous roots with which the plant anchors itself firmly in the ground so that it can bear the considerable weight of the young hanging shoots.

Cultivation

In the growth period, the spider plant should be watered regularly and fertilized once a week. On the whole it is better to water too little rather than too much, since the plant is not particularly fond of standing water and acid soil.

In winter, its rest period, you can stop feeding altogether and cut down the watering, depending on what sort of position the plant has. If it is in dry air, you should water it more than you would in a cool summer. The spider plant can usually tolerate temperatures of 10°C (50°F) and below for quite a time without ill effect.

The plant grows quickly and so should be repotted every two years. Use a mineral-rich, fairly loamy soil in a wide but not too deep pot.

Propagation

The simplest way to propagate the spider plant is to separate the rooted runner from the scape and put it in a pot, keeping it fairly warm at first. After only a few days you can put the new plant in its final position. Young plants should be fed often.

Chlorophytum comosum **'Variegatum'**

CISSUS

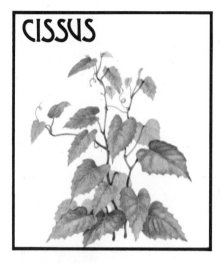

Kangaroo Vine

Evergreen climbing shrub with unremarkable flowers.

Position half-shady to shady, in loamy, humus-rich soil.
Height climbing up to 3 m (10 ft).
Propagation by cuttings.

These shrubs, which originally grew in Australia and the tropical parts of Africa and South America, presumably got their name because many species are outstanding climbers. There are also quite a lot of succulent species of cissus, both climbers and nonclimbers. But they are rarities as house plants.

Species
The most widely distributed species is called the kangaroo vine, *Cissus antarctica.* It is a rapidly growing evergreen shrub which climbs with tendrils. It has broad, pointed leaves with a toothed edge on which the veins are distinctly marked. This slender, green plant is so popular

because it is completely undemanding and can also tolerate considerable fluctuations of temperature. You can keep the kangaroo vine just as well in a heated room as in a cool entrance hall where the temperatures may sometimes drop to around 5°C (41°F).

Cissus discolor boasts leaves with all sorts of designs on them in red, silver-grey or yellowish green. This decorative semievergreen climber should be kept at a steady temperature of 20°C (68°F). It is beautiful as a hanging basket plant.

Cultivation
The cissus must have no direct sun and above all must not 'get their feet wet'. Certainly you should water them well, but never let water collect at their base, especially in winter, or they will get yellow spots on their leaves. The splendidly coloured *Cissus discolor,* with its pointed leaves up to 15 cm (6 in) long, can be made to flower and then produce small blue berries if the temperature of the room is kept constant. From spring to autumn the cissus must be fed once a week. Repotting in the spring is recommended but is often very difficult if the plants are trained up a trellis. If they are not, you should put a few bamboo canes in the bowl for the tendrils to climb along.

Propagation
The propagation of cissus is simple. Take cuttings in spring and keep them under glass or plastic foil where they will soon root. Cuttings of *Cissus discolor* must be kept at at least 20°C (68°F) while those of the kangaroo vine grow well at 15°C (59°F).

Cissus antarctica

CITRUS

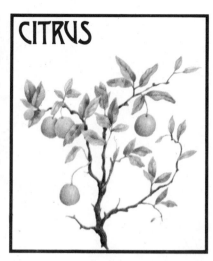

Evergreen tree or shrub with scented flowers.

Position in direct sun or in half-shade. Keep cool and dry during the winter.
Height 30-120 cm (12-48 in).
Flowering in spring.
Propagation by seeds and half-ripe cuttings.

The citrus shrubs and trees have dark evergreen foliage, and the white or yellowish flowers have a penetrating, bittersweet scent. The small fruit of these highly attractive house plants—limes, lemons, oranges or mandarins—cannot of course compare with the citrus fruits in the shops. They are grown for purely decorative purposes, not as a food source for they have no flavour at all, but their scent is lovely.

Species
We have cultivated the orange *(Citrus sinensis)* for a long time. The low trees or bushes, which originally came to Europe from eastern Asia, often have thorns, and oval, scented leaves up to 10 cm (4 in) in length, on long stalks. The white, sweet-smelling flowers are traditionally worn or carried by brides in many European countries. The fruits are round and, not surprisingly, orange-coloured.

The lemon *(Citrus limon)* is a small, thorny tree with light green, oval leaves. The oval yellow fruits are pointed. The commonest house plant of this family is the dwarf orange or calamondin *(Citrus mitis).* Its orange-coloured fruits hang down in bunches between the rather leathery leaves, often beside new flowers. The dwarf orange takes nearly a year to ripen and has a faintly limey flavour.

Citrus mitis

Cultivation

If the citrus trees like plenty of light during the summer, they are just as keen in winter to have a cool, dry position. The winter temperature must not exceed 5°C (41°F) or the plant will immediately shed its leaves. Even the root ball must be allowed to get quite dry then.

You can put citrus trees outdoors or on the balcony in summer, or by an open window. Give them plenty of fertilizer and water until mid-summer; for best results the water should not be too hard. Spray when you see flower buds and when in flower to help set fruit.

Repot the little trees or shrubs in winter only every four to six years as they do not like root disturbance. Choose pots that are not too big, and reduce the old root system a little with a knife. The crown can also be cut back in spring if necessary, but you should wait for at least a year after repotting.

Propagation

You can propagate by seeds, which generally germinate very easily in a mixture of leaf mould and turf, or by half-ripe cuttings. But do not expect too much. You will raise only 'wild trees', as they are called, which hardly ever flower or fruit.

Citrus sinensis

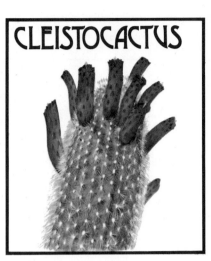

CLEISTOCACTUS

Attractive columnar cactus with many decorative flowers.

Position light to sunny, warm or cool according to the season.
Height up to 2 m (6 ft).
Flowering spring or summer, according to species.
Propagation by cuttings or seeds.

The slender, profusely flowering cleistocacti make popular show pieces in any collection. The genus comprises a number of species that come from the mountainous regions of South America. The columns rise directly out of the ground. In time they grow to as much as 2 m (6 ft) high and have tubular flowers.

Species

The bright red, slightly curved tubular flowers of the species *Cleistocactus baumannii* appear early in the spring. This species grows up to 2 m (6 ft) tall and is densely covered with whitish thorns.

Connoisseurs rate *Cleistocactus strausii* as one of the most beautiful cacti. Its great charm lies in the striking contrast between the snow white spines and the glowing dark red flowers, which can grow as much as 8 cm (3 in) long.

Cleistocactus wendlandiorum (also known as *Cleistocactus flavescens*) is smaller, and the spines are creamy yellow. It has orange-coloured flowers, bent at right angles.

Cultivation

In summer the cleistocactus must be kept as warm as possible. Even direct sunlight does it no harm. The important thing is to give it plenty of water. In winter bring the plants indoors to a light and cool place, watering only a little so that the soil does not dry out.

Propagation

Take cuttings or sow seeds.

Cleistocactus strausii

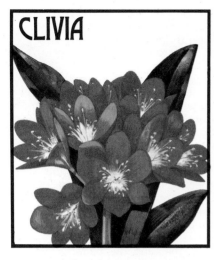

CLIVIA

Evergreen house plant with magnificent flowers.

Position light, but not in direct sunlight, in fairly loamy soil.
Height up to 60 cm (24 in).
Flowering spring or autumn.
Propagation by offsets or by seeds.

Clivia was once a popular house plant, but now we see it less often. It needs a great deal of attention all year round if you want it to flower. Clivia has still not abandoned the lifelong habits of its native South Africa. But the plants are long-lived and can, with the right treatment, often be persuaded to flower twice a year.

Of the three species of clivia we grow only one, *Clivia miniata*. The evergreen leaves, growing at ground level, are slightly broadened at the base and form a funnel with a light throat. Up to twenty orange flowers, of very different sizes, can grow in a single cluster. Clivia does not have a real bulb but a bulbous stem surrounded by dense leaf sheaths.

Cultivation
Clivia is very fussy about its position. Year in, year out, it must stand in the same place and with the same side facing the light. The best place is in a window that only gets direct sunlight first thing in the morning or in the evening. It wants temperatures of about 15°C (59°F) and tolerates dry air well.

If you really want to enjoy clivia flowers, you must be careful about watering. Clivia dislikes standing water. In its rest period, from autumn to winter, it must stand in dry earth. Wipe the leaves with a wet cloth from time to time during this period. Feed every ten days from late winter through summer. Young plants

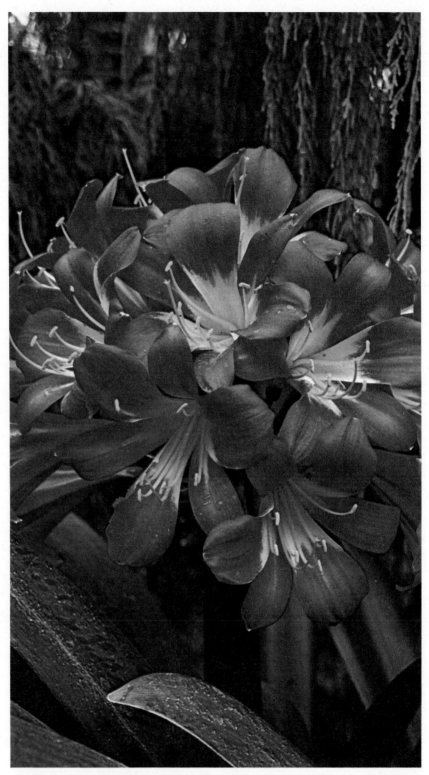

Clivia miniata

should be repotted every year, but old plants only seldom—particularly if you want a dense display.

Do not begin feeding and watering until the flower stem has reached the height of the leaves. At this period you should keep the plant warm at 18°C (66°F), or the flowers will appear inside the funnel of leaves and never blossom fully.

Propagation
A second growth from the seeds that form in the flowers of clivia is unlikely, but you can buy seeds to sow. Or use the abundant suckers. Choose those with four or five leaves and plant them in a mixture of sand and peat.

COCOS

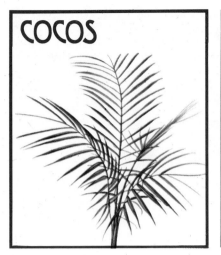

Small, decorative indoor palm with attractive pinnate leaves.

Position shady and warm, in slightly sandy garden soil.
Height up to 150 cm (59 in).
Propagation by seeds.

Even in its natural habitat in Brazil the cocos palm grows no higher than 150 cm (59 in).

Species
Of the two species, we cultivate only one, *Cocos weddelianum,* as a house plant. The plant takes 20 years to reach its maximum height and is usually seen as a small plant about 30 cm (12 in). The short stem is often enveloped by brownish fibres. The flexible leaf stalks bear opposite, narrow pinnate leaves. There will often be as many as 200 of these to a frond. The upper surface is dark green and the underside is whitish.

Cultivation
The cocos palm must stand in a shady, warm place in the window all year round. Even in winter the temperature should never be below 18°C (64°F). Always keep the plant moist and, if possible, keep some water in a dish under the pot. Keep out of draughts.
   The cocos palm thrives best in a high, narrow palm pot. Take the greatest care not to damage the roots when repotting, or the plant will quickly die.

Propagation
Propagation by freshly imported seeds is possible but difficult for the amateur gardener. You must have very high bottom heat and humidity. It is easier to buy young plants from a nursery than to try and raise from seed yourself.

CODIAEUM

Croton, South Sea Laurel

Evergreen house plant with splendidly coloured leaves.

Position in half-shady and warm places with high humidity.
Height up to 1 m (3 ft).
Propagation by cuttings.

Croton is a plant grown exclusively for its foliage. Remove the flowers at once, for they only take strength from the plant. At home in tropical Southeast Asia and the Pacific Islands it reaches a height of 3 m (10 ft). Elsewhere it reaches 1 m (3 ft).
   Codiaeum variegatum, the only species, has endless hybrids of disparate appearance. The leaves of the varieties are quite different both in shape and in colour.
   The colours range from whitish to dark red, and the patterns on the leaves from patches and spots to fine linear designs. The only common

Codiaeum variegatum

factor is leathery surfaces of the leaves.

Cultivation
The croton can safely be put on the ledge of a south-facing window. It needs protection only against glaring sunlight; but a lot of light is necessary if the leaves are to keep their colour and patterns. Also, the humidity must be kept constant. Spray the leaves frequently, and keep the soil ball moist. Feed once a week. In winter the croton needs a room where the temperature is not below 18°C (64°F). Give it a little less water at this time.

Propagation
The chances of successful propagation are not great. But if you want to try, take strong, ripened cuttings in the greenhouse in early spring, dip the tips in powdered charcoal to stem the flow of latex, and insert them in a mixture of peat and sand with high bottom heat and humidity.

Codiaeum variegatum

Codiaeum variegatum

COFFEA

Coffee Plant

Undemanding and rewarding evergreen house plant. Established plants have scented flowers and decorative fruits.

Position half shady and moderately warm, in loamy soil.
Height 80-200 cm (32-72 in).
Flowering summer.
Propagation by seeds and cuttings.

Many flower lovers have no idea that the coffee plant can flourish not only on a plantation but in the living room. You cannot buy them as pot plants, but you can grow fine specimens from fresh seed.

Grown commercially, they reach a height of 5 m (16 ft), but the house plants you grow yourself will rarely grow more than 1 m (3 ft) high. They

Coffea arabica

can reach twice that height after a few years.

Of the 50 or so species, the best known is *Coffea arabica*. Widely distributed as a commercial and ornamental plant, it has shiny sinuate leaves that grow transversely on horizontal branches.

After three or four years the first little white, stellate flowers appear in summer. They smell like jasmine. After the flowers the tiny red berries ripen, each one containing two seeds. Commercially these are harvested as coffee beans; the amateur gardener can use them as seeds for sowing.

Cultivation
The coffee plant must be sheltered from strong sunlight at a steady temperature. It feels best in summer at 16-20°C (61-68°F) and in winter at 14-16°C (51-61°F). Water generously during the hot seasons, less later on, but never let the loamy soil dry out. If the air in the room is dry, spray frequently. Also, in spring and summer, put some fertilizer with low lime content into lukewarm water for watering.

Propagation
The seeds of the coffee plant must be put in moist sand as soon as they are ripe and kept under glass at a temperature of 25°C (77°F) until they germinate. When little plantlets have formed, pot them and treat them the same as older plants. If you already have a coffee plant, you can take stem cuttings in the spring, let them root in moist sand and plant them later.

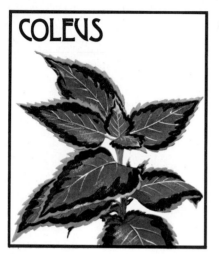

COLEUS

Flame Nettle

Very popular house plant with magnificent ornamental leaves. Generally a perennial.

Position in a sunny room or in a box on a balcony facing south.
Height according to species, from 15-70 cm (6-28 in). Flowering mid- to late summer.
Propagation by cuttings or seeds.

The charm of the flame nettles lies not in their quite insignificant blue or mauve flowers but in their magnificently patterned, brilliantly coloured leaves. Only young plants have these pretty leaves; the leaves of older plants are crumpled and wrinkled and their coloured patterns already faded. The flame nettle has many species of quite different appearance. Some of them are only annuals, some are subshrubs that can form fine bushes.

Species
The *Coleus blumei* hybrids are grown mainly for their wonderful foliage. Different varieties reach heights of from 30-60 cm (12-24 in) and all are perennial. They have angular stalks, woody at the lower end, and oval leaves that come to a point, with all sorts of colour patterns. Since these plants are grown primarily for their foliage, it is best to take off the flowers, which would otherwise weaken the growth. *Coleus fredericii,* from Africa, forms a shrub 1 m (3 ft) high with light coloured leaves. This annual produces dark blue flowers.

Cultivation
The flame nettle needs a light room, but not too warm. In summer it also does well in a windowbox or on the balcony and can even be planted outdoors in the full sun; but in rainy summers a disaster is inevitable. The flame nettle should be put in a fairly rich potting compost and watered and sprayed frequently with tepid, previously boiled water. It easily wilts if it does not get enough water. It should have liquid fertilizer once a week from spring to autumn. Pinch out growing tips regularly to make the plant bushy.

The flame nettle passes the cold weather best in a kitchen window in moist air. Otherwise keep the plants fairly dry, at a temperature of about 10°C (50°F), and cut them back firmly after flowering. Occasionally spray lightly in the morning and put them out in the sun.

Propagation
Do not let flame nettles grow too old.

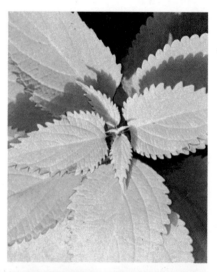

Right: *Coleus blumei* **hybrid**
Below: *Coleus blumei* **hybrids**

It is best to propagate them before they get unsightly. Take cuttings of your favourites, which will grow readily in a mixture of peat and sand kept constantly moist. It is even enough to put the cuttings with their lower ends in a glass of water. They will form roots in as little as 14 days.

Seedlings can be raised from seed in a warm room. But you may get some surprises—hardly any two of the plants coming up will resemble each other.

Plant both cuttings and seedlings separately in small pots with peat-based or standard compost, and pot out gradually until they stand in a 15 cm (7 in) pot. Prune them once or twice to get shapely branching.

Coleus blumel **hybrid**

Coleus blumei

COLUMNEA

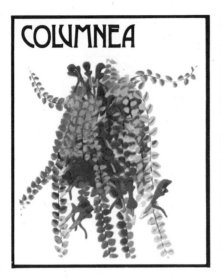

Evergreen, abundantly flowering basket plant.

Position light to half-shady, out of direct sun and draughts.
Height up to 120 cm (48 in).
Flowering at all seasons, according to species.
Propagation by cuttings.

The *Columnea* species, which are at home in the tropical rain forests of Central America, have become quite robust hanging plants, with their leathery thickly growing leaves and brightly-coloured profusion of flowers.

Species
Magnificent red flowers with a yellow spot gleam from the dark green foliage of *Columnea gloriosa* from autumn to spring. The little, hairy, almost round leaves grow on long

Columnea gloriosa

stalks that hang down at an angle. This species must be kept in a conservatory.

Columnea hirta has a long flowering period but is very sensitive to light. The pale red flowers grow on long stems covered with reddish brown hairs.

The *Columnea vedrariensis* hybrid is very robust, flowering at temperatures around 17°C (62°F). You most often find them in nurseries under the name of *Columnea kewensis*. Its narrow, rounded leaves with a little point are brownish green on top and reddish underneath. The bright red flowers bloom from late winter to early spring.

Cultivation
The columnea is intolerant of direct sunlight and especially sensitive to draughts. When the buds begin to form, the plants want temperatures around 20°C (68°F) and high humidity; but after this they want rather lower temperatures. Do not get water on the plant or it will cause yellow spots. Use only softened water and lime-free food. Repot into flat pots after flowering. Like many plants that like a high humidity, columnea may be attacked by the soft-skin mite. Young plants are in particular danger and should be kept from other plants till you have examined them and ensure that they are free from pests.

Propagation
Cut a shoot into several pieces about 5 cm (2 in) long and plant them in a propagator at 20-22°C (68-72°F). Propagation by seeds is difficult and not recommended for the amateur gardener.

CORDYLINE

Cabbage Palm, Flaming Dragon Tree, Scarlet Aspidistra

Difficult indoor shrub with colourful, ornamental foliage and insignificant small flowers that appear only on older plants.

Position half-shady and warm, with high humidity, in sandy soil.
Height up to 2 m (6 ft).
Propagation by cuttings.

In tropical parts of India and Australia some 15 species of the cordyline grow as trees or shrubs. Outstanding examples will sometimes grow to over 4 m (13 ft) in height. They are popular elsewhere as ornamental plants with pretty, brightly coloured leaves. These leaves, narrow and sword-shaped, grow on a small stem and branch out just above the ground to make a

Below: *Cordyline* (right) and its relative *Dracaena* (left)

dense crown. The small, insignificant flowers are found on older plants.

Species
Cordyline terminalis is one of the most beautiful ornamental house plants. Long, stalked leaves grow on the slender stem to a length of 50 cm (20 in). Their original colour is green, but breeders have produced many varieties with particularly beautifully coloured leaves—most of them multi-coloured—in shades of green, red and white.

The white to reddish flowers of the older trees grow in panicles and are succeeded by little red berries. In greenhouses with tropical conditions the shrubs can be grown to 2 m (6 ft). The lower-growing, red-leaved varieties are better suited for a living room.

The fragrant white-flowering *Cordyline australis* with leaves up to 1 m (3 ft) long and the violet-flowering *Cordyline stricta* with broader, shorter leaves are easier to grow and just as attractive as the more temperamental species.

Cultivation
If you want to get lasting pleasure from *Cordyline terminalis,* you must have a warm conservatory with very high humidity. The plants must stand in a light but not sunny place at temperatures between 22-28°C (72-82°F). Keep the soil pretty moist and feed once a week.

The species *Cordyline australis* and *Cordyline stricta* particularly like a half-shady place on the balcony during the summer. Shelter them carefully from draughts, and give them plenty of water. Water them less in winter and keep them away from frost at temperatures of up to 10°C (50°F).

Propagation
You should propagate cordyline only if you have a conservatory or a greenhouse. Top cuttings need very high bottom heat—about 35°C (95°F)—and moist air to make them take root in humus-rich soil under glass.

Crossandra infundibuliformis

CROSSANDRA

Charming, abundantly flowering, subshrub.

Position very light, but not in direct sun.
Height up to 1 m (3 ft).
Flowering spring and summer.
Propagation by cuttings.

Although the crossandra came to Europe from the tropical forests of India and Sri Lanka as long ago as the beginning of the 19th century, it was quickly forgotten again, and it is only in the last few years that interest has revived in it, the main reason being that it was long looked on as a very difficult plant.

Species
Crossandra infundibuliformis is a low-growing plant with dark green leaves that flowers in spring and summer. Its salmon-pink flowers have a distinctly one-sided corolla. The flower stems, 10 cm (4 in) long and growing in the axils, carry green bracts.

'Mona Wallhed' is a particularly easy, robust and compact variety. *Crossandra subacaulis* is still quite rare. It has yellow-white flowers which do not appear until mid-summer.

Cultivation
A first essential for cultivation is enough moisture in the soil and in the air. After the rest period in autumn and early winter feed once a week until late summer. Plants that have filled their pots with their root system should be repotted in standard compost.

Propagation
Take cuttings in winter and keep them under glass; plant them out in summer.

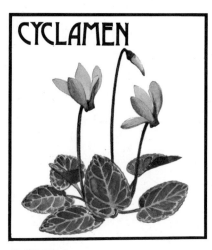

CYCLAMEN

Sowbread

Tuberous plant, one of the most popular and rewarding house plants.

Position in a light, cool room.
Height 10-20 cm (4-9 in).
Flowering in spring.
Propagation by seeds.

The cyclamen is one of the most popular house plants. There are so many different forms of flower among the 14 or so species that a whole battery of cyclamens could never get boring or monotonous.

Species

The famous indoor cyclamen—*Cyclamen persicum* (otherwise *Cyclamen puniceum*, *Cyclamen latifolium*), a tender plant suitable for potting —is a relative of wild flowers that grow in the mountain woods of Iran, Greece and Asia Minor. It has rounded leaves and produces large, attractive rose, salmon pink or white flowers.

There is also a great range of cultivars. You can choose between strangely patterned leaves, large or small, scented or unscented flowers, smooth hoods or fringed heads on the flowers, single or double, bordered and striped blooms.

Cyclamen persicum

Cultivation

When you buy cyclamens, make sure that all the flowers are not already out. There ought to be a good number of buds still hidden among the leaves.

Too much warmth, and an oppressive, dry position are bad for the cyclamen. It likes temperatures around 14°C (57°F), with plenty of light and air.

Water cyclamens carefully with softish water. If possible, water them so that the corm stays dry, or it may rot. Feed with liquid fertilizer every week or two.

Faded, yellowing leaves can be removed by twisting them away from the corm. If you cut them off, the corm easily begins to rot.

Propagation

The corms of cyclamens do not divide or produce others so propagation is possible only by seeds, but it is not too difficult. They should bloom within 12 to 15 months.

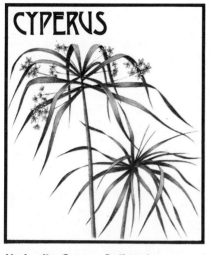

CYPERUS

Umbrella Grass, Galingale

Very tough, moisture-loving, freely growing perennial ornamental grass with pretty flowers.

Position half-shady, cool or warm according to species, in normal or very moist, loamy soil.
Height 30-150 cm (12-60 in).
Flowering spring to autumn, according to species.
Propagation by division or cuttings.

Cyperus is a house plant as unusual as it is long-lasting, notable for the abundance of its graceful leaves. Over 500 different species occur in the tropical and subtropical regions of Africa and America. Some of the species can grow to 5 m (16 ft) in height.

The low-growing species are widespread as house plants. The narrow leaves clustered at the top of the thin, flexible stalk look like a feather duster. Amid these strong heads of foliage small whitish flowers grow in spring and summer in ears, or umbels.

Species
The best known species of cyperus, the umbrella grass *(Cyperus alternifolius)*, comes from swampy areas in the Malagasy Republic. It grows to a height of 150 cm (60 in) and has long, pointed leaves, 20 cm (9 in) long and never more than 1 cm ($\frac{1}{2}$ in) wide.

Very similar, but only about 30 cm (12 in) high, is the dwarf species, *Cyperus gracilis*.

Cultivation
Cyperus alternifolius is among the most versatile of house plants. Being a true swamp grass, it grows well in an aquarium or at the edge of a pool. If you want to put it on the window ledge, you must put its pot into a high-sided container filled with water and spray the plant regularly. The same applies to *Cyperus gracilis*.

All species of cyperus can tolerate temperatures up to 25°C (77°F) but should be kept out of the full glare of the sun. In winter they can do with less warmth, the lower limit being about 10°C (50°F).

Propagation
Cyperus is easy to propagate by division. Divide the plants carefully at the roots and replant. With *Cyperus alternifolius* and *Cyperus gracilis* you can also take cuttings—the head of a leaf with about 5 cm (2 in) of stalk. Plant them in damp sand or lay them in water. When they root, plant them in small pots.

Cyperus gracilis

Harry Smith

DIEFFENBACHIA

Dumb Cane

Extremely poisonous evergreen house plant with attractive ornamental leaves.

Position in light, but not sunny, places with high humidity.
Height up to 1 m (3 ft).
Propagation by cuttings and air-layering.

Dieffenbachia, which comes from the forests of tropical America, is among the most popular house plants in the world on account of its beautifully patterned leaves. It is named after Josef Dieffenbach (d.1863) who was the head gardener at the Vienna Botanical Gardens for many years. Its little flowers, rather like those of the arum lily, are not particularly attractive and can only be seen on older or greenhouse plants.

Take great care with this plant, however, as it is·extremely poisonous. Biting any part of it causes intense pain and prevents speech for several days. Keep hands away from eyes when handling it, and wash hands well afterwards.

Species

Dieffenbachia bausei, a robust species and very widespread, has yellow-green leaves of up to 25 cm (10 in) long, with a lot of dark green spots and rather fewer white ones. There is a narrow green stripe round the edge of the leaves, which tend to darken as the plant grows older.

Dieffenbachia macrophylla has no pattern on the leaves. It is a strong grower, forming a green stem on which the dark green, rather leathery leaves grow. This species does best in deep shadow.

Dieffenbachia maculata (also called *Dieffenbachia picta*) comes from Brazil. It grows a powerful stem sometimes as much as 1 m (3 ft) tall. The oblong leaves are patterned in white and yellow. Many varieties of this species have been grown. The best known are 'Jenmannii', 'Mag-nifica' and 'Julius Roehrs'. Even experts are sometimes hard put to tell the difference between them.

Flat, only slightly arched leaves distinguish *Dieffenbachia seguine*, the original dumb cane. Its leaves and leaf stems are stripy and spotted with white. The best known varieties are 'Irrorata' and 'Nobilis'.

Cultivation

Unfortunately dieffenbachia generally loses its lower leaves when kept in an ordinary room where constant humidity and room temperature are difficult to ensure. Protect the plants from direct sunlight, and from spring on, when they begin to shoot, feed them well and give them plenty of water—a dry root ball results in brown edges on the leaves. In winter the plant can do with a temperature of about 16°C (61°F). The rest period

Left: *Dieffenbachia seguine*
Below: *Dieffenbachia*

starts in autumn, when you should water sparingly and feed hardly at all. Repot every spring.

Propagation
Top cuttings are the best method of propagation, because with the same operation you can rejuvenate older plants that have grown bare at the bottom of the stem. You can also plant or lay stem cuttings, preferably with a leaf on them, in heat of 30°C (89°F). A humus-rich soil is best.

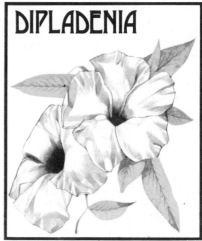

DIPLADENIA

Profusely flowering, creeping evergreen house plant.

Position warm and sunny places with high humidity.
Height on supports, up to 120 cm (47 in).
Flowering spring to autumn.
Propagation by cuttings.

In the last century dipladénia was a favourite house plant, but later became a rarity found only in botanical gardens. Its renewed popularity is due to Danish gardeners, who have succeeded in reducing the luxuriantly climbing plants to a more compact growth.

Species
Dipladenia boliviensis bears white flowers with a yellow throat, growing in clusters, three or four of them together. Bright green leaves, 8 cm (3 in) long, grow on slender stems.

The striking flowers of *Dipladenia sanderi* grow together in pairs. The flowers are up to 7 cm (3 in) across, pink with a yellow throat. You can now buy pretty hybrids of this species, notably 'Amoena', bright pink, and the salmon-coloured 'Rosea'.

Dipladenia splendens produces flowers that are pink inside and white outside; they bloom in summer. The leaves of this species grow up to 15 cm (6 in) long. In cultivation it is usually twined round cane supports as a pot plant or trained on strings or wires against a greenhouse wall. It will flower only when about 20 cm (9 in) high.

Cultivation
These shrubs and subshrubs, which originated in tropical America, need a lot of water but cannot tolerate standing in continuous damp. So

you must ensure that the soil is well drained. Feed them once a fortnight. They have a rest period from autumn through winter, when they should be watered only a little, just enough to prevent the plants from flagging.

It has always proved best to spray the plants from time to time, even in winter. Repot in spring in medium-sized pots to ensure they flower readily.

Propagation
Take cuttings of young lateral shoots in spring or older stem cuttings with two leaves in summer and insert in peat and sand at 16-18°C (61-64°F). When rooted, pot in potting compost. The leaves of the rooted cuttings will be pale at first but take on colour during subsequent months.

Dipladenia splendens

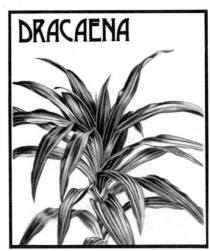

DRACAENA

Dragon Tree

Tropical tree or shrub, kept as foliage plant. It seldom flowers.

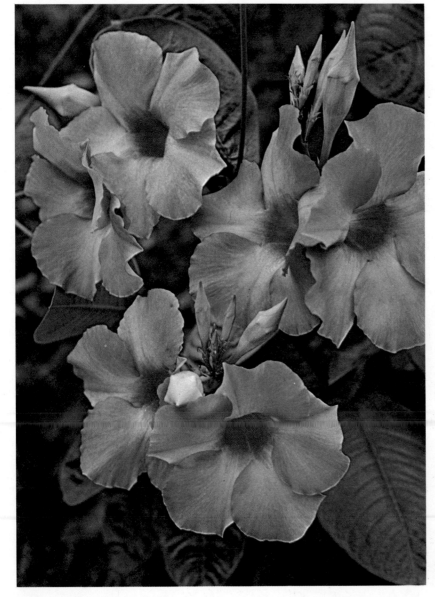

Position half-shady and warm, with high humidity.
Height 2 m (6 ft).
Propagation by cuttings or seeds.

Tourists in the Canary Islands who buy little green foliage trees in the market are usually unaware that these will grow into trees 20 m (65 ft) high. Part of the characteristic scene of the Canary Islands, *Dracaena draco*, the dragon tree, can grow at an astonishing rate. Of course that happens only in the tropics. But with proper care dragon trees indoors will grow to a height of 2 m (6 ft) and live for years. There is a specimen in the Canary Islands said to be over 1000 years old.

Green-leaved species
The true dragon tree · (*Dracaena draco*) is a tall-stemmed tree with grey-green leaves growing close together. They grow to a length of 50 cm (20 in) and come to a sword-shaped point. *Dracaena hookeriana* has a short, often branched stem. The narrow, leathery leaves grow up to 70 cm (28 in) long and have lighter borders. A favourite is the variety 'Latifolia', with leaves up to 8 cm (3 in) wide, as well as the brightly leaved 'Variegata'.

Coloured-leaved species
Dracaena deremensis has long, pointed, shining dark green leaves about 50 cm (20 in) long. At first the leaves stick straight out, but later they hang down a little. This species from East Africa is not so often seen in the nurseries as its bright-leaved varieties 'Bausei' and 'Warneckii', whose dark green leaves have white-green stripes.

Dracaena fragrans develops tall stems; its dark green leaves reach a length of 75 cm (30 in) and are very narrow and drooping, hanging rather crookedly. All the varieties have foliage with white or yellowish stripes or edges.

The shrub-like *Dracaena god-seffiana* comes from Zaire. It is an abundantly branching bush. Its bright green leaves grow together in groups on the upright branches and display curious white spots. This species comes into flower when quite young. The yellow-green, strongly scented flowers give way to pretty red berries. Well known varieties are 'Florida Beauty', with large white spots on the leaves, and 'Kelleri', with marbled leaves.

The smallest species, *Dracaena*

sanderiana, has lovely white-patterned foliage and is popular among flower lovers, because it is easy to look after. This species has narrow leaves up to 20 cm (9 in) long growing horizontally from a thin, short stem; the leaves have stripes of white and silver-grey.

Cultivation
In a normal living room only the green-leaved species and the variety *Dracaena fragrans* 'Rothiana' can be kept without special equipment. They need light and winter temperatures at 12-14°C (54-58°F). The other species and varieties are more awkward to cultivate, because of their temperature and humidity requirements. One exception to this, however, is the shrubby *Dracaena godseffiana*.

Put dragon trees in a light, warm place but remember that they do not like direct sunlight. Rich soil and regular watering and spraying does a lot to make them grow well. During the autumn and winter give them less water. Apart from the species mentioned above and the variety 'Rothiana', do not keep the plants in rooms under 18-20°C (64-68°F). These plants really need to live in the conservatory if they are to be successful.

The dragon tree should be repotted into a medium-sized container every two or three years. Be careful not to damage the root systems during this operation; the plants are very sensitive to root damage. The best soil is a mixture of leaf mould, peat and loam, but you can also use standard rich compost. Larger plants need weekly feeding.

Propagation
Only experts should try to propagate the dragon tree. *Dracaena draco* is grown from seeds. The other species are propagated from stem cuttings put in a propagator at 21-24°C (70-75°F) in a half-peat, half-sand mixture. Enthusiasts with few technical resources are advised against propagating this plant.

***Dracaena draco*, full size**

ECHEVERIA

Succulent annual or shrub, with very decorative flowers.

Position in full sunlight in a rather loamy soil.
Height up to 150 cm (60 in).
Flowering late winter to autumn, according to species.
Propagation by leaf cuttings or shoots, offsets and seeds.

Above: *Dracaena godseffiana*
Below: *Dracaena sanderiana*

In southern Europe you often see echeverias used as ground-cover plants. Their thick, fleshy leaves, arranged in rosettes, are sometimes white and yellow, and sometimes green, or even violet. Certain species have leaves dusted with powder, which protects the plant from the sun's heat. They are easy to grow, spreading to form a thick carpet.

Species

The common species *Echeveria agavoides* is stemless and has light green leaves with rusty brown points. The short, broad, sharply pointed leaves form thick rosettes from which yellow-red, short-stemmed flowers with yellow tips protrude, generally in spring.

Similarly stemless is the *Echeveria carnicolor* with its flesh-coloured flowers and loose rosettes of up to 7 cm (3 in) wide. This attractive plant has small, pointed, blue-grey leaves which occasionally exhibit a red gleam. The yellow-red and bell-shaped flowers appear from late winter to early spring.

Echeveria derenbergii has red-edged leaves covered with bluish powder. In drought the rosettes, some 6 cm (2 in) across, fold up to practically form a sphere. This short-stemmed species remains very small; its bell-shaped, yellow-red flowers are yellow inside and seldom grow higher than the rosettes. It flowers from spring to summer.

Echeveria elegans is a little shrub about 40 cm (16 in) high, whose branches are covered with soft hairs.

The small green leaves form rosettes of about 7 cm (3 in) across at the tips of the shoots. This species produces big, pink bell-like flowers from spring to summer.

Echeveria gibbiflora forms thick rosettes at the tips of its strong branches. The greeny-blue leaves have a red sheen and grow up to 15 cm (6 in) long. This species bears red flowers which look as if they are frosted. More common than the true species is *Echeveria gibbiflora* 'Metallica'. It has blue-green leaves, rather broader and rounder than those of the species and generally covered with a mat of light red-brown hairs.

Echeveria gigantea, a subshrub of about 30 cm (12 in) high, has inflorescences as tall as 150 cm (60 in). Its leaves often have a red border and grow to 20 cm (9 in) long. The inflorescence of many yellow flowers does not appear until the autumn.

Echeveria setosa is thickly covered with white bristles. This fine down is even found on the lovely yellow-red flowers, which appear from spring to summer. The thick, green leaves form tight rosettes and often have a waxy sheen.

Cultivation

Echeveria needs a light position both in winter and summer. In winter, except for the winter-flowering species, they must be kept at temperatures of about 8°C (46°F) and only watered a little. Even in summer

Echeveria gibbiflora 'Metallica'

these plants need little water; too much water causes rot. Feed them once a month during their growth period. The plant does best in rather loamy soil with a mixture of sand. Young plants should be repotted every year; established plants are best left alone.

Propagation

Even beginners will be able to propagate echeverias with no trouble. Old stems that have been cut down will usually send out new shoots from the leaf scars. After letting them dry off for two days, simply plant leaf cuttings or even leaf stalks in the ground and they will root. Use sandy compost and keep them slightly moist.

Propagation is also possible by offsets from the rosettes and by seeds.

Echeveria gibbiflora

EPIPHYLLVM

Orchid Cactus

Perennial house plant with lovely flowers.

Position light place in chalk-free soil; in summer, half-shade outdoors.
Height up to 1 m (3 ft).
Flowering spring to summer.
Propagation by cuttings or seeds.

Orchid cacti grow on trees in the tropical rain forests of Central and South America.

We cannot keep these original species on our window ledges, but we have many splendid hybrids which will almost always grow and thrive. These large-flowering cacti will survive at a minimum winter temperature of 5°C (41°F), but their large showy flowers are produced more frequently if the plants are kept warmer.

Cultivation

During the winter rest period orchid

Below: *Echeveria setosa*

cacti need a light, cool place at temperatures of about 8-10°C (46-50°F) and should only be watered sparingly. After that the plants like a warmer temperature and rather more water of the lime-free, tepid kind. Outdoors from spring to autumn, orchid cacti feel best in a warm, sheltered place in the garden, but out of direct sunlight. There they should be watered freely, sprayed and fed with high-potassium cactus fertilizers.

Do not repot too often or they will not flower readily. Repot only after flowering or, better still, replace the top layer of soil in the pot.

Propagation
Side-shoot cuttings, surfaces thoroughly dried before planting, normally grow well in new soil. Or sow seeds in spring at 21°C (70°F).

Epiphyllum 'London Glory'

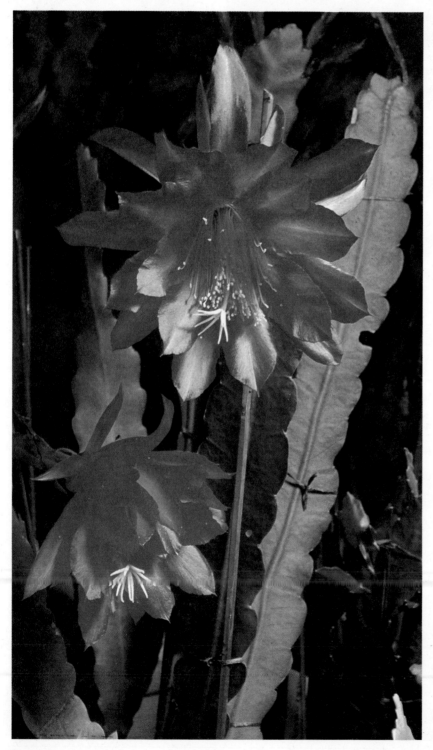

EUONYMUS

Flowering shrub with ornamental leaves and small, decorative fruits.

Position sunny to half-shade and airy, in loamy soil containing peat.
Height up to 150 cm (59 in).
Flowering spring and summer.
Propagation by cuttings.

The dark green, leathery leaves of some species look like laurel leaves. Growing wild, they often reach a height of 8 m (26 ft), but the hard, angular branches of the cultivated species grow only to a maximum of 150 cm (59 in). The ovate leaves, coming to a point at the tip, with slightly toothed edges, are dark green, or in some breeds green with yellow and white patterns. Small white flowers are followed by bright red berries.

The only pot plant is *Euonymus japonicus,* from Japan. Many varieties of this species have been bred, notable mostly for their beautifully patterned leaves. Best known are 'Aureomarginatus', with dark green, yellow-bordered leaves, 'Albomarginatus' with white edges to the leaves, and 'Microphyllus' with leaves in shades of green, yellow and white.

Cultivation
During the summertime the euonymus enjoys the open air of the balcony or terrace. It must have a sunny to half-shady position with plenty of air. In winter return it to a light room at about 5°C (41°F). From spring to autumn give it plenty of water and feed it every fortnight.

Propagation
Take top cuttings in early spring or late summer and root them in warm, moist sand. Then plant them in pots of loamy earth mixed with peat.

EUPHORBIA MILII

Crown of Thorns

Popular and trouble-free semisucculent shrub with showy spurious flowers.

Position light, sunny and airy, in good humus-rich soil.
Height up to 150 cm (59 in).
Flowering winter and spring.
Propagation by cuttings.

Since the crown of thorns was first brought to Europe from the highlands of the Malagasy Republic in the early nineteenth century, this succulent indoor shrub has won countless friends. The plant is ideal for dry indoor air and, with the right handling, will last for decades. The branches, which are as hard as pencils, are brownish green and bear many thorns. Between the thorns lanceolate-obovate, light green leaves occur.

The crown of thorns, like all species of its genus, contains a poisonous sap. From late winter to early summer—occasionally earlier —it produces small flowers, insig-

Euphorbia milii

nificant in themselves but distinguished by very decorative, crimson, kidney-shaped bracts. The plant is inclined to climb.

Cultivation
The crown of thorns needs a sunny place by the window. Above all it is intolerant of humidity. It does not need a cool spot, even in winter, when you can keep it in the living room, but give it rather less water. As a young plant it should be repotted every two years or so.

Propagation
Propagation by cuttings in spring is easy. But you must remember to wear gloves all the time to avoid the thorns. Lay the young shoots in tepid water to draw off the milky sap, or dip in powdered charcoal to stem its flow. Then let the cuttings dry and plant them in a mixture of sand and peat.

EUPHORBIA PULCHERRIMA

Poinsettia

Evergreen indoor shrub with striking red or cream bracts and insignificant yellowish flowers.

Euphorbia pulcherrima

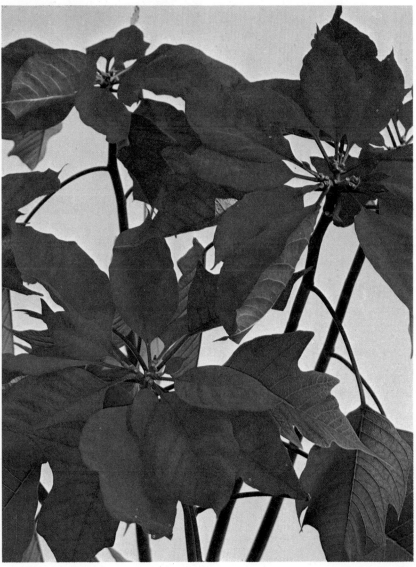

Position light and half-shady, in porous humus-rich soil.
Height up to 1 m (3 ft).
Flowering autumn to early spring.
Propagation by cuttings.

The poinsettia is an evergreen house plant originally from Mexico with striking bright red or creamy white bracts. Its relatively recent popularity is largely due to the intensive breeding carried on, especially in America, which has succeeded in overcoming its original awkwardness as a house plant. Its pointed, slightly curved, white-veined green leaves are totally overshadowed by the bracts. These are grouped round the tiny and insignificant yellowish flowers which appear in winter.

Cultivation
Poinsettia can stand in a room all year round, in a light but not sunny place and at temperatures of 20°C (68°F) or less. During the growth period, spring to autumn, water freely and spray with tepid water. After flowering, water only moderately and cut the plant back. To make the plants flower again, they must be allowed to stand in light rooms for only ten to twelve hours a day for some eight weeks before the autumn flowering period. During this period even street lighting and the occasional switching on and off of electric lights will hold up the formation of flowers. The temperature at this time should be kept constantly at around 17°C (63°F).

Propagation
You can take leaf cuttings in summer. When they stop exuding their milky, poisonous sap, plant the cuttings in flat pots of standard compost, with a bottom heat of at least 25°C (77°F). The cuttings should root in about three weeks.

Right and below:
Euphorbia pulcherrima

FATSHEDERA

Evergreen indoor shrub with light green leaves.

Position light place in a cool room.
Height up to 2 m (7 ft).
Propagation by cuttings.

Fatshedera, a cross between hedera (ivy) and fatsia (an indoor aralia), has only one species, *Fatshedera lizei,* which is an upright shrub with an inherited tendency to climb—but just a little. The stem of the young plant has rust-coloured hairs and the evergreen leaves resemble those of the fatsia but are harder, smaller and more hairy. Only occasionally in late summer does it decide to flower.

Fatshedera lizei

Then it produces close round clusters of green flowers. There is a very pretty ornamental-leaved variety, 'Variegata'.

Cultivation
Fatshedera does not care for the sun, but likes bright light in a cool room. Fresh air suits both the green-leaved and the coloured-leaved variety. The soil—a standard compost—must be moderately watered and manured. The leaves should be carefully washed down each week. A room temperature of 10-12°C (50-54°F) is enough during the winter, when the plants need less water and no food.

Propagation
Propagation is possible only by cuttings. You can use the head, with three or four leaves, and you can also cut up a shoot and plant pieces on which one leaf remains. Plant the cuttings in little pots filled with sand mixed with leaf mould—the top cutting by itself, the stem cuttings three to a pot. Cover them with an inverted glass cover or a plastic bag to ensure the required humidity. Whatever you do, do not let the pots stand in the sun. At moderate temperatures of about 18°C (64°F) rooting and the formation of buds at the leaf shoulders will go ahead quickly. You can propagate at any time except in winter. Growing three cuttings in one pot will produce particularly healthy and bushy plants.

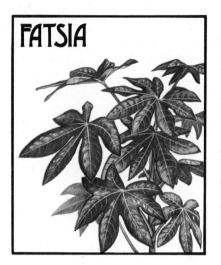

FATSIA

Fig Leaf Palm

Evergreen indoor shrub with big, impressive leaves.

Position shady and cool, in loamy earth.
Height up to 2 m (6 ft).
Propagation by seeds or cuttings.

The fig leaf palm is one of the best known of all foliage plants. (You will often hear it called the castor oil plant, but this is not correct.) With due care it will grow many years old, and in the course of time will form strong, slender stems. These, together with the huge palmate leaves, give it a most attractive appearance. At home in Japan these shrubs quite often grow 5 m (16 ft) high. As house plants, however, they seldom grow more than 2 m (6 ft). Their great virtue is that they do well in dark corners of the room or entrance hall without losing any of their beauty.

There is only one species of fatsia, *Fatsia japonica*. But many attractive varieties have been developed from it. The stems of young plants are thin and flexible. Dark green palmate leaves, not unlike maple leaves, grow on smooth stalks; they are deeply lobed and can develop up to nine 'fingers'. The young leaves are about 15 cm (6 in) across, brown, with a rough upper side. Later they grow as much as 40 cm (16 in) wide and are smooth and leathery.

When the fatsia matures, umbels of greeny white flowers appear in mid-summer and autumn, forming thick little clusters. Quite often small black decorative berries grow from them.

The most popular variety, 'Variegata', has whitish or yellow patterns on the leaves. 'Moseri' is compact and low-growing.

Cultivation
The fatsia gives very little trouble. It can stand in the cool and dark, indoors or (in summer) outdoors.

Fatsia japonica

Water it well and feed once a week, from spring to autumn. Give less water from then on, and let the plant overwinter at about 8°C (46°F). Wash the great leaves down with a damp cloth once a month.

Propagation
There is no difficulty in propagating from imported seed, which you must sow at a warm room temperature in ordinary seed compost as soon as it ripens. With coloured-leaved varieties you can also propagate by cuttings, but the new plant will most probably do less well than the parent. If you are propagating by cuttings, a minimum bottom heat of about 25°C (77°F) is best. The cuttings will usually strike in wet sand at this temperature.

Fatsia japonica 'Variegata'

FICUS

Indian Rubber Tree, Weeping Fig, Fiddle Back Fig, Creeping Fig

Evergreen shrub or tree with leathery leaves. Some species are climbers.

Position in a not too light place.
Height 2-4 m (7-13 ft).
Propagation by cuttings or air layering.

Indian rubber trees divide open-plan offices into individual rooms, break up our living rooms and cheer up our entrance halls, staircases and corridors. In the tropical regions of Asia at least two thousand species grow wild to reach a height of 30 m (100 ft).

Species
Ficus benjamina (weeping fig) is a pretty ornamental shrub. It has slightly drooping branches and oval, pointed leaves 6-10 cm (2-4 in) long.

A rather more spreading shrub is

Ficus elastica '**Decora**'

Ficus cannonii, which can grow as tall as 4 m (13 ft). Its short-stemmed bronze foliage, red on the underside, is very striking. This plant grows quickly, and if you want to confine it in a heated room, you had better prune it back severely every year. If you plant the pruned-off pieces in warm soil, they will root like cuttings.

The leaves of *Ficus deltoidea* are only a little smaller. The charm of this species lies in its greeny yellow fruit, only 1 cm (½ in) long. You often get a lot of fruit even on young specimens. This plant comes from the Azores, and grows 50 cm (20 in) high.

Ficus edulis, a shrub with hardly any branches, from New Caledonia, bears edible fruits about the size of peas. Its leaves are bright red when they first appear, later turning brownish green. It needs a rather warm spot and will not bear fruit until well established.

The best known of all is *Ficus elastica*, the true rubber tree, whose

**Right: *Ficus elastica* 'Doescheri' (front) and *Ficus benjamina*
Below: *Ficus elastica* 'Variegata'**

brilliant, oval and pointed green leaves grow up to 40 cm (16 in). Young leaves are often covered by red stipules, which soon fall. The commonest are the cultivar 'Decora', with shining, dark green leaves and brightly coloured stipules, and the 'Variegata' varieties, with whitish, yellowish or even greyish spots on the leaves.

Ficus lyrata or *pandurata* (the violin case rubber tree or fiddle back fig) has even bigger leaves of up to 50 cm (20 in) long. They are dark

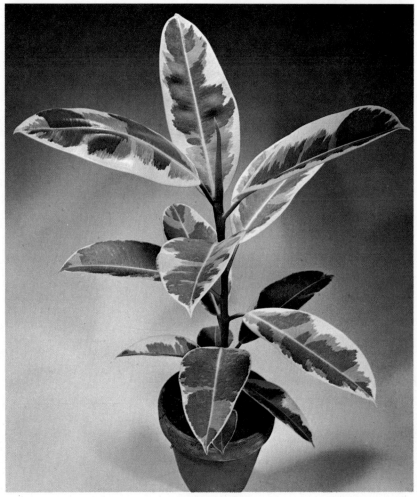

green with light veins. This species is a really high- and wide-growing plant.

If you have a trellis partition in your room, *Ficus pumila* (also called *repens* or *stipulata*) will easily climb up it to a height of 4 m (13 ft). This plant, the creeping fig, has strong tendrils which enable it to climb brick, even concrete, walls. It also makes a good hanging plant. Its leaves are narrow, kidney-shaped and arched. The form 'Minima' has white-green, rather smaller leaves.

Besides the climbing variety, another fine species for decorating a trellis is *Ficus radicans*. This has long, pointed leaves some 5 cm (16 in) long, and roots growing at the leaf nodes with which the shrub clings to the frame.

Ficus rubiginosa (also called *australis*) will thrive even in cold rooms. Its leaves, some 10 cm (4 in) long, are rusty red at first, hairy on the underside and dark green and leathery on top. The form 'Variegata' has yellowish white patches.

Cultivation

Ficus benjamina likes a warm environment—even in winter the room temperature should not fall below 18°C (64°F). In summer it must be shielded from the sun and liberally watered, and it must be sprayed in high temperatures and dry air to prevent the leaves drying out. Fertilize it twice a week, except in winter.

A moist atmosphere in a warmish room is what *Ficus deltoidea* needs; it can tolerate a good deal of sunlight but should be sheltered from the sun in the middle of the day. Spray the plant regularly and from spring to autumn feed it with house plant fertilizers every two months.

Ficus elastica cannot stand cold

water and the other species also prefer being watered and sprayed with tepid water. *Ficus elastica* must also be kept out of draughts. Its ornamental-leaved varieties particularly like a light position. Do not let it get cooler than 10°C (50°F) in winter. It needs plenty of food during the growing period, but little water.

The violin case rubber tree or fiddle back fig can be kept in any normally warm room, but since it does best in a humid atmosphere, spray it often. Maturer plants need fertilizer every fortnight, but not in winter. Their position should be light but not sunny.

The climber *Ficus pumila* will tolerate full sun—though not in the middle of the day. It will also thrive in a dark place. It must have plenty of water in summer, with a tepid spray once a week, and some manure. In winter, it requires less water and no manure at all. It will still require spraying.

All species of the genus *Ficus* grow well in loamy, nutritious soil.

Scale insect and red spider can be a threat to them, and leaf spot diseases can appear as a result of too low a temperature, fluctuating temperatures or draughts. Yellow patches on the edges of the lower leaves are due to excessive cold or damp.

Propagation

Propagation is difficult. Propagation by seeds is more or less out of the question because the seeds will not become fertile, and propagation by cuttings is dubious because of the excessive care required. In the spring, take a cutting from a runner, stem or side shoot, with from two to four leaves, and keep it in a bottle of water in front of a sunny window until it roots. You can also plant the cutting in a mixture of peat and sand and keep it in a bowl on the radiator until it strikes. Put a plastic cover over the top so that the cuttings can root in a constantly humid atmosphere. *Ficus benjamina, elastica* and *lyrata* can also be propagated by air layering.

Left: *Ficus pumila*
Below and right: *Fuchsia*

FUCHSIA

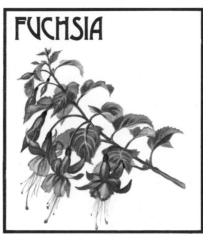

Shrub with very lovely flowers. Popular plant for the balcony.

Position half-shady, in light humus-rich soil with no lime.
Height between 15 cm (6 in) and 5 m (16 ft).
Flowering all seasons, according to species.
Propagation by cuttings.

The fuchsias are shrubs—in rare cases small trees—that come from the upland forests of South and Central America.

We grow only very few of the many species, but experts have reckoned that just those must contain over two thousand varieties. We differentiate between upright and hanging varieties. The upright varieties may be grown as bushes, standards or against walls, as pot plants in a cool greenhouse, or outdoors, the latter as plants for hanging baskets.

Fuchsias are chiefly grown for their attractive pendulous flowers, which consist of a tube ending in four spreading sepals and four overlapping petals forming a bell.

Species
This splendid little tree with a magnificent scent, fuchsia or lilac fuchsia tree (*Fuchsia arborescens*), produces a great many little rose-coloured flowers in hanging panicles from winter to spring. This plant, which looks very attractive growing in a tub, needs unheated rooms during its flowering period, with temperatures of between 8°C and 12°C (46 and 54°F). During the summer it should be planted out in the garden, where it needs nutritious soil.

A rarity among the fuchsias is *Fuchsia corymbiflora*, which blooms on half-shady balconies from mid-summer to autumn. The widely opened flowers, like the reflexed bracts, are brilliant carmine red.

Even in cool climates you can grow *Fuchsia magellanica* in the garden, in the shade of deciduous trees. Even if the upper parts of the plant are killed by frost, they will produce new shoots next season. This species will grow to 1 m (3 ft) high and has long, pointed leaves with reddish veins. The deep red flowers grow on long stems in the leaf shoulders. Seedsmen have developed some lovely varieties of this species. 'Gracilis' is a thin-stemmed, soft-haired plant, not more than 80 cm (32 in) high, with very long purple flowers. 'Madame Cornelissen', which grows to 50-60 cm (20-24 in), has dark green leaves; strange white flowers grow above its brilliant red bracts. 'Riccartonii' has drooping branches with beautiful red pendulous flowers under dark violet bracts.

The dwarf among the fuchsias is the variety 'Tom Thumb', which grows to only about 25 cm (10 in) and is to be found everywhere in the rockery and on the balcony.

Fuchsia procumbens has a low, almost creeping growth; it is one of the few species of this shrub that come from New Zealand. Exceptionally, its flowers have no petals. The long, bluish corolla makes an attractive contrast with its yellow-brown bracts.

Fuchsia triphylla has dark, bronze-coloured leaves and striking orange-red tubular flowers. It is from this species that the racemose fuchsias (*Fuchsia triphylla* hybrids) have been developed. They do well in sunny positions. They bloom from mid-summer to autumn in many combinations of colours, but must be brought indoors before the first frost.

You can enjoy the fuchsia hybrids —also called garden fuchsias—all year round. They are characterized

Below: *Fuchsia procumbens*

as having upright or hanging growth, and as bearing robuster single or double flowers.

Cultivation
Outdoor fuchsias should always have a half-shady place and be mulched in winter to protect the stem and roots from severe frost. Fuchsias on the balcony and indoors also need a half-shady place in summer, but a little morning sun will do no harm. Keep them in light positions in unheated rooms in winter, but do not let the temperature fall below 10°C (50°F) for any length of time. Fuchsias want dry soil in winter, and you should not begin to water them liberally until they begin to shoot. It is a good thing to syringe them frequently in their growth period and flowering period. All fuchsias, indoors or on the balcony or in the garden, are glad of a powerful dose of mineral fertilizer or organic manure in spring.

Propagation
Fuchsias are propagated by cuttings which should be taken six months before you want flowering plants. The cuttings should be kept at about 20°C (68°F).

GREVILLEA

Silk Bark Oak

Evergreen indoor tree.

Position light and cool, in lime-free soil; outdoors in summer.
Height up to 2.5 m (8 ft).
Propagation by seeds or cuttings.

As a house plant, grevillea does not have a particularly silky bark; the

Grevillea robusta

common name really applies more to the mature trees in their natural habitat in Australia. Its leaves, astonishingly like fern fronds, have a silky sheen on the underside, especially when young. They grow about 20 cm (9 in) long, doubly pinnate, green and smooth on top and having silvery hairs below.

Grevillea robusta grows as high as 50 m (164 ft) in Australia, and even in the Mediterranean region there are 20 m (66 ft) specimens. We think of it as no more than an elegant, undemanding pot plant, reaching a height of 2.5 m (8 ft).

Cultivation
A silk bark oak growing in a bowl or tub in the living room or hall during the winter will do best in temperatures between 12-20°C (56-68°F). It likes a light position, but not direct sun because its fern-like leaves fade very easily. If you keep it at temperatures below 15°C (59°F), it will become stunted, but with high temperatures will simply shoot up. If you do not prune it, it will not grow new shoots.

You can stand this decorative, elegantly shaped plant outdoors in the summer in half-shade. Water it

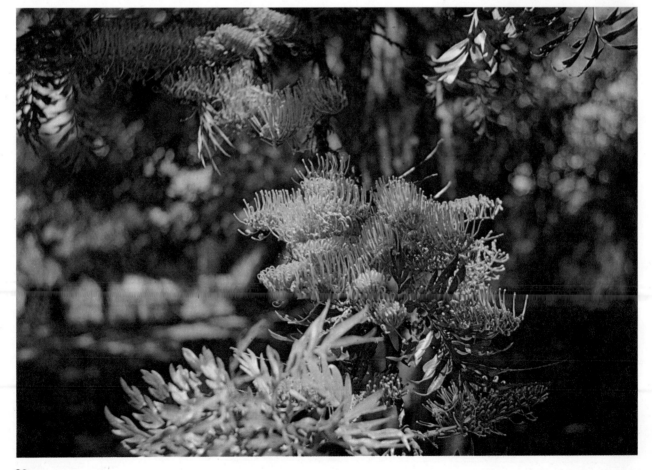

regularly and spray it with the syringe all year round. Repot young plants every year. The ideal soil consists of a mixture of three parts leaf mould, two parts old cow manure, one part coarse sand and some loam. Or simply use a lime-free potting compost.

Propagation

Grevillea is propagated by seeds or cuttings. Sow them in the spring in sandy leaf mould with some peat. Young side shoots are planted in sandy soil in summer.

GUZMANIA

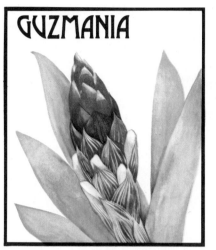

Foliage and flowering evergreen perennial for the conservatory.

Position shady and warm, high humidity, in loose, humus-rich porous soil.
Height up to 60 cm (24 in).
Flowering all seasons.
Propagation by suckers or seeds.

Guzmania comes from the tropical

Left: *Grevillea banksii*
Below: *Guzmania lingulata*

rain forests of South and Central America and cannot normally be raised as a house plant. It has green coloured, elongated and pointed leaves that form a funnel-shaped rosette. One inflorescence grows from each funnel, and according to species it may form a head, a cylinder or a spike. The bracts are often bright red.

Species

During the last decades a number of very beautiful guzmania hybrids have been developed by crossbreeding.

The most common form other than hybrids is *Guzmania lingulata,* which forms leaf rosettes up to 80 cm (32 in) wide. The leaves, 5 cm (2 in) wide, have undersides with reddish brown lines. This species has an erect shape bearing dark red bracts and white flowers.

Guzmania minor has small rosettes made from a large number of narrow green leaves which come to a point and often have a reddish tinge. The white head of flowers is surrounded by bright red bracts.

Guzmania monostachya has an upright inflorescence which grows straight up from the thick, rather spreading rosette of narrow, greeny yellow leaves. The bracts are dark red to blackish at the bottom, becoming bright red further up with pure white flowers which last only a few days.

Guzmania musaica, a native of Colombia has many-leaved rosettes of up to 50 cm (20 in) high. The foliage has a pattern of fine, red-brown lines on the upper side and brown dots underneath. It bears yellow-white flowers enclosed within orange bracts.

Cultivation

These natives of tropical forests need moist, warm air, light without sun, plenty of water and plant food once a fortnight, room temperatures that never fall below 18°C (64°F) even at night, and high humidity.

Guzmania needs to be sprayed frequently, and the pot, containing broken crocks, should stand in a 'footbath'. Before the flowers develop, top up the leaf funnel with water, but stop when the flowers begin to develop.

Propagation

Detach the rooted suckers which will root only in high room temperatures and great humidity. Enthusiasts with few technical resources are advised not to try to grow plants from seed.

GYNURA

Subshrub with decorative foliage and pretty fruits; one climbing species.

Position as light as possible and warm, in nutritious humus-rich soil.
Height up to 1 m (3 ft).
Flowering in autumn, or sometimes in late winter.
Propagation by cuttings.

Gynura comes from the tropical rain forests of Africa and India. Its purple foliage—found only on young plants —has made it very popular, though when in flower it has a disagreeable smell. Gynura is a composite with

Gynura scandens

angular stems on which large, toothed, velvety leaves grow opposite one another.

Species
Gynura aurantiaca is a subshrub of up to 1 m (3 ft) high, thickly covered with purple hairs, especially on the underside of the leaves. The clusters of yellow flowers do not appear until late autumn.

Gynura scandens, a climbing and hanging subshrub, looks lovely trailing over a bamboo frame. It has dentate leaves on which violet hairs and orange flowers appear.

Cultivation
Gynura prefers as light a position as possible and can even be put out on the balcony in summer. In winter the plants need temperatures of between 15-18°C (59-64°F) with a minimum temperature of 12°C (54°F) at night. Give them plenty of water, and from spring to autumn a generous feeding once a month will ensure lively growth. If they get too much warmth and not enough light, the plants will begin to lose their violet colouring. Make them bushy by repeated cutting back.

Propagation
Cuttings will root easily at any time. Since older specimens lose their colour, it is best to plan for a second growth each year.

HEDERA

Ivy, Pot Ivy, Persian Ivy

Evergreen climbing shrub, ornamental on walls and tree trunks.

Position in half-shade or shade.
Height climbs up to 30 m (98 ft).
Propagation by cuttings.

The ancient Greeks and Romans used to look on ivy as a symbol of gaiety, friendship and fellowship. Even today the darkest, dullest wall looks more friendly with ivy climbing over it, and for this reason this climbing plant has become very popular.

Species
Persian ivy *(Hedera colchica)* has bright triangular or oval leaves 10-25 cm (4-10 in) long, with a dull green, leathery upper surface. The berries are black and round.

The common ivy *(Hedera helix)* has a profusely branching stem. It creeps along the ground or prefers to climb up trees, walls or fences with the aid of aerial roots. As long as the ivy climbs with youthful vigour, its lobed leaves, dark green, and often with

Hedera colchica 'Dentato-variegata'

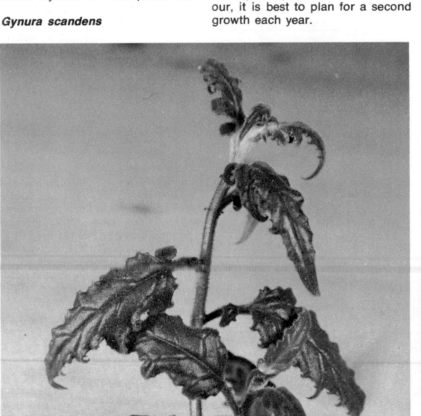

Harry Smith

84

white veins, will have from three to five points. Its size ranges from 4-10 cm (1-4 in). As soon as climbing ceases, the leaves will change to their alternative form and become larger and fuller. On the flowering shoots the leaves are oval or diamond-shaped, and duller in colour on the sunny side. These shoots have no aerial roots which will not appear until the plant is eight to ten years old.

There is a wide selection of pot ivy varieties. They include climbing or trailing varieties of the young *Hedera helix*, with leaves between 3-7 cm (1-3 in) long. There are as many leaf patterns as there are varieties: yellow or white spots, or even all-white or yellowish white on a background of green or grey-green.

The white-flowering form of *Hed-era canariensis*, 'Gloire de Marengo', is among varieties suitable for fairly large conservatories.

Cultivation

In the open air ivy creeps along the ground to form a thick carpet. If it meets an obstacle, it simply climbs up it with the aid of its aerial roots. It is easily satisfied. Any soil is suitable as long as it is not too dry. It must have damp soil if it stands in the full sunlight. Ivy grown in a room will thrive even in a shady position.

Leggy plants must be cut back every year at the beginning of the growth period.

As a house plant, ivy makes a good plant for the conservatory, but it also does well in a darker room. If the air

Hedera helix

is dry, you must look out for two pests to which ivy is most susceptible—aphids and red spider.

The ornamental-leaved forms of indoor ivy need rather more warmth than the green. Water them moderately as soon as the soil is dry. Spring to autumn, feed them every three weeks. Pot ivies will overwinter at about 12°C (54°F) in a dryish environment and need only be watered from time to time.

Propagation

You can propagate by planting cuttings from tips of shoots in ordinary garden soil. For a climbing plant take cuttings from the runners, for a bush, cuttings from adult growth. They grow very quickly. Cuttings from pot ivy are more delicate. Keep them under transparent polythene at first.

HIBISCUS

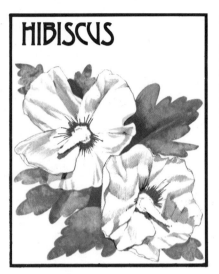

Rose Mallow

Profusely flowering tender evergreen shrub.

Position sunny to half-shady and warm, in loamy soil.
Height up to 2 m (6 ft).
Flowering spring through autumn.
Propagation by shrubby cuttings.

Hibiscus rosa-sinensis **hybrids**

Of all the hibiscus species, *Hibiscus rosa-sinensis* has won a special place among our house plants. A native of South China, it is a rather spreading, evergreen shrub with pointed, bright green leaves and abundant, large trumpet-shaped flowers. Usually these last for only a day, but since the plant goes on producing new buds endlessly, a hibiscus remains in flower from spring to autumn.

Countless hybrids have been bred from *Hibiscus rosa-sinensis,* differing mainly in the shape and colour of the flowers. You can get them with white, yellow, orange, red and pink flowers, and some in double forms. The variety 'Cooperi' is especially well known; its leaves are variegated with dark green, cream, and crimson.

Cultivation
Shelter young hibiscus shrubs from

Hibiscus rosa-sinensis

the full glare of the sun, but let the older specimens enjoy full sun and great warmth, without which they do not flower long. Give them plenty of water and spray them frequently from spring until well into autumn. You can also put them out on the terrace in the rain. During the growth period, from late winter on, feed them every week or their bud formation will be affected. Repot older plants every two or three years, younger plants every year in late winter.

Propagation
You can propagate the hibiscus in early spring by shrubby cuttings, which must be kept under glass with air and soil temperatures at around 25°C (77°F). But be careful to take cuttings from stems that have not yet become completely woody. In autumn you can also begin to propagate by stem cuttings. Take only cuttings without buds.

HIPPEASTRUM

Amaryllis, Barbados Lily

Bulb plant with impressive flowers.

Position light and sunny during the growth period, outdoors in summer.
Height 30-60 cm (12-24 in).
Flowering according to species, mostly winter or early spring.
Propagation by offsets.

Flower lovers know the hippeastrum as Barbados lily or more commonly amaryllis, which is incorrect. Hippeastrum comes from America, growing wild in the tropical and subtropical regions, but the house plant is the result of years of breeding.

The result can be seen in *Hippeastrum reticulatum* 'Stratifolium' and in *Hippeastrum vittatum* hybrid which blooms more abundantly than its American ancestors and bears new, bigger, but neater flowers. But in one respect it resembles its American forebears: once a year it must have its rest period, without which the plant will not yield its magnificent flowers. The growth period that follows must also be strictly observed, when it needs plenty of feeding. Each bulb should produce two scapes with four flowers on each. The flowers should point straight out.

Cultivation
During the rest period in autumn, the plant should not be watered, and it needs a warm place where the temperature does not fall below 16°C (61°F). As soon as the first flower shoots appear on the bulb, in winter, put the pot in a light place in the window with a temperature of about 22°C (72°F), but do not start watering until the scape is some 25 cm (10 in) high. By then the hippeastrum can tolerate a rather cooler position,

17-18°C (63-64°F). During or after flowering, the plant produces tall, narrow leaves. The number of scapes produced the following season depends on the number of leaves.

After flowering, cut down the flower scapes just above the bulb, and then you can repot. Do not sink the bulb too deep in the soil; it is best to leave the top half of the bulb uncovered. Whether it is on the window ledge or out of doors, the plant needs a light and sunny position with at least 12°C (54°F) of warmth during the growth period. Water regularly until late summer and, as soon as enough roots have formed, feed twice a week with a complete fertilizer solution. Keep feeding after the flowers have gone and until the leaves begin to yellow and die. Only after this should you stop feeding and gradually reduce watering in autumn. When the three-months-long rest period begins, the plant will have lost its leaves.

Propagation
There is only one method of propagation that can be recommended to the layman, and that is by offsets. New bulbs often form on the bulbs of old pot plants, which, when rooted, can be separated and planted out.

Hippeastrum reticulatum **'Stratifolium'**

HOWEA

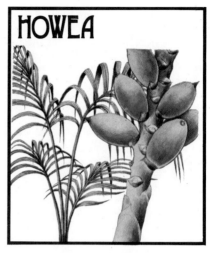

Curly Palm, Thatch Leaf Palm, Kentia Palm

Undemanding indoor palms with bushy pinnate leaves growing close together.

Position shady and moderately warm, in loamy garden soil.
Height up to 3 m (10 ft).
Propagation by seeds.

Howea is a native of the Lord Howe Islands in the Pacific Ocean where it sometimes grows as a mighty tree 15 m (49 ft) high. But the howeas we see in pots and tubs do not generally grow more than 2 m (6 ft) high and rarely as much as 3 m (10 ft). Their orderly, narrow, pinnate leaves grow on slender stems and attract attention by their symmetrical, thick growth. Howeas growing wild develop long flower stems after a number of years, but indoor specimens hardly ever flower.

Species
We know two species of the genus *Howea* which at first glance aren't easy to distinguish. There is probably some interbreeding. *Howea belmoreana* has strongly ribbed pinnate leaves, straight or slightly curved, on short stems.

Howea forsteriana—the curly palm or thatched palm—has a slender stem and long-stemmed leaves. At the bottom of the stem the leaf segments hang down, but farther up they grow out sideways. Their underside is slightly scaly.

Cultivation
The howeas do not need much light

Howea forsteriana

and will thrive even in deep shadow. You can keep them in a room all year round, young plants at about 20°C (68°F), older at 18°C (64°F). In winter the temperature should stay at about 15°C (59°F).

Water liberally, especially in summer, when you must also feed once a week. Give less water from autumn through winter, but do not let the soil dry out. The fronds should be regularly cleaned with a damp cloth and sprayed from time to time.

Propagation
Experts regard raising howeas in a room as difficult. If you want to try, buy some freshly imported seeds in late winter or early spring. Soak them in water at 30°C (86°F) and after two days lay them in a flat bowl of seed compost at a room temperature of 30°C (86°F). When the plantlets are about 5 cm (2 in) long, insert them in small pots and keep them shady, humid and warm. From mid-summer on repot them in bigger pots, but accustom them slowly to the sun. Never water with alkaline water.

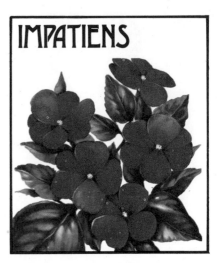

IMPATIENS

Busy Lizzie, Touch-Me-Not

Perennial, abundantly flowering pot plant. Very popular for the balcony.

Position light, but not in direct sunlight, in slightly sandy humus-rich soil.
Height up to 50 cm (20 in).
Flowering the whole year.
Propagation by cuttings.

Impatiens walleriana

Impatiens glandulifera

Busy lizzie gets its name from its ability to flower abundantly all year round. In summer you see this tireless plant in boxes on the balcony and bowls in the garden, but do not fail to bring it indoors in winter, for it is very sensitive to cold and will suffer damage from temperatures below 12°C (54°F).

Busy lizzie is the bushy shrub *Impatiens walleriana,* a species of touch-me-not. It has much-branched, fleshy and rather translucent stems and pointed, slightly toothed, light green leaves. Many varieties—and busy lizzie has a great number—have leaves with white patterns. The flat-shaped flowers, which have the spine found in all species of *Impatiens,* for example *Impatiens glandulifera,* grow densely above the foliage and shine in every shade of red.

Well known varieties are 'Firelight' with orange flowers, 'Petersiana' with bronze foliage, and 'Variegata' with white-bordered leaves.

Impatiens walleriana varieties

Cultivation
Busy lizzie likes a warm position but not direct sun. Half-shade is best for it in winter too, when the plant must be kept at temperatures of about 20°C (68°F). If it gets cooler, it will shed its leaves and stop flowering. You should water it liberally, but the root ball should be moist rather than wet or the stems will rot. Despite its continual flowering, the plant needs feeding only during the main growth period, from spring to autumn, and even then only once a week. Repot when it seems to be necessary in light humus-rich earth. Discard the plants when they get too leggy, using the best part of the existing plant to make new plants.

Propagation
You can propagate busy lizzie at any time of the year by cuttings, about 10 cm (4 in) long, which root easily in water or sandy soil. Replant them separately in pots and within four months you will have a new young plant. Pinch out the growing points to encourage bushy growth.

KALANCHOË

Succulent annual or subshrub with abundant flowers.

Position sunny to shady, airy, in loamy garden soil.
Height 10-50 cm (4-20 in).
Flowering winter through spring.
Propagation by seeds or cuttings.

Tropical shrubs or annuals, kalanchoë are notable for the unusual shape and colour of their leaves and flowers. The thick, fleshy leaves mostly grow opposite each other along a strong stem. The white, yellow or red flowers are only small, but they grow in crowded clusters, which gives the impression of luxuriant growth. The species we keep as pot plants grow no more than 50 cm (20 in) high, but become very bushy.

Species
A most popular species is the profusely flowering *Kalanchoë blossfeldiana,* a subshrub some 30 cm (12 in) high with bright red clusters of flowers that grow on such a long stem that they are often used as cut flowers. You can also get a number of

Kalanchoë tomentosa

Kalanchoë blossfeldiana

varieties with yellow, orange and deep red flowers, of which the best known are 'Compacta Liliput' and 'Orange Triumph'.

The abundantly growing *Kalanchoë marmorata,* an annual about 50 cm (20 in) high, flowers in great snow-white clusters. The big, ovate leaves have brownish spots and a jagged edge.

The tiny leaves of *Kalanchoë rhombopilosa* also have red-brown spots. It grows to a maximum of 10 cm (4 in).

The subshrub *Kalanchoë tomentosa,* up to 50 cm (20 in) high, has particularly attractive foliage. The very fleshy leaves, about 6 cm (2 in) long, are covered with a silvery green-grey down, and the jagged edges are speckled with dull red.

Cultivation
The plants must have a light, warm place at a temperature of about 20°C (68°F). They need an airy position and must be kept good and moist. Water them less in winter and keep them at about 10°C (50°F), though *Kalanchoë blossfeldiana,* exceptionally, must overwinter at 15°C (59°F). Between spring and autumn feed the plants every fortnight.

Propagation
The plants can be propagated by seeds in early spring; let them germinate under glass at about 20°C (68°F). You can also take cuttings in the spring or summer; let them dry for a day or two before putting them to root in moist sand and later plant in loamy garden soil.

LAVRVS

Bay Laurel, Sweet Bay

Evergreen ornamental shrub, with occasional tiny flowers.

Position sunny and warm, in sandy soil.
Height 2-3 m (6-10 ft).
Propagation by cuttings.

You will find laurel trees all over the world: in gardens, on terraces, in halls or rooms. It is generally cut to form a pyramid or sphere or a tall-stemmed bushy crown.

The bay laurel grows wild in most Mediterranean countries, where it reaches a height of 15 m (49 ft). As a pot plant it will grow to only 2-3 m (6-10 ft). It has decorative, thick, shining foliage. The yellow-green clusters of flowers are insignificant.

Laurus nobilis

Species
Our commonest species is *Laurus nobilis.* Its short-stemmed, oval leaves come to a point at both ends, feel leathery to the touch and have a shiny, dark green surface. The whitish clusters of flowers appear on older specimens in spring.

Laurus azorica, a native of the Canary Islands and the Azores, has bigger, broader leaves. Its foliage is more yellow and less thick.

Cultivation
Laurel trees flourish if they get plenty of air and warmth, so it is best to put them in the garden or on the balcony in late spring and summer. Keep them moist, and spray frequently or the shining leaves will become yellow and dull. In spring and summer feed once a week.

In winter the plants must stand in a light room at about 5°C (41°F). Water meagrely to ensure that they do not form any shoots.

It is usually enough to cut laurel shoots that are growing too long back to the right length at any time, but if, after some years, the plant gets too big for the room, you can cut it back to the desired height in early spring.

Propagation
Laurel trees can be propagated by cuttings; put them to root in moist sand at about 18°C (64°F), autumn to spring. After about a month you can plant the young plants in a pot of sandy garden soil. It will be several years before you get a tree worth looking at.

MARANTA

Arrowroot, Prayer Plant

Difficult luxuriant perennial house plant with strikingly beautiful patterns on the leaves.

Position shady and warm, with high humidity, in porous garden soil.
Height up to 30 cm (12 in).
Propagation by division or cuttings.

Marantas are among the most popular indoor foliage plants because of the extravagant range of colours found on their leaves. Found mainly in the rain forests of Brazil, they bear broad, oval leaves either spread flat over the ground or standing upright. Like its hybrid relatives, the maranta seldom grows to more than 30 cm (12 in).

Only two species are found as house plants, but many attractive varieties have been bred from them. The short-stemmed leaves mostly have strong ribs and are spotted or striped with every conceivable shade of green, red and brown.

Species
The pretty, oval, short-stemmed leaves of *Maranta bicolor* grow up to 15 cm (6 in) long and as much as 11 cm (4 in) broad. The dark green surface is patterned on both sides of the prominent midrib with as many as six dark brown spots. In between, a light green stripe runs along the leaf. The underside of the leaf is coloured red-brown to violet.

Maranta leuconeura has rather narrower leaves, though they still grow up to 15 cm (6 in) long. The upper side of the light green, white-veined leaves has spots of white and dark green. The underside has a bluish green to reddish sheen. The variety 'Kerchoveana' has leaves with

striking patterns: the sea green upper side has regular dark spots on each side of the midrib. The underside is greenish blue spotted with red. The white-ribbed leaves of the variety 'Massangeana' are rather smaller and less pointed, brown spotted on top and red underneath.

Cultivation
A true plant of the tropics, the maranta needs as high a humidity as possible and a constant temperature of 18-22°C (64-72°F) in winter. Always keep the plants moist with tepid water and feed once a fortnight from spring to autumn. Spray frequently.

Propagation
You can separate the rhizomatous roots of luxuriant marantas with a sharp knife at the beginning of spring, and plant them in peat-based compost. Propagation by cuttings is also possible; cut young shoots with two or three leaves from the base of the plant and let them root in damp sand and peat.

Maranta leuconeura 'Fascinator'

MIMOSA

Sensitive Plant, Humble Plant

Decorative subshrub with small flowers.

Position sunny to half-shady, in constantly moist, standard compost; cannot tolerate draughts.
Height 40 cm (16 in).
Flowering in summer.
Propagation by cuttings or seeds.

What florists sell you as mimosa is usually a species of acacia. Mimosa is a decorative, but short-lived, sub-shrub kept all too seldom as a house plant. The leaves of these easy-to-

care-for plants from South America droop at a touch, and assume the so-called sleeping position. They resume their former position after a short period if left undisturbed. This characteristic will occur only if you keep the plant at a room temperature of 20°C (68°F) and is a daytime only phenomenon.

Mimosa pudica, the humble or sensitive plant, a subshrub just 40 cm (16 in) tall, is the only species in general cultivation. Other varieties need greenhouse care. This attractive plant bears clusters of small, tufted ball-like violet to reddish flowers in summer. Its light green leaves are bipinnate, composed of numerous narrowly elliptic leaflets.

Left and below: *Mimosa pudica*

Cultivation

Mimosa should be kept at temperatures around 20°C (68°F) in summer and some 15°C (59°F) in winter. Water it regularly. It is also sensitive to draughts and smoky rooms. Give it some weak liquid fertilizer about once a week from spring through autumn.

Propagation

Mimosa is propagated by cuttings, which you put under glass in spring, or by seeds, which you lay in little pots in spring and keep at about 20°C (68°F). The seedlings must be kept under glass until established, which should be by about the beginning of summer. Do not prune seedlings, as is often recommended; feed them well instead.

MONSTERA

Swiss Cheese Plant, Shingle Plant

Resistant, evergreen climbing house plant.

Position light, warm but not in direct sunlight, in humus-rich soil.
Height up to 10 m (33 ft).
Propagation by top cuttings or air layering.

The Swiss cheese plant, so called because its leaves are perforated like Gruyère cheese, is perhaps the commonest of all house plants. You will hardly ever see an office or conservatory that does not have one of these semiepiphytic climbing shrubs with evergreen, deeply lobed, perforated leaves standing out on long stalks. This robust and graceful house plant comes from the rain forests of South and Central America, where it generally grows on the branches of trees. It will not grow so big as a house plant as it does in its natural environment, but you will see occasional specimens in botanical gardens, in halls and on landings which are as much as 10 m (33 ft) high.

Mature specimens form smooth, rope-like aerial roots, whose outer layer, the velamen, consists of a spongy tissue that stores up water, and with which the plant can absorb moisture from the air at any time.

You must not on any account cut off the aerial roots. You should either lead them back to the soil in the same pot or lead them into another, where they will immediately turn into ground roots. Or pack damp moss around them to encourage the plant to grow more vigorously. Or simply leave them alone.

Species
Monstera deliciosa grows very strongly. The stem of this shrub very quickly forms wood. The big, dark green, rather leathery leaves grow on long, bare stalks of up to 60 cm (24 in) long. Older plants bear decorative clusters of flowers almost every year; they are surrounded by a creamy spathe almost 20 cm (9 in) long. When the flowers ripen, they produce large numbers of violet, strongly scented, hexagonal berries, which are edible.

The variety 'Borsigiana' grows more quickly than others, and is rather more delicate. Its leaves are not so deeply lobed and less perforated.

Monstera obliqua has long, pointed leaves which have a continuous chain of holes along the border.

Cultivation
Monstera likes warmth, humidity and a light position, but not direct sun. Ideally the room temperature should be between 12-20°C (54-68°F), but brief fluctuations will not do the plant any harm.

If you put the plant in too dark a

Monstera

position, or if the temperature rises too high, the leaves will not develop their characteristic shape. Also, if the highest leaves on a plant are in constant rising warm air, they will not produce the lobes and holes. To restore them to this characteristic shape, transfer the plant to a cooler place.

Water the plant according to its size and give it a frame to climb up in good time. Do not give it much water in winter but feed well in summer. It is a good idea to wipe the big leaves with a damp cloth.

Propagation
If you want to have a fine, bushy indoor plant, remove the top shoot. You can then propagate the plant by air layering. Alternatively you can remove the top cutting, about 1 m (3 ft) long, and plant it in a fairly large pot of garden soil. Do not cut the aerial roots off even the cuttings. The soil should be rich and very coarse and kept good and moist. Stem cuttings laid in damp peat and kept at a temperature of about 30°C (86°F) will quickly root.

MYRTUS

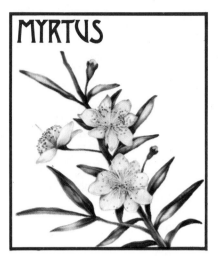

Myrtle

Evergreen ornamental shrub with beautiful, scented flowers and aromatic foliage.

Position sunny and airy, in loamy, lime-free soil.
Height 20-50 cm (9-20 in); rarely, as much as 2 m (6 ft).
Flowering summer and autumn.
Propagation by cuttings.

Myrtle has been a symbolic plant from time immemorial. In olden days it stood for fertility, later for chastity and purity. You may still see brides carrying sprigs in their bridal bouquets.

Most species are natives of the Mediterranean countries where they

Myrtus communis

reach as high as 5 m (16 ft). The only species at all common as a house plant is *Myrtus communis*, common myrtle, whose lanceolate, leathery leaves grow opposite each other on erect branches. They have a shiny, dark green surface and a slightly spicy smell. Large numbers of pretty, short-stemmed flowers appear in the leaf axils in summer and autumn. Numerous yellowish white stamens stand out above the white petals. On older specimens, which can reach 2 m (6 ft) high, little blue-black berries appear in the autumn.

Cultivation

Since myrtles should stand in a sunny, airy, but not too warm place, they do very well in the open air in summer. In winter bring them in to a cool room, with temperatures between 2-10°C (37-50°F). Feed established plants with weak liquid manure at fortnightly intervals during the summer. Water freely in summer, less in winter according to room temperature, giving them just enough to stay moist. Do not let them stand in water or let the root ball dry out. Prune only straggly shoots from the base in spring.

Propagation

You can take cuttings of lateral non-flowering shoots in summer and put them to root in sand under glass. Pot on first in small pots with sandy soil, then in larger pots with loamy soil the following spring. Frequent nipping out of the tips of shoots ensures bushy growth.

NEPHROLEPIS

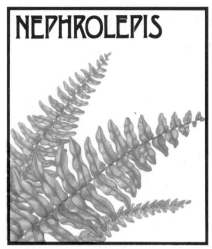

Ladder Fern, Sword Fern

Bushy indoor fern with decorative pinnate leaves.

Position half-shady and airy, in humus-rich soil.
Height up to 80 cm (32 in).
Propagation by runners or by spores.

Ferns have always been popular as house plants. Still among the favourites is nephrolepis, the bushy ladder or sword fern with its filigree pinnate leaves. This tropical and subtropical perennial bears light to dark green leaflets on more or less curved fronds which are generally wavy or even crinkly. In older plants they often grow over 1 m (3 ft) long.

Species

The most attractive varieties have been developed from the species *Nephrolepis exaltata*. The individual breeds are mainly distinguished by the variously formed pinnate leaves, which can either be quite smooth or heavily wrinkled.

The best known variety, 'Bostoniensis', has dark green, lanceolate leaves which are simply pinnate. 'Boston Dwarf' has leaves of the same shape but considerably shorter. 'Rooseveltii' has long, wavy leaves, strong and lasting. The bushy variety 'Whitmannii' attracts attention by its prettily crinkled, compound pinnate, light green leaves.

At first sight the species *Nephrolepis cordifolia* is hard to tell from *Nephrolepis exaltata*, but you can recognize it by the tiny storage bulbs growing on long runners. The slender, crowded leaves are generally dark green and have a particularly large number of leaflets in the pinnate leaf.

Cultivation

From spring to autumn the ladder fern must stand in a half-shady, airy place. A north window is ideal. The temperature should not exceed 20°C (68°F), and in winter should not fall below 15°C (59°F). Water freely in summer, less in winter. To prevent the root ball from drying out, put the pot from time to time up to its rim in a basin of water and leave it there for a few hours. Take off dead leaves.

Young plants grow very strongly and must be repotted every year. Repot older plants only every two or three years, preferably in spring. Take great care not to damage the delicate root system when repotting.

Propagation

Detach strong runners from luxuriantly growing ferns and plant them in humus-rich soil. The best periods are spring or early autumn. Or, to ensure strong growth, separate nascent plantlets from the runners (stolons), and pot in peat and sand at greenhouse temperatures of 13°C (55°F).

Many ladder ferns can also be propagated by spores, but this is best left to professionals.

NERIVM

Oleander, Rose Bay

Tender evergreen house plant with fascinating flowers.

Position sunny and airy, in sandy loam.
Height growing wild, up to 4 m (13 ft).
Flowering in summer.
Propagation by cuttings.

If you have ever had a holiday near the Mediterranean, you will know the abundant, scented flowers of the wild oleanders. These bushy shrubs grow up to 4 m (13 ft) high in their own country. They bear white, yellow, pink or red clusters of flowers between shining, bright green, long, pointed leaves.

Indoors, the oleander grows less abundantly. Nor does it flower often, and in rainy summers it scarcely flowers at all.

If you take cuttings for a second growth, be careful! All parts of it are poisonous.

Of the three species, we can grow only one as a pot plant, *Nerium oleander*. When young, its lanceolate-leaved stems are flexible, but later become woody. The delicate clusters of flowers, which appear in summer, are generally pink, but there are also white, yellow or red varieties, some of which bear large double flowers.

Cultivation

The best guarantee of a good show is an airy position in full sun, so in spring and summer you should keep your oleander on the balcony or terrace as much as possible. But the plants cannot tolerate heavy rainfall or the first night frosts. The oleander needs a lot of water and must be fed once a week.

Put the shrubs in a light, airy place all through the winter. Minimum room temperature is 7°C (45°F). Water less in autumn and winter, but do not let the plant dry out.

Propagation

Take stem cuttings in summer, which will root in water or moist sand if protected from the light. Pot on in small pots with sandy loam. Prune flowering shoots frequently to encourage bushy growth.

Left: *Nephrolepis exaltata*
Below: *Nerium oleander* hybrid

Nerium oleander

NERTERA

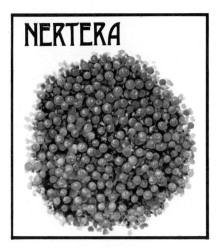

Bead Plant, Fruiting Duckweed

Creeping, mat-forming perennial herb with striking berries.

Position half-shady, airy and cool, in sandy loam.
Height up to 10 cm (4 in).
Flowering in spring.
Propagation by division.

The bead plant is one of the few house plants grown purely for its ornamental fruits.

The genus includes only a few species, and of those we grow only the South American *Nertera granadensis*. It forms a dense cushion up to 10 cm (4 in) high. The stems are some 20 cm (9 in) long, with tiny oval leaves growing closely along them. This carpet is covered in spring with tiny greenish white flowers.

The bead plant really comes into its own in late summer, when it produces round, scarlet berries which often last well into the winter.

Cultivation
The bead plant will get through the summer unharmed as long as it stands in a light, half-shady, cool and—above all—airy position. A place by an open window, or on the balcony, suits it best. The temperature should not be higher than 16°C (61°F). In winter the plants need a light room with a temperature of about 8°C (46°F). Water regularly, but not too much, in summer, and rather less in winter. Spray frequently, except when the plant is in flower.

Propagation
The plants can be cut into several pieces in late summer or early autumn. Plant these cuttings in small pots with sandy loam. A bit more bottom heat next spring will stimulate abundant fruiting.

NIDULARIUM

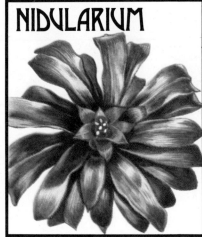

Bird's Nest Bromeliad

Low-growing perennial with beautifully coloured leaf rosettes.

Position half-shade and warm, in loose humus-rich soil.
Height up to 30 cm (12 in).
Flowering spring to autumn.
Propagation by offsets.

In its Brazilian homeland nidularium grows in the forks of trees. Indoors it is grown as a hanging or basket plant. The species we cultivate are comparatively small. The narrow leaves of the widely fanned-out rosette seldom grow longer than 30 cm (12 in). The middle of the rosette is often red, and forms a little nest in which the white, blue or reddish flowers grow closely together.

Species
Nidularium fulgens has marbled dark green leaves with brown edges. The inner leaves of its erect rosette range from white to red, and between them a cluster of up to 40 small blue flowers can gather together.

The loosely arranged leaves of *Nidularium innocentii* gleam blue-black but become red at the centre of the rosette. They have toothed edges, and their underside is reddish. The flowers are greeny white.

Cultivation
The rosettes form well in a humid hothouse atmosphere, but will also thrive in a half-shady place in a warm room with high humidity. In summer they need temperatures of at least 22°C (72°F), in winter of at least 15°C (59°F). As with many bromeliads, the soil needs only moderate watering, but some water with the chill off should always stand in the funnel of the rosette. Spray in summer.

Propagation
Older specimens form offsets at the foot of the rosette. To propagate you can cut these with a sharp knife and plant them in loose humus-rich soil. Growth takes place best with some bottom heat and very moist air.

Nidularium innocentii 'Lineatum'

OPHIOPOGON

Undemanding indoor perennial with grass-like evergreen leaves.

Position shady, in loamy soil.
Height 15-80 cm (6-32 in).
Flowering in summer.
Propagation by division.

Perhaps the most striking feature of the ophiopogon is its thick, luxuriantly growing, grass-like leaves.

Species
The evergreen leaves of the species *Ophiopogon jaburan*, which comes from Japan, grow up to 40 cm (16 in) long and about 1 cm ($\frac{1}{2}$ in) broad. Above the thick heads of older specimens there sometimes appear in summer as many as nine racemes of white or violet flowers. There are several varieties with firm, yellow foliage or with leaves striped and spotted with white and yellow.

Ophiopogon japonicus grows more bushy but considerably lower. Its dark green leaves grow only 15 cm (6 in) long. They are hard and stand erect and close together. The variety 'Variegatus' has white and yellow-striped leaves. Both species and varieties flower white or violet. Small blue-green berries quite often occur.

Cultivation
Ophiopogon does equally well in cool rooms or in warm. Even dry air does it no harm. All that matters is that you should protect it from the full glare of the sun. Water regularly in summer, but just keep the soil slightly moist in winter.

Propagation
The plants of the ophiopogon can be easily divided in late winter or early spring. Plant in small pots of loamy soil.

OPUNTIA

Prickly Pear

Cactus with pretty flowers. Some are hardy.

Position hot and sunny, on rich, open soil.
Height between 5 cm and 5 m (2 in and 16 ft).
Flowering spring and summer.
Propagation by cuttings and seeds.

Even the real cactus experts have not yet managed to classify the immense number of prickly pear cacti or even to make an estimate. There are too many species, too different in size, in appearance, in flowers and in the conditions they need for growth. But they do have one troublesome characteristic, and that is their glochids—tiny spines with a sort of hook at the tip, which break off at a touch and stick in the skin.

The prickly pears originated in America. Today they grow wild in every warm part of the world. The stems are branching and of different shapes—flat, circular stems, for instance, cylindrical stems and globular stems, some erect, some prostrate.

Species
Even as a young plant, *Opuntia azurea* produces a marvellous, fiery red flower. The stems of this species have very few glochids and vary in colour between blue-grey and rusty brown. They have a remarkable long, dark central spike, with a white tip growing from the areoles at the ends of the joints.

Opuntia bergeriana has a red flower 5 cm (2 in) wide that blooms in summer. This plant will grow up to 2 m (6 ft) high in a tub and has broad joints up to 25 cm (10 in) long.

Opuntia microdasys often produces branching shrubs up to 1 m (3 ft) high. The joints are rounded, about 15 cm (6 in) long. The pale yellow flowers, 5 cm (2 in) across, are not so striking and often fail to appear in cultivation.

Cultivation
The prickly pear needs a porous, preferably sandy, loamy soil and a sunny position. Water freely while the plants are growing in spring and summer, and on hot summer days spray as well as water. In the rest period—it generally begins in autumn when the flowers have fallen—reduce watering or even stop it altogether. In winter put the house plants in light, airy, but always cool places at about 8°C (46°F).

Propagation
All species of opuntia can be propagated by cuttings without trouble. Cut a side shoot off in the spring, let the cutting dry a little, then put it in a pot of very sandy soil. Propagation by seeds is possible but calls for a lot of patience as the seeds take a long time to germinate. Soak them in water a day or two before planting.

Opuntia

OXALIS

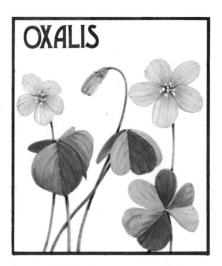

Perennial for the room and balcony with abundant flowers.

Position half-shady, moist and cool, in sandy, loamy humus-rich soil.
Height up to 20 cm (9 in).
Flowering autumn or, if forced, also in winter.
Propagation by offsets.

A popular plant, because of the superstition that a four-leaved clover brings luck. *Oxalis deppei* looks rather like a four-leaved clover. It is a bulbous perennial with a long, juicy root, originally from Mexico. Its leaves grow on a stem 20 cm (9 in) long and have a brownish patch on each of the four leaflets; the underside of these 'clover leaves' is a silvery grey-green. If you just let the plant grow normally, it will flower in a room or on a balcony in early autumn.

Gardeners have managed to get this 'lucky' flower to bloom in winter. To obtain these flowers, put several offsets in small flower pots in autumn and cover them with about 1 cm (½ in) of sandy loamy humus-rich soil. Given a temperature of 8°C (46°F) and moderate watering, they soon root, and by early winter the rapidly growing plant will have produced tubular, yellow-throated flowers.

Cultivation
Oxalis deppei is generally kept too warm. You should put it on the north side of the house, preferably in an unheated room or an entrance hall, but in the light. Water regularly in growing and flowering periods. The plant has its rest period in spring, when, if you want to grow it as a normal indoor foliage plant, you can detach the offsets and replant them. After flowering, store the detached suckers until next spring at a temperature just under freezing point.

Propagation
Divide the plants after flowering.

PACHYSTACHYS

Bushy indoor perennial with abundant flowers and brilliant bracts.

Position half-shady, but light and airy, in ordinary garden soil.
Height up to 50 cm (20 in).
Flowering spring to autumn.
Propagation by cuttings.

These shrubby perennials are about 50 cm (20 in) high, with long, pointed leaves on which the veins are distinctly indented. Growing up from the leaves are a number of erect flower stems, of up to 15 cm (6 in) long. The white flowers last only a short time and then fade, but the golden bracts shine on for weeks.

Cultivation
Pachystachys lutea, the yellow beloperone, needs a light and airy position, but one that is sheltered from the summer sun. Keep the ordinary garden soil moist, and water with lukewarm water.

During the growth and flowering periods, from late winter through autumn, the plants need liquid fertilizer every fortnight. During the rest period give no fertilizer and hardly any water.

Propagation
You can take cuttings 8-10 cm (3-4 in) long in spring and summer. First put them in water, then plant them in sandy soil. Keep the shrubby cuttings under glass or protect them with plastic foil. Repot the young plants in loose garden soil.

Oxalis deppei

PANDANUS

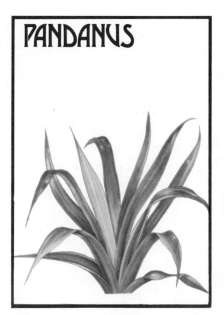

Screw Pine

Evergreen house plant with adventitious roots and attractive leaves.

Position light and warm, in loose, humus-rich soil.
Height up to 150 cm (59 in).
Propagation by seeds, suckers or offsets.

You cannot fail to recognize the screw pine by its long narrow leaves growing spirally up the stem. After about five years the plant lifts itself up out of the ground on strong adventitious roots or aerial roots.

Of more than 500 wild species, some of which grow as high as 20 m (66 ft), only three are common as house plants. They have sword-shaped, variously patterned leaves, some of them growing erect, others bending over to a greater or lesser extent.

Species
The dark green leaves of the shrub *Pandanus sanderi* have white, yellow or light green stripes, and their edges have little red spines. They grow up to 1 m (3 ft) long and 6 cm (2 in) wide.

The spiral growth shows particularly clearly in the leaves of *Pandanus utilis*, which grow 150 cm (59 in) long and 8 cm (3 in) wide. The stiff, blue-green leaf-swords of this indoor tree bear long, red prickles on their edges.

The shrub *Pandanus veitchii* grows equally bushy. The leaves, dark green in the middle with silver margins towards the edges, have only a few spines.

Cultivation
The screw pine needs plenty of light all year round, but no full sun, and high humidity. The right temperature for its position in summer is between 20° and 25°C (68° and 77°F). Water freely in spring and summer, and feed once a week. Give it less water in autumn and winter, and a minimum temperature of 13°C (56°F). Repot mature plants in spring.

Propagation
You can get freshly imported seeds for all species to germinate at 28°C (82°F). *Pandanus sanderi* and *Pandanus veitchii* can also be propagated by offsets. Take cuttings about 20 cm (9 in) long in spring and let them root in sand at 22°C (72°F) until they are well established.

Paphiopedilum callosum

PAPHIOPEDILUM

Slipper Orchid

Evergreen orchid, also suitable as cut flowers and hardy enough to thrive in a temperate room.

Paphiopedilum insigne

Position light and airy, in peat.
Height up to 30 cm (12 in).
Flowering according to species, autumn to spring.
Propagation by division.

While most orchids are hothouse plants, paphiopedilum will often thrive in a temperate room. There are 50 wild species and a number of hybrids.

One part of paphiopedilum's attractive flower, the lip, stands out like a little slipper. Behind this there is a big, vertical spathe, from which two smaller inner spathes grow down sideways. The flower stands at the top of a long scape between leathery, spear-shaped leaves.

Species
The big, brightly coloured flowers of *Paphiopedilum callosum* appear in early spring, growing at the top of a slender scape 30 cm (12 in) high. Behind the rust red lip there is a white spathe with red stripes along it. The side spathes are green, turning to red in the middle and spotted with black at the edges. The blue-green leaves have spots of dark green.

The especially hardy species *Paphiopedilum insigne* will flower throughout the winter if properly looked after. These brilliant orchids, up to 10 cm (4 in) across, have a greeny yellow lip speckled with brown. The vertical spathe, green with a white point, is covered with reddish brown spots. The narrow side spathes are light green, the veins marked out in brown. A number of cultivated varieties have been developed from this species, among which are 'Chantinii' and 'Harefield Hall'.

Cultivation
Paphiopedilum must stand in an airy, light spot, but not in the sun. Night temperatures for *Paphiopedilum callosum* must not fall below 25°C (77°F) in summer or 18°C (64°F) in winter. Cold-house species like *Paphiopedilum insigne* need night temperatures of only 18°C (64°F) in summer and 12°C (54°F) in winter. Always keep the plants well moistened with lukewarm water, and syringe them every day in summer. Water sparingly for three weeks after flowering.

Propagation
Plants that are growing well can be divided in the spring. Plant in loamy leaf mould and in the early stages spray them several times a day.

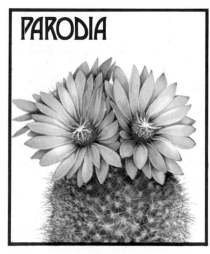

PARODIA

Globe cactus with brightly coloured spines and magnificent heads of flowers.

Position sunny and warm in loamy soil.
Height up to 20 cm (9 in).
Flowering spring and summer.
Propagation by seeds.

The parodias, which come from South America, have coloured spines, and even as young plants often flower with unusual abundance. There are numerous species, some globular, some growing as straight or twisted columns. Their ribs bear a number of tubercles, from which curved spines often grow. In spring and summer red or yellow flowers, mostly star-shaped and often in groups of two or three together, grow from the top of the cactus.

Species
Parodia aureispina is a globe, 6-8 cm (2-3 in) across, with tubercles on the ribs, which have soft white bristles at the edges and curved yellow spines at the centre. The bright yellow flowers grow to 3 cm (1 in) in diameter.

The species *Parodia chrysacanthion,* 10 cm (4 in) high, grows globular at first but elongates later. The soft, covering spines are golden-yellow and grow to 3 cm (1 in) long. Little yellow flowers grow on the white, downy top of the cactus.

Parodia maasii grows 20 cm (9 in) high and 15 cm (6 in) wide. The yellow-brown spines grow in all directions, with a sharp curve in the middle. The flowers, up to 5 cm (2 in) across, are red brown, red or salmon pink.

A common species is *Parodia microsperma*, a globe cactus 10 cm (4 in) across. Between the light-coloured

thorns at the edge of the tubercles grow red-brown central thorns, some of which are long and hooked. This species blooms yellow or orange.

Parodia sanguiniflora is certainly among the loveliest species. The big globe, up to 8 cm (3 in) in size, is covered all over with little tubercles, from each of which grow a great many border spines and four red central spines. The flowers are of various colours—orange, scarlet, red.

Cultivation
Parodia cacti must be kept sunny

and warm in summer, and in winter the temperature must not fall below 10°C (50°F). Water freely in the warm season, preferably with lime-free water. Keep very dry in winter.

Propagation
The parodias can be propagated by seeds, but not with ease. The tiny little seeds must be kept completely in the dark until they germinate. Transplant the seedlings in loam. Keep them under glass at first.

Right: *Passiflora caerulea*
Below: *Parodia aureispina*

PASSIFLORA

Passion Flower

Splendidly flowering, evergreen climbing shrub with twining stems.

Position sunny and airy, in sandy soil.
Height up to 2 m (6 ft).
Flowering spring to autumn.
Propagation by cuttings.

The passion flower is popular for its twining foliage and fascinating flowers. There are over 400 tropical species in the wild and some cultivated species which, when grown as house plants, must be supported by a trellis.

Species
The wide-open stellate flowers of *Passiflora caerulea* have a dense central corona of blue filaments. An extraordinary feature is the protruding triple, dark red style. The broad, stalked leaves have five or seven lobes. Well known varieties are the ivory 'Constance Elliott', and 'Empress Eugénie' with big, reddish or violet flowers.

The big, red flowers of the Brazilian species *Passiflora racemosa*, 10 cm (4 in) wide, grow in loose clusters. The filaments, growing like a wreath, are in shades of blue and white.

Cultivation
After early spring, the best place for a passion flower is in the light and sun of a windowsill. From late spring to autumn you can even put the plants out on the balcony, and during this

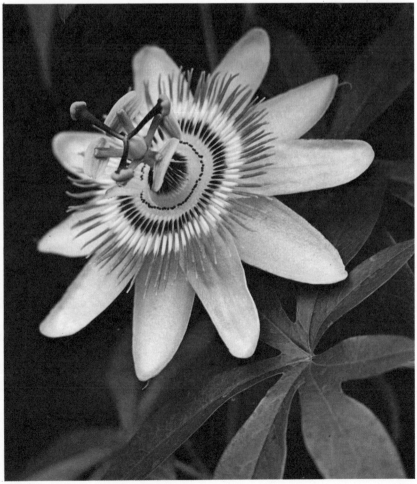

time you must water freely and feed once a week. Spray frequently. In winter the soil should be only slightly moist. *Passiflora caerulea* should then be kept as cool as possible, at about 5°C (41°F), but *Passiflora racemosa* needs an overwintering temperature of some 18°C (64°F).

Propagation
Take top cuttings in early spring, and let them root in warm sand under glass. After about eight weeks pot on in sandy soil.

Far right and right: *Pelargonium grandiflorum* **hybrids,** *Pelargonium zonale* **hybrid**
Below: *Passiflora caerulea* **fruits,** *Pelargonium*

Geranium

Perennial shrub or subshrub for house and balcony, as popular for its foliage as its flowers.

Position airy and warm in sun and half-shade, in fairly moist humus-rich soil.
Height up to 2 m (6 ft).
Flowering spring through autumn.
Propagation by cuttings.

There is hardly a hanging basket, window box, or balcony in which geraniums do not appear. With their many quite different species and abundance of cultivated varieties, the geranium can be kept as a cold-house plant, a plant for the living room and as a half-hardy garden plant.

The name 'geranium' is botanically incorrect. What we insist on calling a geranium is a pelargonium in correct botanical terminology.

The genus has too many species, varieties and hybrids to sort out here. Our common house and balcony

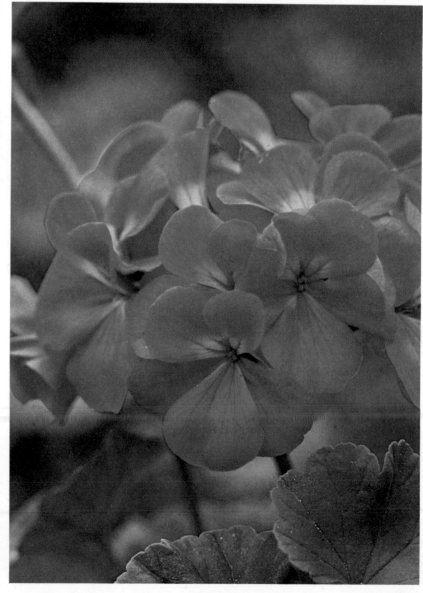

plants are not true species but hybrids or crosses.

Regal species

The *Pelargonium grandiflorum* hybrids, also known as regal pelargoniums, are kept indoors all year, though they can summer on the balcony if well sheltered. They have light green, kidney-shaped leaves as big as a hand and slightly toothed at the edges. Plants with a single shoot and usually woody stem, they bear flowers of up to 5 cm (2 in) across, which form dense clusters of pink, red or white with dark spots. Older specimens, from say the fourth or fifth year, slacken their flowering and should be exchanged or renewed from cuttings.

Cultivation of regal species.

These geraniums like moist soil but no standing water. Feed about twice a month as long as they are growing.

THey need light positions both in summer and winter, but should be kept out of the full sun at midday. Keep them cool in winter, at about 12°C (54°F), but do not put them in the cellar as you would with geraniums from the window box.

Propagation of regal species

When the flowers begin to wilt, propagate the hybrids by ripened cuttings, put into sandy soil broken up with peat. Not until then do you give the young plants a warmer position —if possible at temperatures not exceeding 15°C (59°F).

Ivy-leaved species

The *Pelargonium peltatum* hybrids, with their trailing or drooping stems, are ideal for flower baskets or for boxes on the balcony. You can keep them in the open air in summer. They are called ivy-leaved geraniums or pelargoniums on account of their rather thick, smooth and shiny leaves, which look a bit like ivy leaves. They grow on long brittle stalks and are green to greeny brown. They range in colour from white to violet, and in some species the flowers are double. All share a long-lasting inflorescence, usually from spring through autumn.

Cultivation of ivy-leaved species

During their growth period the ivy-leaved geraniums need plenty of water and should be fed about once a fortnight. Remove dead flowers immediately. After the flowering period, cut these subshrubs back a little and then store them dry in a light cellar until late winter. Be careful not to damage the root ball when you come to repot them.

Propagation of ivy-leaved species
Propagate ivy-leaved geraniums in late summer by cuttings; plant them in slightly sandy humus-rich soil and keep them in the shade. They only need very little water. The young plants must be kept light and cool during the winter at about 10°C (50°F).

Zonal species
Most of the geraniums you find on balconies and in gardens are *Pelargonium zonale* hybrids or, otherwise, zonal geraniums. They get their name from the semicircular, brownish mark on their leaves. These little subshrubs have upright, succulent stems which grow woody in older specimens. The little bushes are strongly branched and have round leaves with slight indentation. The characteristic geranium scent is unmistakable; you get it when you rub the leaves between your fingers. Zonal geraniums bear round clusters of flowers in all shades of red, from rose pink to fiery red or violet. Famous varieties include the light pink 'Jean Billis'.

Cultivation and propagation of zonal species
As for ivy-leaved geraniums.

Succulent species
Among the 250 or so species of geranium there are a few succulents, which laymen would hardly expect to see classified as such. They are grown less for their tiny flowers than for their dense foliage. Of these, good examples are *Pelargonium crassicaule,* with a thick, short stem, on the upper half of which grow needle-like leaves, and *Pelargonium ferulaceum*, whose many leaves have silky hairs.

Cultivation of succulent species
Both species are true house plants, preferring a light position and temperatures of between 10° and 15°C (50 and 59°F). During the rest period after flowering, these species should be kept quite dry.

Propagation of succulent species
They are readily grown from seed in sandy, loamy soil.

Nonsucculent species
The rose geranium *(Pelargonium*

Pelargonium peltatum

graveolens) is grown for its scented leaves. This sturdy shrub has five-lobed, hairy blue-green leaves, which smell like roses. This species is kept as a house plant, like the species *Pelargonium radens*, also known as rose geranium. The leaves of *Pelargonium odoratissimum*, the lemon geranium, give off a marvellous scent of lemons. Their attractive, velvety leaves grow on long stems. The light pink flowers of this species, like those of the rose geraniums, are very small.

Propagation of nonsucculent species

The best way to propagate these nonsucculent species is by cuttings, taken in the spring. They develop quickly and soon can be put out in sheltered positions on the balcony. Although they are really house plants, they can be planted out, but must be brought inside in autumn and left to overwinter in a cellar.

Right: *Pelargonium peltatum* **hybrid**
Below: *Pelargonium* **'Mac Mahon'**

Pelargonium **'William Walker'**

Pelargonium zonale (upright),
Pelargonium peltatum (hanging),
Petunia, Lobelia

PEPEROMIA

Pepper Elder

Evergreen, sometimes epiphytic indoor plant with beautiful leaves of varying contours.

Position half-shady and warm in sandy garden soil.
Height up to 20 cm (9 in).
Propagation by cuttings.

The pepper elder has become one of the most popular foliage plants. The genus originates in the tropical forests of South America where many of the 400 or so species live on the branches of trees.

Their fleshy leaves, ornamental or green, smooth or wrinkled, are heart-shaped, round or lobed and grow on a long stalk.

Species
The rounded leaves of the *Peperomia argyreia* grow on red stalks 12 cm (5 in) long. They are greeny brown on top with silvery stripes, and reddish underneath.

Peperomia caperata has small, heart-shaped wrinkled leaves, marbled light and dark green on top. It bears thin clusters of yellowish white

Peperomia argyreia

flowers on long, red speckled stalks. *Peperomia glabella*, with its twining branches, is often used as a hanging plant. The green leaves are oval.

The long, white leaf stems of *Peperomia griseo-argentea* have a striking red pattern. The densely growing leaves, roundish to heart-shaped, are irregularly cambered with wavy edges. The upper side gleams silver-grey, the underside is greeny white.

The broad, oval leaves of *Peperomia obtusifolia* are particularly stiff and leathery. They have a short, red-spotted stem and white flower spikes.

Cultivation
The pepper elder needs a light, warm position out of the sun. Ornamental-leaved species must overwinter at a minimum temperature of 18°C (64°F), the others at about 15°C (59°F). Water regularly but not too much in the summer growth period, feed once a fortnight, and keep the atmosphere moist. In the winter rest period give the plant just enough water to keep the root ball from drying out.

Propagation
You can take stem or leaf cuttings all year round—but only stem cuttings for the ornamental-leaved species. Let them root in peat and sand under glass at 20°C (68°F), and later put the young plants in peat-based compost.

Peperomia griseo-argentea

PHILODENDRON

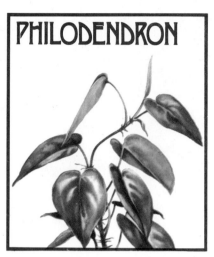

Sweetheart Vine

Evergreen, climbing foliage plant.

Position half-shady to shady, but light and warm in nourishing humus-rich soil.
Height up to 5 m (16 ft).
Propagation layering or cuttings.

We have many cultivated species of philodendron which differ from one another widely in appearance and in the shape of the leaves. Moreover, these shrubs and trees acquire quite different features as they mature. Many can only be kept as young plants, because later they get too large to keep in a room or to climb. They rarely flower as house plants, but the inflorescence and the brightly coloured surrounding spathe are very attractive.

Species

Philodendron bipinnatifidum needs plenty of room. It has broad, slightly heart-shaped young light green leaves with long stems. Later the leaves become irregular in shape. These are not climbing plants. They have a short, upright stem dotted with the scars of fallen leaves.

Enormous, thin leaves, deeply lobed, and growing on long, spotted stems, distinguish the quick-growing *Philodendron elegans*. This climbing plant from the rain forests of Brazil has aerial roots which you must in no circumstances cut off.

The red-stemmed *Philodendron erubescens* has a great many small aerial roots. This climbing plant has leaves of an elongated heart shape, which on the young plant are reddish. As the plant grows older, the underside of the leaves remains reddish while the upper side changes to dark green. The flowers are particularly beautiful. The characteristic spadix is snow white with a rusty brown spathe behind it.

Philodendron martianum, a non-climbing species with leathery, dark green, shiny leaves, soon grows too big for an ordinary room, but you can often see it as a splendid foliage plant in a conservatory.

The easily cultivated *Philodendron scandens*, or sweetheart vine, is a climbing plant with long, thin stems bearing dark green leaves that are heart-shaped at first and round out as the plant grows older. This plant will quickly twine up a stake padded with moss. Without such support it makes a pretty basket plant.

Cultivation

Philodendrons need positions that are light to half-shady, warm and giving maximum humidity. During their rapid growth they need feeding once a week and plenty of lime-free water. Spray the big leaves frequently and wipe them with a wet cloth once a week. When the plants are resting in winter they do not need much water. Repot younger plants every two years, putting them in open humus-rich soil. Older plants can be repotted at longer intervals.

Propagation

You can propagate older specimens by air layering, which is easier than trying to raise the plants from imported seeds. Propagation by cuttings is difficult, because you have to keep the cuttings under glass, preferably in late spring, for weeks at a temperature of around 30°C (86°F).

PHLEBODIUM

Evergreen perennial fern.

Position shady and warm with high humidity, in coarse compost.
Height up to 150 cm (59 in).
Propagation by division.

When botanical nomenclature was rearranged, one species was with-

Right: *Phlebodium aureum*
Below: *Philodendron erubescens,*
Philodendron scandens

drawn from the old fern genus *Polypodium* and established as a genus on its own.

Species

This huge fern, *Phlebodium aureum*, from the Brazilian rain forests has remarkable blue-green leaves. They grow on stalks 50 cm (20 in) long and themselves reach a length of 1 m (3 ft) or more. The evergreen plants grow well in baskets, especially when young.

Besides the true species, there are also two varieties: 'Glaucum crispum' with dark blue, very wrinkled leaves and 'Manalanum' with wavy, deeply lobed pinnate leaves.

Cultivation

Phlebodium plants thrive best in warm rooms or a conservatory. They like high humidity and winter temperatures of not below 20°C (68°F). Always water them with previously boiled water at room temperature.

Propagation

For the indoor gardener the best method is to divide the plants when repotting.

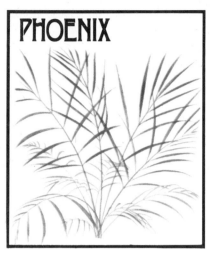

PHOENIX

Date Palm

Evergreen house palm, grown in tubs on the balcony or terrace.

Position sunny and airy, in nutritious, loam-rich soil.
Height outdoors, up to 5 m (15 ft).
Propagation by seeds.

Date palms are easily-cared-for tub plants which do as well indoors as on the balcony or terrace. But keep them away from frost in winter, for these trees from the tropical and subtropical parts of Asia and Africa can only tolerate temperatures of under 10°C (50°F) for a short time. Of the numerous species, including those in botanical gardens, we only keep three. Their stems are covered with the scars of fallen leaves. The evergreen, irregularly pinnate leaves fold inwards and curve backwards and give the trees bushy tops.

Species
Tourists visiting the Canary Islands and seeing the trees of the *Phoenix canariensis* growing up to 15 m (49 ft) tall might not believe that these were the very same plants that they had growing on the balcony at home. This species generally has thick, short trunks and dark green, curved fronds, whose pinnules are folded and somewhat twisted. It needs an airy position in summer so that it can ward off a patchy fungus.

The true date palm, *Phoenix dactylifera,* has a tall stem and blue-green fronds with stiff, strongly folded pinnules. The dwarf date palm, *Phoenix roebelinii,* is a convenient house plant, with short stem and dark green leaves. Its soft and narrow pinnules are arranged on the

Phoenix canariensis, full size

fronds in two rows. This species cannot tolerate direct sunlight and needs high humidity all year round.

Cultivation
Apart from the dwarf date palm, all species need sunny positions, with some shade in summer, and plenty of fresh air. Water freely with softened water during the growth period from early spring through summer, and once a week add liquid fertilizer to the water. Wipe the fronds with a damp cloth fairly often, and do not

allow the root ball to dry out. In the rest period in winter give the plant less water and either move it somewhere cooler or arrange for higher humidity in a warm room. The dwarf date palm, exceptionally, needs no cool place to overwinter.

Repot younger specimens every two years into loamy soil, older plants every four. Do this in the spring, and scarcely water at all for a week afterwards.

Propagation

If you really want to grow a date palm yourself, put fresh imported seed to soak in warm water for two days and then sow them in a flat bowl under very little soil, keeping the bottom heat at 25-30°C (77-86°F). When the seedlings appear, lift the seed out carefully and put in small pots, pressing the seedlings down firmly; then put them in a warm, damp place out of the sun. Plants sown in late winter will have advanced far enough by late summer to be transplanted into a tub.

Phoenix dactylifera

Phyllitis scolopendrium

Hart's Tongue Fern

Strong, evergreen perennial fern.

Position half-shady and shady, in moist soil.
Height 20-40 cm (9-16 in).
Propagation by spores, division or leaf cuttings.

The hart's tongue fern is so robust that you can safely keep it in an unheated hall, and it can even overwinter on the balcony. It does equally well in a moderately heated room, but dislikes direct sunlight.

A great number of varieties have been developed from *Phyllitis scolopendrium*. All have blunt leaves, some 40 cm (16 in) long and 5 cm (2 in) wide. The different surfaces of the leaves distinguish the varieties: 'Undulata' has a wavy surface; 'Crispa' has very wrinkled edges to the leaves; and on 'Marginata' the borders of the leaves are patterned. Dark lines of spores can be seen on the underside of the fronds.

Cultivation

The soil for the hart's tongue must always be moist, and in summer the plant should be sprayed frequently. During the growth period add some liquid fertilizer to the water once a month. Give less water in winter. In spring repot in garden soil.

Propagation

Propagate by division in spring. Only the true species can be propagated by spores, and it is a difficult task. The best method of propagating is by leaf cuttings. Tear the bottom ends of leaf stalks from the rhizome and keep them at a constant temperature of about 20°C (61°F). They will not strike for eight or ten weeks.

Left: *Phyllitis scolopendrium*

PILEA

Artillery Plant, Aluminium Plant, Gunpowder Plant, Pistol Plant

Evergreen house plant with patterned leaves but dull flowers.

Position half-shade to shade, in ordinary garden soil.
Height up to 30 cm (12 in).
Propagation by cuttings.

Pileas get their popular names from a curious characteristic: when the small flowers are watered, the ripe buds of the male flowers discharge a cloud of fine pollen all round them. The many species belong in the tropics. They are kept as house plants for their beautiful, oval leaves, which grow transversely on long stems. The plants look prettiest when they are young and bushy. By the time they are three years old they have lost their profusion of leaves.

Species
Pilea cadierei, the aluminium plant, can grow as high as 30 cm (12 in). The dark green upper side of the leaves is speckled with silver; the underside is light green. Insignificant white flowers grow in the leaf shoulders.

Pilea microphylla, the gunpowder or artillery plant, grows 15 cm (6 in) high. Its bright green, elongated leaves grow on branching stems, the light coloured flowers in umbels.

Cultivation
This foliage plant thrives in the half-shade or shade; it can go on the balcony in summer. Let it overwinter in cool or warm rooms at between 8°C and 20°C (46° and 68°F). Keep moist in summer and feed it each week. Give it less water in winter.

Propagation
Put top cuttings about 5 cm (2 in) long into moist warm sand at about 20°C (68°F) to root.

PIPER

Pepper

Undemanding evergreen climber.

Position half-shady and warm, in ordinary garden soil.
Height climbing, up to 2 m (6 ft).
Propagation by cuttings.

Everybody knows about the spice, but the pepper plant is also an attractive house plant. Some species are especially suitable for climbing up walls or for growing in hanging baskets on account of their lengthy, twining shoots, and big, sometimes colourfully patterned leaves.

Species
Black pepper, *Piper nigrum*, is grown commercially in the tropical regions of Asia. Black peppercorns are the round berries of this plant dried while they are still unripe, and white peppercorns the same berries, ripened and peeled. We can grow this species only as an ornamental house plant: it seldom produces its insignificant flowers, and never fruits. The bright green leaves, growing opposite each other on twining stems, are up to 15 cm (6 in) long.

The ornamental pepper, *Piper ornatum*, has heart-shaped, stalked leaves, spotted pink and white on the upper side, red below.

Cultivation
Pepper cannot tolerate full sun, but does well in even a shady place at ordinary room temperatures. *Piper nigrum* must overwinter at not less than 12°C (54°F), *Piper ornatum* at not less than 16°C (61°F). Water normally, but cut down a bit in winter. Feed once a fortnight from spring to autumn, and spray frequently.

Propagation
Group several cuttings together under glass in very light soil in spring and summer. The temperature must be around 25°C (77°F).

PITYROGRAMMA

Gold Fern, Silver Fern

Very ornamental indoor fern.

Position light and half-shady, in humus-rich soil, not too damp.
Height up to 50 cm (20 in).
Propagation by spores.

Pityrogrammas do not need much moisture. They secrete a gold and silver powder which prevents excessive transpiration, and this makes them particularly suitable for keeping in heated rooms. The powder forms only on the underside of the fronds, but drops down on to the other fronds until the whole plant is covered with the resinous dust.

Species
Pityrogramma argentea, a native of South Africa, forms a silver-white powdery deposit under its leaves. These plants, of bushy habit, have red-brown leaf stalks 15-20 cm (6-9 in) long, with fine dark green leaves.

Pityrogramma calomelanos has fronds up to 60 cm (24 in) long, dark green on the upper side and tinged with gold underneath; the triangular leaves grow on black stalks.

The commonest is *Pityrogramma chrysophylla* which has triangular, dark green leaves powdered with golden-yellow underneath. They grow on dark green to black stalks of up to 50 cm (20 in) long.

Cultivation
Pityrogrammas like a lot of light but dislike direct sun. They keep best in a room with temperatures at between 12-15°C (54°-59°F). Only water them if the soil feels dry. Feed every week in summer, every four in winter.

Propagation
Propagation is a job for the experts.

PLATYCERIUM

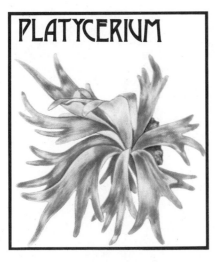

Stag's Horn Fern, Elk's Horn Fern

Exotic fern with big antler-like leaves. A basket plant.

Position a shady place in the room or conservatory, with a constant temperature and air that is not too dry.
Height 40 cm-2 m (16 in-6 ft).
Propagation by spores or division.

Characteristic of the 20 species of platycerium is the cushion formed by its sterile fronds, which grow in great numbers at the base of the fertile fronds. They die and create a cushion of humus where roots form, fed by the water stored there. The long, narrow, strap-shaped antler-like leaves first stand erect, but later hang down. They are much forked, with a leathery surface, and carry the store of spores.

Species
Platycerium bifurcatum or *alcicorne* comes from Australia. The species which has been subdivided by botanists nowadays appears as *Platycerium bifurcatum, Platycerium stemaria* and *Platycerium vassei*. The fern is covered with a fine white and light grey down which partly disappears as it grows older. The round, sometimes overlapping, sterile fronds, called scale leaves, have a diameter of up to 40 cm (16 in). The antler fronds are doubly or trebly forked; those lowest down grow erect, while those at the top hang down. Spores are stored at the ends of the leaves, which can grow as much as 70 cm (27 in) long.

Platycerium grande grows much bigger. The scale leaves reach a length of 60 cm (24 in). The antler-like leaves hang down as much as 2 m (6 ft) and are many times divided. The spores are found in a big, kidney-shaped area at the base of the first fork.

Cultivation
You can plant stag's horn ferns in baskets or wooden tubs; also in a hole in the side of a biggish bit of moss-filled cork. It is best to hang the containers up with copper wire. Important requirements are porous soil (cow manure, peat, moss, even standard compost), and regular spraying, watering and feeding with a complete fertilizer. The stag's horn fern needs a lot of feeding; you should even push little bits of lightly-manured peat under the scales.

What suits the plants best is a firm position in shade or half-shade, away from draughts, in a normally heated room where the temperature does not fall below 15°C (59°F). It likes humid air, but will tolerate dry temperatures.

Propagation
Propagation by spores is difficult and calls for expert knowledge. Propagation by division is much easier and can be successful at any time of year.

PLECTRANTHUS

Perennial house plants for cool or warm rooms.

Position sunny or half-shade, in rooms, staircases, offices or entrance-halls.
Height 60-100 cm (24-40 in).
Flowering according to species, early spring or autumn.
Propagation by cuttings.

It is not easy to get hold of a plectranthus. A relatively easy way is to arrange a swap with another enthusiast. There are 120 species growing in Africa and eastern Asia, but only two are common in Europe.

Species
The Germans call *Plectranthus fruticosus* the moth king, not because it attracts moths but because its smell is said to drive them away. Its heart-shaped, toothed leaves give off a strong smell when rubbed. *Plectranthus fruticosus*

Left: *Platycerium bifurcatum*
Below: *Plectranthus oertendahlii*

flowers in light blue panicles in early spring.

Plectranthus oertendahlii is of lower, drooping habit and so makes a good basket plant. The leaves are oval or round, light green and white-veined. Violet flowers appear in short clusters in autumn.

Cultivation

Plectranthus fruticosus will do well in any nutritious soil and grows throughout the year. It flourishes particularly in places such as halls, landings and corridors, where the temperature may drop to about 5°C (41°F). If you wish, though it is not essential, you can put it out on the balcony or the terrace in summer. *Plectranthus oertendahlii,* however, should stay in warmer rooms in the shade. Water freely during spring and summer, but keep the plants just moist in winter.

Propagation

Both species are easily propagated by cuttings: shoots 6-10 cm (2-4 in) long are put in a little bottle of water. They will produce roots in just a few days.

Below and right: *Plumbago auriculata, Plectranthus oertendahlii*

PLUMBAGO

Leadwort

Flowering ornamental shrub which must overwinter in the warm.

Position light, sunny, as sheltered as possible.
Height about 150 cm (59 in).
Flowering in summer.
Propagation by cuttings or seeds.

It is not too easy to grow plumbago, but the plant will repay your care with endless flowering. In summer, even longer in mild, sunny years, the five-petalled, plate-shaped flowers will go on growing together in clusters. Depending on its size, you can grow the plants in pots, baskets, tubs, window boxes or beds. Plumbago is naturally bushy and branching, but by cutting back the side shoots you can train it to grow as a shrubby plant which will take two years to form a crown.

Species

The commonest species grown is *Plumbago auriculata* or *capensis,* which comes from South Africa. It is an upright shrub, but also a climber, with leaves of up to 5 cm (2 in) long. Its weak, floppy stems usually need tying to supports. Its sky blue flowers, with long, viscid calyxes, occur from spring to autumn. The variety 'Alba' bears white blooms. *Plumbago indica* has pink clusters of flowers as does *Plumbago rosea.*

Cultivation

Until they get too big, plumbagos should be kept indoors all year round. Even in winter, when it has lost its leaves, it should stay in the light. You can then cut back and repot in early spring.

In spring and summer it can go out in the open air—on the balcony or terrace—or can be planted out in a flower bed. It does particularly well in the sun, so long as it is well sheltered from the wind. Water it freely at this time and feed once a week with liquid fertilizer. In autumn you must bring the plumbago back into the house to overwinter at 6-8°C (43-46°F). During the winter keep the plants just moist.

Propagation

Propagation is long and wearisome, both by seeds and by cuttings. Amateur gardeners expecting quick results in return for their efforts are advised to leave this plant to those with much greater reserves of patience.

POLYSTICHUM

Shield Fern

Evergreen, hardy fern with luxuriant filigree fronds.

Position half-shady and airy, in moist garden soil containing peat and sand.
Height up to 1 m (3 ft).
Propagation by division or cuttings.

The numerous species of the shield

Polystichum setiferum

fern are at home in almost every part of the world. Most grow as evergreen, hardy outdoor plants, but some are grown as pot plants. The erect fronds of the polystichums, up to 1 m (3 ft) long, grow closely together from thick, scaly roots, and branch out to form compound pinnate leaves with a filigree effect.

Species

The species *Polystichum aculeatum* has hard, lanceolate leaves up to 80 cm (32 in) long, growing on short stalks with brown-red hairs, mostly double pinnate and bright green.

The luxuriant, ovate leaflets of *Polystichum setiferum,* with finely toothed edges, are outstandingly beautiful. There are several varieties with particularly fine, shaped leaflets. Best known are the dark green 'Plumosum Densum', with very delicately constructed, feathery leaves, and 'Proliferum', with very narrow, compound pinnate leaves on which grow small suckers.

Cultivation

Besides a half-shady position in the window, as airy as possible, the shield fern needs a lot of water. Never let it dry out. In winter the temperature must not fall below 10°C (50°F).

Propagation

Propagation is very simple: divide older plants with a sharp knife in autumn and replant. You can take cuttings in autumn from varieties with suckers. Let them root in warm, moist peat at about 20°C (68°F).

Below, left and right: *Primula obconica*

PRIMVLA

Fairy Primrose, Chinese Primrose

Perennial house plant with many species, all flowering abundantly.

Position half-shady and cool, in porous soil.
Height up to 40 cm (16 in).
Flowering all the year.
Propagation by seeds.

Primula means 'first' and gets its botanical name because some of the outdoor species, like *Primula auricula,* are among the first plants to flower in the year. While most species are garden or wild flowers, a few can also be kept as pot plants in the living room or on the balcony.

Because one species, *Primula obconica,* contains the hormone primin, the entire genus is regarded with some reserve. Primin induces an allergic reaction in many people, in the form of a skin rash. Although varieties without primin have been bred from *Primula obconica,* they are not as beautiful as the other cultivated forms or as the true species.

Primulas have leaves that form rosettes at ground level, while the shape and colour of the flowers vary. Four species are grown exclusively as house plants but many outdoor species can be grown in pots.

Species

The fairy primrose, *Primula malacoides,* is an annual with many varieties which flower in winter and early spring. The flowers grow in whorls at different heights on long, thin stems. It has mid-green leaves with deckled edges; those by the ground are heart-shaped, while those growing higher up are round. This species flowers in white, pink and crimson and in shades of red to purple violet.

Primula **and other spring blooms**

Primula obconica can be cultivated to flower at any time of year. It has long-stemmed, soft leaves with a slight down (the source of primin). Umbels of colourful flowers grow on scapes of up to 25 cm (10 in) long. The many varieties have mostly red or blue flowers.

The Chinese primrose *(Primula praenitens* or *sinensis)* has a great many varieties with widely varying flowers. Breeders have even raised Chinese primroses with pink blooms like carnations, but mostly they are cup-shaped with an inflated calyx. The long-stemmed, big, round leaves are toothed at the edges. An outstanding feature is that the whole plant is covered in soft hairs.

Primula × kewensis, an annual obtained by crossing *Primula floribunda* with *Primula verticillata,* bears flowers of plain canary yellow, which grow on long scapes. The plants are covered with a white powder.

Cultivation

Indoor primulas like light but not full sun. The fairy primrose and *Primula obconica* want winter temperatures of not more than 12°C (54°F), the Chinese primrose and *Primula × kewensis* should be kept at about 15°C (59°F). All of them are susceptible to overwet soil and to the root ball drying out. Water them every day. Once the flower stems start to lengthen, give regular weekly liquid feeds. If primulas are kept too warm in winter, they will only flower for a short time. *Primula obconica* should be discarded after flowering, although they can be grown on.

Propagation

Primulas are propagated by seeds. Sow them under glass in seed compost during the growth period, and maintain a temperature of about 16°C (61°F).

Reinwardtia trigyna

REINWARDTIA

Tender evergreen subshrub with many short-lived flowers.

Position half-shady and airy, in sandy garden soil.
Height up to 80 cm (32 in).
Flowering autumn to spring.
Propagation by cuttings.

This subshrub makes no great demands as a house plant. Its display of yellow flowers is charming during the winter. The little flowers grow in clusters in the leaf axils of the upper branches. Although the individual, delicate, stellate flowers last only a few days, the flowering period lasts for several weeks. As soon as one flower withers, the next begins to open.

Species

Reinwardtia tetragyna flowers from autumn to spring. Its bright green, ovate leaves grow opposite each other on the stems.

The light yellow flowers of *Reinwardtia trigyna* reach a diameter of 3 cm (1 in). They grow in the axils of the lanceolate leaves from winter to spring.

Cultivation

The plants must be protected from glaring sunlight and should stand in as airy a position as possible. In summer you can put them out on the balcony. In winter the room temperature must not fall below 10°C (50°F). Water and spray regularly.

Propagation

Take cuttings in early spring, to root in a mixture of peat and sand at 14°C (57°F). Put the plantlets in sandy soil in summer. Pinch out tips in first growing season to make plants bushy.

RHAPHIDOPHORA

Evergreen climbing plant with ornamental leaves.

Position light to half-shady, in porous, humus-rich soil.
Height on a frame, several metres (feet).
Propagation by cuttings.

Botanists have only recently made up their minds about some species of rhaphidophora, and classified the gold-flecked climbing plant.

Whatever the botanists may have called it in the past, this evergreen climbing shrub has long been a popular foliage plant. The rhaphidophoras are very good climbers on a trellis and have pretty, golden-yellow spots or stripes on their leaves, which on older specimens can attain a breadth and length of 50 cm (20 in). Despite intensive efforts, the plants cannot be made to flower—why, no one knows.

Cultivation
Rhaphidophora aurea needs a light position away from direct sun, with plenty of warmth and high humidity. From spring through autumn water moderately and syringe the leaves frequently; occasionally wipe down the leaves of older specimens. During rapid growth the plant will be glad of plenty of fertilizer. In the winter rest period water little and do not feed at all.

Repot young specimens in spring each year, older plants less often. They need good porous soil and a layer of broken crocks in the pot.

Propagation
Rhaphidophora is propagated by cuttings of ripe growth, which will grow best if cut in spring and planted under glass at temperatures of over 20°C (68°F).

RHIPSALIDOPSIS

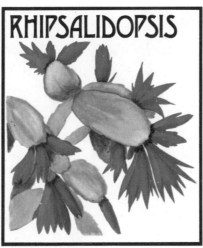

Easter Cactus

Abundantly flowering cactus with leaf-like joints.

Position half-shady, but light and warm, in porous, humus-rich soil.
Height up to 40 cm (16 in).
Flowering spring.
Propagation by cuttings.

The Easter cacti have pendent stems with flat, broad joints which mostly have bristles in their indentations. The little flowers have no crown tube, but radiate fringed petals. In its Brazilian homeland it grows on the branches of trees. Elsewhere it is cultivated mostly as a pot plant.

Species
Rhipsalidopsis gaertneri really forms tiny trees. It is much branched, and its joints are 5 cm (2 in) long and just 2 cm (1 in) wide. It generally flowers in spring, with bright red flowers of up to 4 cm (1½ in) long growing from areoles at the ends of the joints. There are generally several flowers at a time.

Rather more decorative than *Rhipsalidopsis gaertneri* is its hybrid, *Rhipsalidopsis* × *graeseri*, which bears stiff bristles on the areoles at the ends of its leaf joints. The flowers, which appear in spring, are edged with brilliant red and pink in the middle.

The third, smaller, species, not often grown, is *Rhipsalidopsis rosea,* whose flowers are all pink. It has short, flat leaf joints and at 20 cm (9 in) tall is only about half as big as the other species.

Cultivation
The Easter cactus has a resting period from the fall of its last flower until late summer—or even later for late-flowering plants. During this period put the plant in half-shade and give it little water. The rest period begins when the joints begin to shrink. When these plump out again, begin to water freely and to give the plant repeated doses of cactus fertilizer. The plant will want a warm place at 24-28°C (75-82°F) from now until early winter. Then, until the first buds begin to form in mid-winter, keep the plants cool, preferably on the windowsill in an unheated room, and give them less water. As soon as buds begin to form, water freely again and take the plant back into a heated room. Make a light mark on the plants and do not change their position again. It is quite normal for some buds to fall if a lot of them are forming. Instead of repotting, take up the top layer of soil from the pot and put new soil over the uncovered roots.

Propagation
Unless you are a real cactus expert you should stick to the tried and true method of propagating by cuttings. Plant strong joints in very sandy standard compost and keep the pots under glass at a temperature of around 25°C (77°F). Pot on the plantlets after two months, put them in a warm place and do not give them too much water.

Rhipsalidopsis gaertneri

Rhipsalidopsis rosea

RHODODENDRON

Indoor Azalea, Indian Azalea

Popular evergreen shrub which can be made to flower continuously.

Position until late spring in a cool, light room, then outdoors in a half-shady place, in lime-free soil.
Height 1-2 m (3-6 ft).
Flowering winter or spring.
Propagation by cuttings.

Botanists no longer call these plants azaleas, but prefer rhododendron. Amateur enthusiasts, however, can be expected to stick to the old name.

Indoor azaleas are a special breed. They generally cast their leaves like an old dress, although they are soon replaced. But there are pot azaleas that also do well in the open and will even survive a winter outdoors if planted in a sheltered position. Belgian and German breeders have been especially successful in breeding azaleas as pot plants.

The original plant came from eastern Asia, where it grows in areas of heavy rainfall, covering mountain slopes with great areas of blossom.

The vast number of cultivated hybrids and varieties are known under the general name of 'Indian Azaleas', although the ancestors of our present-day pot plants come from Japan and China. Even the plant's namesake, the true *Azalea indica* (now called *Rhododendron indicum),* came not from India but from Japan, though that was not known when the plant was named.

Cultivation
The azalea needs an acid, damp and porous soil. A good mixture is light,

The rich hues of rhododendron blossoms make it a rewarding house and terrace plant.

lime-free compost and peat. During the flowering period, in winter or spring, the azalea can stand on a window ledge in a living room. But it will thrive only if it is regularly watered with lime-free water.

After flowering, they must go into a cool, light room in which the temperature never exceeds 10°C (50°F). In spring, the plant can be put outdoors in its pot. A few hours of sun during the day will not do it any harm. On very hot days azaleas must be sprayed several times. Take them indoors again in cooler weather into a light, cool room with temperatures of about 5-10°C (41-50°F), and move them back into the living room before they flower.

Repot after flowering every two or three years, but only if the plant is becoming pot-bound. After flowering, feed once a week until the middle of summer, and start again when the plant begins to form its new buds, usually in autumn.

Propagation
After flowering, take half-ripe cuttings and insert in peat and sand at 16°C (61°F). Keep humidity high. The cuttings are often slow to root.

RHOEO

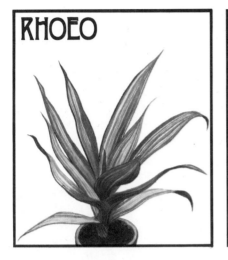

Boat Lily

Evergreen house plant with erect-growing leaf rosettes and insignificant flowers.

Position shady, airy and warm, in ordinary garden soil.
Height up to 30 cm (12 in).
Propagation by seeds or cuttings.

Only one species of this plant from tropical America is at all widespread.

Rhoeo spathacea has narrow lanceolate leaves that grow up to 30 cm (12 in) long and 6 cm (2 in) wide. They grow closely together to form an erect rosette; after a time the lowest leaves bend down a little. The shiny upper sides of the leaves are olive green, the undersides shine reddish violet.

The leaves of the particularly beautiful variety 'Vittatum' are also striped with light yellow. Clusters of little white flowers, framed by slender bracts, grow in the lower leaf axils from late spring to early summer.

Cultivation
The plants are at their best in a shady, warm place. In spring and summer they need comparatively high humidity and very moist soil, and require feeding once a week. In winter they need very little water, otherwise they easily begin to rot. The room temperature in the cold season must be at least 15°C (59°F).

Propagation
You can propagate rhoeos by seeds, which germinate quickly in warm soil at 18-21°C (64-70°F). Propagation by top or stem cuttings is also simple; plant them in moist, warm sand to root and then pot on in standard compost.

RHOICISSUS

Grape Ivy

Evergreen climbing plant with shiny leaves.

Position half-shady and light, in loamy humus-rich soil.
Height climbing 2-3 m (6-10 ft).
Propagation by cuttings.

The grape ivy is one of those house plants that can be kept as well in a centrally heated living room as in a cool entrance hall. It will thrive magnificently as long as the temperature does not fall below 8°C (46°F).

Botanists have kept changing their minds about *Rhoicissus capensis,*

Rhoicissus capensis

the only species that we have and which comes originally from South Africa. Consequently we find this evergreen climbing house plant often called by its old botanical name, *Cissus capensis,* and so included not among the vines but among the wild grapes.

The grape ivy has woody shoots covered with brown hairs, and slightly toothed, heart-shaped, bright green leaves growing on long stalks. In mature specimens these grow 15-20 cm (6-9 in) in size, with some brownish hairs on the underside. Flowers appear only on mature specimens, and form red berries.

Cultivation
If you keep the grape ivy in a warm room, you must give it plenty of water; and because it grows so fast it needs a lot of feeding. Plants in cooler rooms can be watered less. You can put the plants out on the balcony in summer, but not in direct sunlight. Repot younger specimens in humus-rich soil every year in the spring—for older specimens this is only necessary every three or four years.

Propagation
You can propagate at any time of the year by taking a green stem cutting as long as your finger and planting it in a very sandy standard compost. It is best to keep the pot under glass at temperatures of 16-20°C (61-68°F).

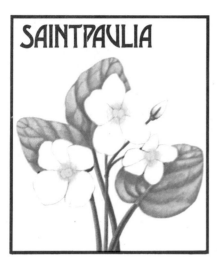

SAINTPAULIA

African Violet

Evergreen house plant with numerous flowers.

Position shady, in loose lime-free humus-rich soil at temperatures not below 15°C (59°F).
Height 5-10 cm (2-4 in).
Flowering the whole year.
Propagation by leaf cuttings.

In 1890 a German colonial officer, Walter von Saint Paul-Illaire, discovered the blue-flowered plant saintpaulia in the forests of what is now Tanzania. Since then, in its many varieties, it has become one of our favourite house plants under the name of African violet. The short-stemmed leaves of this evergreen perennial form rosettes at ground level. The flowers grow in loose cymes on short stems only just above the leaves.

Species

Saintpaulia ionantha is almost the only species we have as a house plant. It has thick, fleshy, slightly hairy leaves, shiny green on top and with a reddish gleam below. They grow on short, reddish brown stems and form firm rosettes about 25-30 cm (10-12 in) across. This species flowers violet-blue all year round.
　Less common is *Saintpaulia confusa*, with violet flowers and thin, green leaves slightly toothed at the edges. Many cultivated forms have been produced by crossing the above two species, some with single, some with double flowers. They bloom in various shades of blue, red and white.

Cultivation

A plant from the tropical rain forest, the African violet cannot tolerate direct sunlight. Keep them in shade, but with plenty of indirect light—a north window is best. Temperatures should be kept at about 18-20°C (64-68°F) all year round and never under 15°C (59°F). Water the roots with lime-free, tepid water, but never sprinkle the leaves and flowers.

Propagation

Even beginners will easily be able to propagate African violets. You can pull off mature leaves complete with stalk at any time of the year and simply insert them at an angle in sandy soil. Young plants will develop in four to six weeks and you can transplant them singly into small pots. Provide sufficient humidity and invert a jam jar or a transparent plastic bag over the leaf cuttings.

Below: *Saintpaulia ionantha*
Bottom: *Saintpaulia confusa*

SANSEVIERIA

Mother-in-law's Tongue, Snake Plant

Very popular evergreen house plant.

Position sunny or half-shady in a warm room, in loamy, nutritious soil.
Height 20-100 cm (9-40 in).
Propagation by leaf cuttings or division.

The snake plant is the undemanding evergreen that you can see on almost every window ledge, waiting room table or hotel reception desk. It is virtually indestructible so long as the room is kept at temperatures about 10°C (50°F). Sansevieria is stemless and has a creeping rootstock. The tough fibres of its long sword-shaped leaves were once used in tropical Africa to make bowstrings.

Species
The species most commonly seen is *Sansevieria trifasciata,* which sometimes develops several leaves on one shoot; the lower leaves are quite small, the upper look like little swords. They can grow up to 100 cm (40 in) long and 7 cm (3 in) broad. They are green with alternate light and dark transverse stripes. The whitish yellow flowers are strongly scented and attractive and grow in spiky panicles on long stems.

There are many forms of this species: 'Laurentii' has broad, golden-yellow borders to the leaves; 'Hahnii' is grown as a dwarf plant, the leaves growing 20 cm (9 in) high and 35 cm (11 in) wide; 'Golden Hahnii' and 'Silver Hahnii' are equally tiny, with broad golden-yellow or white borders to the leaves.

You can tell *Sansevieria metallica*

Sansevieria trifasciata

by its flat leaves, a good deal broader than other varieties and growing obliquely or horizontally. Its leaves are dark green, edged attractively with orange-brown.

Sansevieria cylindrica has three or four leaves to a shoot; they are round in cross section and can grow to 100 cm (40 in). These leaves are also green and have dark green and whitish grey transverse bands.

Cultivation
All species of mother-in-law's tongue should have a light position in the room. They can even stand in the full light of the sun. Do not keep them in the shade or they will grow too tall too quickly.

Sansevieria tolerates dry, centrally heated air very well, but the lower the temperature the less water you should give the plants.

Water regularly in summer, but never water in the hollows of the stems or the rosettes, or the leaves will begin to rot. To prevent rotting the water should also be a little higher than room temperature.

Propagation
The green varieties of sansevieria are propagated by leaf cuttings. Cut the leaves into sections 10 cm (4 in) long and dip them in powdered charcoal before inserting them in a mixture of coarse sand and peat.

Sansevieria cuttings must always be kept warm—20°C (66°F)—or the propagation will not succeed.

Coloured varieties must be divided. If you try to propagate them by leaf cuttings, only green varieties will grow.

SAXIFRAGA

Saxifrage, Mother of Thousands, Roving Sailor

Low-growing perennial with flowers in long-stemmed panicles.

Position half-shady and airy, in humus-rich soil.
Height up to 50 cm (20 in).
Flowering spring through summer.
Propagation by runners and division.

In its mountainous homelands the saxifrage grows very tall. Of the many wild species we have cultivated only a few, mostly as ground-cover plants in rock gardens.

Although they are outdoor plants, some are also kept as pot plants. They differ from one another considerably in leaf shape and in habit, and their flowers, too, are quite different.

Species
Saxifraga cotyledon has fleshy

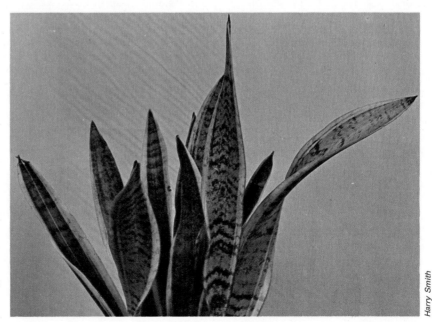

Harry Smith

133

leaves of oval or kidney shape. They form several rosettes up to 20 cm (9 in) wide. In summer a number of pointed spikes of small white, stellate flowers spread over them like a roof. The flowers of this hardy perennial, also often grown as a house plant, can grow to 50 cm (20 in).

Saxifraga stolonifera, known as mother of thousands or roving sailor, attracts attention by its long, drooping runners, which look like thin, red threads and bear new plantlets at the end. The big, hairy leaves of the mother plant grow flat, forming a thick cushion. The upper side of the leaves is grey-green and interlaced with light veins; the underside is dotted with red. The small white, red-tipped flowers grow in panicles of up to 40 cm (16 in) tall. The smaller and more tender variety 'Tricolor' is especially colourful, with cream, red and green variegated leaves that have bright red undersides.

Cultivation
The saxifrages cannot stand direct sun, but need plenty of light and air if the leaves are not to grow dull. The plants will do well on a balcony in summer; in winter the temperature must be kept at least 8°C (46°F) for the mother of thousands, but *Saxifraga cotyledon,* being originally an outdoor plant, is more robust. Water the species normally, the varieties a bit more freely. Spray from time to time. Always take off dead heads immediately.

Propagation
Mother of thousands produces well-developed young plantlets on its runners. Cut several of them off and insert them together in a pot in humus-rich garden soil. Propagate *Saxifraga cotyledon* by division.

Schefflera actinophylla

SCHEFFLERA

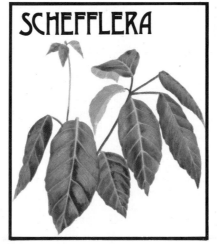

Evergreen, indoor shrub with radially divided leaves.

Position half-shady and warm, in loamy garden soil.
Height up to 150 cm (59 in).
Propagation by seeds.

In the tropics scheffleras are magnificent trees. The genus comprises over 100 different species in which deeply lobed palmate leaves are characteristic.

Only one species has been developed as a house plant, *Schefflera actinophylla,* from Australia. In its homeland the tree will grow to a height of 40 m (131 ft), but if confined to restricting indoor tubs will attain only 150 cm (59 in) and so is suitable as a house plant.

It is common to find 16 separate leaves, as much as 30 cm (12 in) long, growing on a single stalk. The little red flowers appear on their short stems in spring.

Cultivation
If you want the beautiful foliage to last, you must make quite sure that it is growing at the right temperature: in summer between 12-20°C (54-68°F), in winter preferably 15°C (59°F) and certainly not above 18°C (64°F). Give the plants a light and airy spot, but keep them out of direct sunlight and draughts. They can pass the summer in a sheltered place on the balcony. Water freely from spring to autumn, spray frequently and feed once a week. Water less often in winter, but do not let the root ball dry out.

Propagation
Propagation is possible with freshly imported seeds, but they will only germinate with a bottom heat of 21-24°C (70-75°F).

SCILLA

Squill, Wild Hyacinth

Evergreen house plant with delicate racemes of flowers.

Position sunny and airy, in loamy garden soil.
Height up to 50 cm (20 in).
Flowering spring.
Propagation by division.

You will meet most species of the genus growing as pretty spring flowers out of doors. Almost the only species grown as a house plant is the South African *Scilla violacea,* with its beautifully coloured leaves.

Up to 50 cm (20 in) high, *Scilla violacea* grows short-stalked, broadly lanceolate leaves from a bulb growing above ground; their grey-green upper side is spotted with dark green, the shiny underside is deep red. Little yellowish flowers with purple stamens appear in spring, about 20 flowers sometimes growing together on a single delicate, ornamental spike.

Cultivation
This scilla is very little trouble. It just needs a sunny, airy place at temperatures of between 10-20°C (50-68°F). Keep it good and moist throughout the summer.

In autumn the leaves shrink. Set the bulb with its bottom quarter in light, loamy soil to overwinter either cool or warm. Give it only a little water; then, as soon as the first leaves appear, water a little more.

Propagation
Scillas can be easily propagated by division. Carefully separate young offset bulbs from the plant and put them in loamy soil, where they will soon develop.

SCINDAPSUS

Ivy Arum

Evergreen climbing and hanging plant with colourful leaves.

Position warm room, in light garden soil.
Height 2 m (6 ft).
Propagation by cuttings.

Scindapsus climbs like ivy and has borrowed its popular name from it. Its big, heart-shaped leaves are patterned with silver-white spots.

The only common species is *Scindapsus pictus*. This speckled ivy arum does well as a basket plant.

Cultivation

Ivy arum belongs in a warm room, but dislikes too much light. It cannot tolerate sunlight. Even in places where most plants would die for lack of light, the ivy arum still flourishes. The long, oblique stems can either hang down or can be trained up a frame; ideally it should be a moss-covered stake.

It prefers standard compost, or a humus-rich, porous soil mixture. Water with lukewarm water only when the soil feels dry—too much and too cold water can cause brown spots on the leaves. Overwinter the plants at a temperature of 10-13°C (50-55°F).

Pot on every second or third year in the spring if larger plants are wanted. Give a weak liquid feed once a month regularly during the summer.

Propagation

Not only new shoots but any part of the plant bearing a couple of leaves can be used as cuttings. Insert in peat and sand at a temperature of 21-24°C (70-75°F).

Selaginella martensii

SELAGINELLA

Creeping Moss

Evergreen, fern-like indoor plant.

Position shady and airy, in sandy garden soil.
Height 5-30 cm (2-12 in).
Propagation by division or cuttings.

These evergreen, ornamental perennials belong botanically to the sub-group of moss ferns of which there are over 800 species. Most grow along the ground in the tropical rain forests, but they are also to be found in the Canadian tundra. The creeping mosses are valued as house plants for their foliage. The much-branched stems are covered with tiny leaves. Delicate leaf heads grow at the ends of the branches.

Species

Selaginella apoda grows as a mat-like trailer only 5 cm (2 in) high. An undemanding creeping moss of greeny yellow, it is also well suited to cultivation in the cold greenhouse.

The leaves of *Selaginella kraussiana* are bright green. The stems grow to 25 cm (10 in) long, but creep close to the ground. Particularly pretty varieties are the yellow 'Aurea' and 'Variegata', whose leaves have white tips.

Selaginella martensii has erect growing stems of up to 30 cm (12 in) long. The leaves of the species are green, with a shiny surface. A very popular variety is 'Watsonia', with silver tips to the leaves.

Cultivation

All species of creeping moss need a shady, airy place. The species mentioned above can thrive at temperatures of between 5-20°C (41-68°F). *Selaginella apoda* can stand in a fairly cool spot; *Selaginella martensii* prefers more warmth, from about 12°C (54°F). Water with water as free from lime as possible; keep the plants not too moist and not too dry, and spray fairly often to raise humidity. Feed every fortnight in the summer growth period.

Propagation

Propagate *Selaginella apoda* by division. Take cuttings from the other species and put them to root in damp, warm soil. Replant divided parts or new plantlets in sandy soil.

Harry Smith

SENECIO

Cineraria, Dusty Miller

Flowering house plant, generally only annual.

Position in the sunlight, with plenty of water.
Height 40-50 cm (16-20 in).
Flowering spring.
Propagation by seeds.

Cinerarias come originally from the wet, cool hills of the Canary Islands.

Senecio cruentus has large round or heart-shaped leaves with toothed edges and a blue-grey tinge on the underside. The velvety red composite flowers, with red or, less often, yellow centres, grow in clusters.

Its many hybrids flower in every conceivable colour—blue, red and white. They vary tremendously in size, but have the common characteristic that none is worth cultivating after it flowers. Generally the plants die off and have to be thrown away.

Cultivation
Cinerarias prefer a light position but as cool as possible. You can even put them in front of the window as long as there is no frost. In warm, closed rooms they are a positive magnet for aphids and are also susceptible to grey mould and mildew. You will be able to enjoy them longest if you keep them at temperatures of about 15°C (59°F). Keep them even cooler before the flowering period.

Propagation
Cinerarias are only annuals as a rule —even if the experts often write about· them as perennials. Seeds, either collected from the plant or simply bought, will give you young plants without any trouble. Sow them in summer, prick them out once and then insert them in pots of 13 cm (5 in) diameter.

SINNINGIA

Gloxinia

Perennial house plant with brilliant, velvety flowers and soft, hairy leaves.

Position light and half-shady, in loose standard compost.
Height 3-30 cm (1-12 in).
Flowering all the year round, depending on species.
Propagation by seeds and cuttings.

Imported from Brazil at the beginning of the last century, the gloxinia commemorates two important botanists: Benjamin Per Gloxin, who lived in the 18th century and wrote a standard contemporary work on botany; and Wilhelm Sinning, a gardener of Bonn University, who studied how to breed this tuberous plant.

It is only through breeding that the original small-flowered plants have developed into the extensive collection of large-flowered, attractively leaved varieties which are now so popular as house plants.

Species
Sinningia barbata, a perennial of upright habit with very attractive foliage, blooms at all seasons. The leaves, dark green and shiny on the upper side and red-brown underneath, grow up to 20 cm (9 in) long. It does not lose its leaves in winter. The white bell-shaped flowers are reddish inside.

Sinningia eumorpha is a decorative house plant with almost round, dark green, shiny leaves. It has creamy bell-shaped flowers with a purple and yellow pattern inside. It flowers in summer and autumn.

Most of the gloxinias we see on window ledges and in nurseries are the so-called garden gloxinias or sinningia hybrids. The common name is deceptive; they are not outdoor plants but house plants. From spring to autumn, they flower white, pink, red, blue and violet, and the blossoms often have patterns of stripes or spots. The plants also have ornamental foliage. The hairy leaves of up to 25 cm (10 in) long are dark green and feel silky to the touch. Florists sell early-flowering, mid-flowering and late-flowering varieties.

Sinningia pusilla is a dwarf gloxinia. These little flowers, just 3 cm (1-2 in) high, have tiny round leaves and equally minute violet bell-like flowers with a white throat. Plant clusters of this species together in bowls to show them off to effect.

With its brilliantly coloured leaves and flowers, *Sinningia regina* is the queen of all gloxinias. The rust red, velvety leaves have striking white veins. The flowers, up to 6 cm (2 in) across and nodding from long stems, are mauve, ornamented with a creamy stripe and dark red spots. Most garden hybrids have been crossed between *Sinningia regina* and *Sinningia speciosa,* the original Brazilian plant.

Cultivation
You can keep gloxinias in the living room all year round, provided that you treat them properly. Put the plants in a light place in the room, with high humidity during summer. There is no harm in opening the window on warm summer days to let the plants get some fresh air.

Give them plenty of water during the growth period, but be careful not to leave any standing water in the pot or the roots will start to rot. Cut down watering from after flowering until the leaves have fallen. Then, until mid-winter, put the pot with the tuber in a light, dry place with temperatures of around 15°C (59°F). Finally, take out the old tuber, remove the root system and the old soil, and insert the trimmed tuber in moist peat at 21°C (70°F). Cover it with a shallow layer of soil and water only for a short time. Do not water it again, and then only sparingly, until the first small leaves appear.

Propagation
Sinningias are propagated by seeds, but only with difficulty. It is much easier to buy plants already in flower and then to cultivate the tuber. Propagation by leaf cuttings is also difficult. Put them with their stalks into moist sand and keep them in the shade at temperatures of about 20°C (68°F). Plantlets will develop after about four weeks.

SKIMMIA

SMITHIANTHA

Species
Most hybrids have been developed from *Smithiantha zebrina,* which bears red-yellow flowers, and from the white-flowering species *Smithiantha multiflora.* The juicy leaves are green, often with a pattern of rusty red. But what has made the hybrids so popular is the luxuriant flowering, which lasts to late summer. The flowers are red, pink or yellow, with darker spots on their light-coloured interiors. The best known hybrids are 'Discolor', 'Golden King', 'Nana' and 'Splendens'.

Hardy evergreen, flowering shrub with brightly coloured ornamental berries.

Position sunny to half-shady, in loamy soil.
Height up to 150 cm (59 in).
Flowering spring.
Propagation by cuttings.

Both growth and leaves are reminiscent of the laurel bush. Of the different species that grow wild, only one, *Skimmia japonica,* is cultivated as a house plant. The leathery, lanceolate or oval leaves of this shrub grow alternately on the much-branched stems. Up to 10 cm (4 in) long, they are light green on top and yellowish green underneath.

Skimmia, up to 150 cm (59 in) high, blooms in spring in long, pale yellow panicles.

If you have both a male and a female plant, round, bright red but inedible berries ripen in the summer, growing in bunches at the end of the branches. They often last until well into the autumn.

Cultivation
Skimmia prefers a light, airy place, but cannot tolerate bright sunlight. You can put it out on a shaded balcony in summer, where you should spray it now and then, and water regularly with lime-free water. In winter keep the plant cool, but away from frosts, and water more sparingly.

Propagation
Take cuttings of half-ripe lateral shoots in autumn, leave them to root in moist, warm sand, then plant in loamy soil.

Skimmia japonica

Tender plant admired as much for its foliage as for its flowers, but which shrivels in autumn.

Position shady, in humus-rich garden soil.
Height up to 70 cm (27 in).
Flowering late summer.
Propagation by division or cuttings.

Like many flowers, smithianthas first attracted attention as house plants when breeders began to crossbreed hybrid forms, distinguished as much by their magnificent foliage as by their flowers. Both species and hybrids have stalked, low-growing, rather downy leaves, growing from tuberous rhizomes. The heart-shaped leaves shrivel in the autumn. The slender blossoms hang down, with an upturned fringe, forming loose clusters above the brownish green stems.

Cultivation
Smithianthas must have a light but shady position, if possible with high humidity. It is important to keep them out of draughts. Keep them at a constant temperature and water moderately with lukewarm water. When the leaves begin to shrivel in the autumn, leave the rhizome to overwinter in dry soil at at least 12°C (54°F). In early spring put the rhizome in new, humus-rich soil and cover it to a depth of at least 2 cm (1 in). Keep in as warm a place as possible—at least 20°C (68°F)—until the plant flowers. During this period feed every fortnight.

Propagation
The rhizomes can be cut into pieces of about 5 cm (2 in) long and left to root—several pieces to one small pot. Later, pot on in a larger pot with humus-rich soil.

Propagation by leaf cuttings is also possible. Let the stalkless leaves root in warm sand, then replant the young plants in soil.

SOLANUM

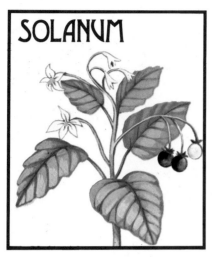

Winter Cherry, Jerusalem Cherry

Subshrubs and shrubs with bright ornamental berries. A good plant for pot or tub.

Position sunny and airy, in loamy or ordinary garden soil.
Height up to 1 m (3 ft).
Flowering summer.
Propagation by seeds or cuttings.

Many of this numerous and universal genus are cultivated as important food crops. The two best known are the potato and the tomato. The brightly coloured berries are pretty but inedible.

Species
The subshrub *Solanum capsicastrum,* the winter cherry, comes from South America. Its light grey, hairy branches, up to 50 cm (20 in) high, bear elongated leaves with slightly wavy edges. In the variety 'Variegatum' they are marbled with white. Densely growing clusters of flowers precede the ripe, round, orange-red fruits which appear in winter.

Solanum pseudocapsicum, the Jerusalem cherry, grows up to 1 m (3 ft) high. The stalked, lanceolate leaves grow separately on green branches. Small, slightly drooping flowers generally hang in groups of three. The round fruits are orange.

Cultivation
The plants like plenty of sun and air. In summer they will do well on the balcony, and even if they get somewhat unsightly in winter, they will revive by the following summer if you keep them in a light place at about 8°C (46°F) and water them less than in summer. Feed and spray in spring and summer to encourage fruiting.

Propagation
Let the seeds germinate at about 18°C (64°F), in late winter or spring. Or take cuttings of side shoots in spring or summer and insert in a mixture of peat and sand at 13-16°C (55-61°F).

Left: *Solanum capsicastrum*
Below, left and right: *Solanum pseudocapsicum, Sparmannia africana*

SPARMANNIA

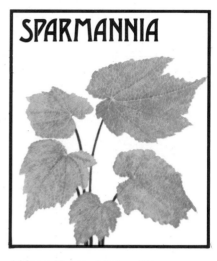

African Hemp, Linden Tree

Evergreen, flowering indoor shrub.

Position half-shady and light, in nutritious, porous soil.
Height 60 cm (24 in).
Flowering late winter and spring.
Propagation by cuttings.

African hemp is an extravagant indulgence, not because it is expensive, but because these evergreen shrubs grow quickly, last for years and require a great deal of room.

We cultivate only one species, *Sparmannia africana,* whose hairy, lime-green leaves of up to 60 cm (24 in) long grow on long stalks. Properly looked after, it will flower winter and spring. The white, stalked flowers grow in cymes and are remarkable for their groups of yellow and rusty brown stamens. If you touch the stamens gently, they will automatically open out.

Cultivation
African hemps are strong growers, and so need nutritious soil manured every fortnight. Their large leaves lose a lot of water by transpiration, so during their growth period, from late winter to autumn, water them liberally. Give them less water in the three months of the rest period, but be careful not to allow the root ball to get dry.

In summer African hemps want a warm, half-shady but light position. You can put them out on the balcony, but be careful to shield them from draughts. In winter keep the plants in unheated rooms at temperatures of around 10°C (50°F). Repot after flowering every two or three years. If they are getting too big you can prune the plants after the flowering period.

Ventilate freely during the spring and summer to ensure that the atmosphere is not too humid.

Propagation
Take shrubby cuttings with three or four leaves from flower stems and put them in sandy soil. To stop the cuttings drying out, trim the leaves a little. Put the cuttings in their pot under glass at temperatures of around 20°C (68°F) and stand them in half-shade. The cuttings form roots after about two weeks and can be potted on after two weeks more. Even as young plants, African hemp must always stand in the light or the leaves will turn yellow or actually drop. Revive the plants by restoring proper treatment.

Spathiphyllum floribundum

Stephanotis floribunda

SPATHIPHYLLUM

Peace Lily

Evergreen house plant with brilliant spathes and scented flowers.

Position warm, but not in sunlight.
Height 25-80 cm (10-32 in).
Flowering at any season.
Propagation by division and seeds.

Spathiphyllum has become a popular house plant due to its brilliant spathes. Small, scented, white or green flowers grow on greenish or pale yellow stems. Brilliant white spathes half enclose the spadix. It flowers mostly in spring and summer, but also at other seasons.

Species
Spathiphyllum cannifolium has rounded, evergreen leaves some 20 cm (9 in) long. It grows well in shade, but the temperature must not fall below 18°C (64°F). The spathe is greenish on the outside and white on the inside. The spadix, 10 cm (4 in) long, is green and yellowish.

Spathiphyllum floribundum only grows about 30 cm (12 in) high. Its leaves are a velvety green, and the curved spathe is pale yellow as are the flowers on the green spadix.

Spathiphyllum kochii has thin leaves, growing on long, light-speckled stalks. The spathe, greenish at first, later white, half encloses the 6 cm (2 in) long spadix with its yellow flowers.

Cultivation
Spathiphyllum does best in the greenhouse at temperatures of between 18-20°C (64-68°F), if the humidity is high.

Propagation
You can propagate by division in the spring, or by seeds under glass at temperatures of around 30°C (86°F).

STEPHANOTIS

Madagascar Jasmine, Clustered Wax Flower

Evergreen climbing shrub with highly scented flowers.

Position half-shady and warm, in sandy loam.
Height up to 4 m (13 ft).
Flowering summer and autumn.
Propagation by cuttings.

The supple stems of this long, climbing and twining plant make an attractive decoration for a flower wall or trellis.

Stephanotis comprises only a few species, and only one, *Stephanotis floribunda,* is cultivated. It comes from the Malagasy Republic (formerly Madagascar). Its short-stemmed, opposite-growing leaves are up to 9 cm (3 in) long and 5 cm (2 in) wide. The foliage is leathery, with a shiny green surface, and often comes to a thorny point. Stephanotis produces stellate, highly scented flowers. They may be as much as 5 cm (2 in) across, with white, waxy petals. They are very much like jasmine, both in colour and in scent.

Cultivation
Stephanotis needs a lot of light, but no strong sunlight, and plenty of fresh air. Water freely in spring and summer, feed every two weeks and spray frequently. In winter give it less water, and do be careful about the temperature, which on no account should fall below 14°C (57°F). Always leave the pot in the same place and avoid draughts and fluctuations of temperature.

Propagation
Stem cuttings are best taken in late winter at a heat of at least 25°C (77°F) to make them root. After about a month you can put the plantlets in sandy loam and keep them at about 12°C (54°F).

Stephanotis floribunda

STRELITZIA

Bird of Paradise Flower, Bird's Tongue Flower

Evergreen house plant with attractive flowers.

Position sunny and airy, in sandy loam.
Height up to 2 m (6 ft).
Flowering winter through summer.
Propagation by seeds or division.

In South Africa and the Canary Islands some strelitzias grow into tall splendidly flowering trees. In a cool climate they will only flourish as fine trees in greenhouses. One particu-larly beautiful flowering species makes a very good pot plant for the living room. This is the bird of paradise flower, *Strelitzia reginae*, which can grow to 2 m (6 ft) high. Its large, oval leaves grow on long stems and have a leathery upper surface. Up to eight flowers grow in a greeny reddish spathe that sticks out horizontally like a little boat. The outer bracts are yellow to orange, the narrower, inner bracts bright blue. The flowers will last for weeks.

Cultivation
The bird of paradise flower thrives best in sunny, airy rooms at temperatures of 8°C-14°C (46-57°F). Water it freely all year round and feed frequently until it flowers. If you want the flowers to open early, put the plant somewhere cooler in the autumn and water sparingly.

Propagation
Use only freshly imported seeds for sowing to ensure fertility. If you make sure that the seedbed is always kept at a high bottom heat of 20-25°C (68-77°F), you will get the first flowers after some three years.

Propagation by division is simpler. It is most successful if done in spring or summer.

Strelitzia reginae

STREPTOCARPUS

Cape Primrose

Abundantly flowering evergreen tender perennial.

Position light, but not in direct sunlight, and out of draughts.
Height up to 35 cm (14 in).
Flowering spring and summer.
Propagation by seeds or leaf cuttings.

There are nearly 80 tropical species in the rain forests round the Indian Ocean, but we grow only naturalized hybrids as house plants.

There are many cultivated forms, flowering in all colours from white to violet, but not in yellow; there are

Streptocarpus **hybrid**

also many bicoloured varieties. The flowers are bell-shaped or tubular, and generally with a deckled edge. The leaves form rosettes immediately above the ground, while the flowers grow on long scapes. The pods are twisted like corkscrews.

Cultivation
While it is in flower, the cape primrose prefers warm, half-shady places. It needs high humidity and cannot tolerate draughts. The best potting soil is a mixture of loose humus and peat and sand. Water the plant freely while it is in flower, but in the rest period in late autumn and winter give hardly any at all. During the winter, put it in a cool room with a temperature of 10°-12°C (50-54°F). Repot yearly.

Propagation
Propagation by seeds is difficult because the seeds are very fine and must be pricked out several times. Sow them on top of the soil 18°C (64°F) and do not cover them. Sowing in late winter gives flowers in mid-summer. To get early flowers you must sow in the summer of the previous year. Water seedlings only sparingly. Propagation by leaf cuttings is simpler.

Streptocarpus hybrid

SYNGONIUM

Evergreen climbing shrub with big leaves.

Position half-shady and shady, warm with high humidity, in porous, humus-rich soil.
Height climbing, up to 2 m (6 ft).
Propagation by cuttings.

The leaves and stems of syngoniums contain a harmless, milky sap. It is a long-lived foliage plant, which you can train up a frame or have hanging from baskets. At the nodes of the shoots the plants form aerial roots which you must on no account remove. A remarkable thing about these plants is that the leaves of young plants are lance-shaped, but

Syngonium podophyllum 'Albolineatum'

as they grow older the plants begin to develop complex lobed leaves.

Only established plants flower. As in all members of the arum family, the spadices are framed by spathes, basically of purple-red.

Species
Syngonium podophyllum has a slender stem. The leaves of older plants have long stalks, often enclosed in a sheath. The light green leaves have up to 11 lobes. In contrast, *Syngonium vellozianum* has a much-branched stem and less pale, green leaves; those on the older plants have only five lobes. This species has thick leaves on very long stalks.

Cultivation
Syngonium podophyllum is a foliage plant for warm rooms with high humidity. The best place for it is in a north-facing conservatory, for the plants must not have any direct sunlight. Water freely with lime-free, lukewarm water, and feed once a week to stimulate growth. Reduce the water a little in winter. Repot every year in spring. Use a big pot to accommodate the roots and coarse, porous, humus-rich soil.

Propagation
To propagate syngoniums, take top cuttings in the spring, which will root quickly in sandy compost at temperatures of around 25°C (77°F). Put the young plants in a big pot and keep them at a temperature of 20°C (68°F) under glass. They must be gradually accustomed to the normal temperature of the room.

THUNBERGIA

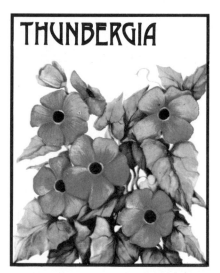

Black-eyed Susan

Climbing plant with attractive flowers.

Position sunny, in loamy soil.
Height up to 2 m (6 ft).
Flowering spring and autumn.
Propagation by seeds or cuttings.

Most species can be seen only in botanical gardens. These climbers and shrubs all need the sort of climate that prevails in their African or Asian homeland. However, there are exceptions. They are handsome flowers which are composed of a distinct tube expanding into five rounded, petal-like lobes at the mouth.

Species
Black-eyed Susan, *Thunbergia alata*, is a common plant for the balcony. This annual, which is just as popular as a climbing or hanging plant, comes in a number of varieties, with different-coloured flowers. The colours range from white through bright yellow and orange to brick-red. The stems will climb up to 2 m (6 ft) and bear long-stalked, round or heart-shaped leaves with prominent veins. The black or chocolate brown spot always shining in the middle of the flower gives the plant its name.

Another species, the evergreen climber, *Thunbergia laurifolia,* has recently made its appearance as a house plant. Its flowers are pale violet and cluster in the axils of long, pointed leaves.

Cultivation
Thunbergia alata needs a warm, sunny position. The plants require a well-lit position, but should be lightly shaded during the hottest summer months. It thrives particularly on the balcony, for it likes fresh air. If it has to stay indoors during the summer, ventilate the house when the temperature exceeds 16°C (61°F). It is generally only grown as an annual, but you can get it to overwinter in a light room at about 12°C (54°F), pruning severely in late winter. *Thunbergia laurifolia* can only be grown in light, warm conservatories. Both species must be watered regularly during the growing period and fed once a week. Water *Thunbergia alata* more sparingly in winter keeping the plant just moist. Train these self-clinging climbers against strings or wires

Propagation
Thunbergia alata is sown in late winter at about 20°C (68°F). Prick out seedlings and put them in little pots of loamy soil. If possible, put them on the balcony from spring on. Flowering will begin after three months.

Cuttings taken from *Thunbergia laurifolia* will root in warm, moist sand under glass. Later, put them in little pots, or plant them out in the conservatory.

Thunbergia alata

Tillandsia cyanea

TILLANDSIA

Decorative evergreen house plant.

Position half-shady and warm.
Height up to 30 cm (12 in).
Flowering summer.
Propagation by suckers or division.

Of the tillandsias suitable as house plants, most do best if grown on a branch or stake.

Species
Tillandsia cyanea is valued for its attractive flowers. Pink and mauve bracts grow on a short stem, overlapping one another like scales, and between them, one after another, the great blue flowers appear. Narrow green leaves with red stripes form a rosette around the flowers.

Tillandsia lindenii looks much like *Tillandsia cyanea.* But you can distinguish it by the flower spike standing a long way clear of the leaf rosette, and the light orange bracts.

Another species is Spanish moss or *tillandsia usneoides.* This epiphyte has no roots but twining, thread-like stems with very small, narrow leaves covered with silvery scales and bright yellow-green flowers.

Cultivation
All tillandsias, grown in pots or as epiphytes on a stake, must be kept half-shady and warm, with high humidity. In winter the temperature must not fall below 15°C (59°F), or 12°C (54°F) at night. Give the pot plants plenty of water in summer, less in winter.

Propagation
Some tillandsias form suckers, which you can carefully separate from the mother plant and pot. All species can also be propagated by division.

TOLMIEA

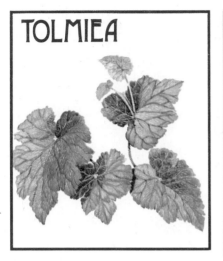

Piggyback Plant, Youth-on-Age

Hardy indoor perennial with tubular flowers.

Position shady and cool in humus-rich soil.
Height up to 30 cm (12 in).
Flowering late spring and early summer.
Propagation by cuttings, air layering, or division.

Every amateur gardener, no matter how inexperienced, can get pleasure from tolmieas. This little North American woodland plant will last for many years by producing young plants of its own accord.
  The only species, *Tolmiea menziesii*, more popularly piggyback plant or youth-on-age, continuously produces little buds in the indentations of its long-stemmed, round leaves. When the leaves of the main plant start to wilt, young plants with roots of their own are already forming from the buds. Loose brownish orange flowers cluster between the sappy green leaves.

Cultivation
Tolmiea cannot tolerate sunlight and prefers temperatures of around 10°C (50°F) if it is not to be attacked by lice. The plant needs plenty of water and weekly feeding during the summer. Water less in winter and keep it somewhere cooler but free from frost.

Propagation
The buds on the already developed plantlets can be separated from the mother plant and potted in humus-rich soil. Or stems can be pegged down and cut off when rooted. Older plants can also be propagated by division.

TRACHYCARPUS

Chusan Palm, Fan Palm

Hardy evergreen, slow-growing fan-shaped palm.

Position light and half-shady, in rich, peaty loam.
Height up to 4 m (13 ft).
Propagation by seeds or suckers.

In districts with a mild climate you can take the risk of growing a chusan palm outdoors. It will even tolerate a few degrees of frost.
  Of the six species of these fan palms native to central and eastern Asia, we cultivate only one, *Trachycarpus fortunei*. The stems are covered with little, pointed knobs, and a big, almost circular leaf, 80-100 cm (32-40 in) wide, grows at the end of each. These leaves are divided into segments some 50-60 cm (20-24 in) deep, which form fans. The little yellow flowers grow in branching panicles.

Trachycarpus fortunei

Harry Smith

145

Cultivation

Palms, especially in small tubs, must be fed regularly from late winter through summer with organic or chemical fertilizers. They need enough water to ensure that the root ball is always fairly moist and never dries out.

The chusan palm is only seldom attacked by pests and diseases.

Propagation

Soak seeds, which must be as fresh as possible, in warm water at 30-35°C (86-95°F) for two days. Then put them in a mixture of sand and leaf mould and keep them constantly moist and warm. The germination period may differ according to the age of the seeds. Carefully pot the seedlings with the seeds still adhering to them; standard compost is best, but after a week or two you must transfer them to a mixture of old leaf or hotbed soil with loam and some sand and horn meal.

Remove suckers with two or three leaves in spring. Pot up in standard compost and root at a temperature of at least 13°C (56°F).

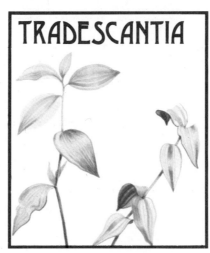

TRADESCANTIA

Wandering Jew, Spiderwort, Widow's Tears, Creeping Sailor, Little Ship

Evergreen flowering perennial.

Position sunny to shady, in sandy standard compost.
Height up to 40 cm (16 in).
Flowering spring.
Propagation by cuttings.

The hardy species are valued in the garden as spiderwort; the house plants, on the other hand, are known as tradescantia. These indestructible, mostly creeping evergreens are suitable for cultivation in baskets and bowls. Their slender, fragile, sappy stems bear oval pointed leaves which partly clasp the stem at the lower end. The leaves grow alternately on nodes. The flowers, surrounded by little bracts, are not particularly striking in themselves.

Species

Tradescantia albiflora, the wandering jew, creeping sailor or widow's tears, has simple green leaves. They grow without stalks on flat stems or hang down from baskets. The white flowers are infrequent. Prettier than the true species is the variety 'Aureovittata', whose leaves have yellow stripes.

Tradescantia blossfeldiana is notable for its hairy leaves, brown hairs on top and red underneath. This plant, generally growing upright to a height of 20 cm (9 in), bears pink flowers with white interiors.

Among the loveliest tradescantias is *Tradescantia crassula,* an upright plant that reaches a height of 40 cm (16 in), with big, shiny leaves and fine white flowers.

Tradescantia fluminensis, similar to *Tradescantia albiflora,* is of creeping or drooping habit. Its little oval leaves are dark green with a slight blue tinge, and violet on the underside. The variety 'Albovittata' is better known; its narrow leaves have white longitudinal stripes. It does well in hydroponics.

Tradescantia navicularis, the 'little ship', is a pretty climbing plant with mauve folded leaves which look like boats. This succulent variety grows slowly and bears pink flowers.

Cultivation

All these species need a warm, light place, but not in direct sun. The colourful species and varieties like more warmth. All want a lot of lime-free water and a humus-rich standard compost. Feed with liquid fertilizer every fortnight while they are growing quickly.

Propagation

Propagation is child's play. Take cuttings at any time of the year and insert them either in soil containing peat or in a container of water.

***Tradescantia fluminensis* 'Variegata'**

VALLOTA

Scarborough Lily

Tender, long-lasting, bulbous plant with lovely funnel-shaped flowers.

Position sunny and warm, in sandy loam.
Height up to 40 cm (16 in).
Flowering spring and summer.
Propagation by offsets or seeds.

Vollota speciosa, the Scarborough lily, from South Africa, bears leaves up to 40 cm (16 in) long and 3 cm (1 in) wide, which grow up from a brown, round or oval bulb and spread out like a fan. In late spring and summer a scape some 30 cm (12 in) tall rises from the middle of the leaves, crowned by a magnificent umbel often containing as many as 10 of the great red trumpet-like flowers. Best known of the different var-

Below: *Vallota speciosa*
Right: *Veltheimia capensis*

ieties is 'Alba', with white flowers.

Cultivation
The plants need a lot of warmth and sun, with regular watering and weekly feeding until the end of the flowering period. After that, keep light and cool at 5-8°C (41-48°F) and water only a little. Unlike other bulbous plants, the leaves must not be allowed to wither.

When you repot the new young plants in the spring, say every four years, be careful to see that the bulb is only two-thirds covered with soil.

Propagation
Small new bulbs form on the bulb, and in the spring you can carefully detach these and plant them in small pots of sandy loam. If you are sowing, use only fresh seeds and let them germinate in warm soil.

VELTHEIMIA

Undemanding, richly flowering bulbous plant.

Position light and cool, in sandy loam.
Height up to 50 cm (20 in).
Flowering late winter to spring.
Propagation by offsets or seeds.

The South African veltheimia is a genus of few species, and only one, *Veltheimia capensis*, is at all common. It is a 'short-day' flower whose blossoms appear in the cold season and last for weeks.

The little tubular flowers are yellow and green with red dots. They grow in a dense cluster on a tall, bare scape some 50 cm (20 in) high rising straight up from the bluish red bulb between the slightly curved leaves, which are wavy at the edges. They grow up to 25 cm (10 in) long and 10 cm (4 in) wide. In the spring the leaves of this bulbous plant die off.

Cultivation
Veltheimia will produce its loveliest flowers in light, cool rooms at about 12°C (54°F). It needs very little watering—hardly any during its resting period from spring to autumn.

In early autumn clean the bulbs and plant them two-thirds down in sandy loam. After that, water fairly frequently and feed from time to time.

Propagation
When you come to replant the bulbs, carefully remove the small new bulbs and plant them in small pots. They will often flower the same year. Fresh seeds are sown in spring, in warm soil. But if you choose this method of propagation, you will have to wait three years for the first flowers to appear.

147

VINCA

Periwinkle, Band Plant, Cut Finger

Evergreen subshrub with large flowers. Rewarding basket plant.

Position sunny to shady, in humus-rich garden soil.
Height up to 25 cm (10 in).
Flowering spring.
Propagation by cuttings or division.

In the Mediterranean countries and the tropics this evergreen is a widespread ground-cover plant. Of the few existing species, we mostly cultivate two as plants for the hanging basket and for the balcony. Many hybrids have been produced.

The creeping or hanging branches grow densely and bear oval leaves, elongated in some species, rounded in others. They are leathery to the touch and their upper surface is shiny. Large, tubular flowers in various shades of blue grow on stalks at the leaf shoulders in spring.

Species

Vinca major, called the band plant, cut finger, or greater periwinkle, has branches that grow up to 25 cm (10 in) long. Besides the true green-leaved species there are the varieties 'Reticulata' with yellow-veined leaves, and 'Variegata' whose leaves are bordered or spotted with white.

Vinca minor, lesser periwinkle, tolerates sun as well as shade and is not particularly sensitive to temperature. You can put it out on the balcony in summer when it should be watered freely. Keep it away from frost in winter, at temperatures around 10°C (50°F), and water less.

Propagation

Both these species can easily be propagated by division. You can also take cuttings from *Vinca major* at the end of summer for rooting under glass. *Vinca major* and *minor* often form new roots on their stems.

VRIESEA

House plant with decorative leaf rosettes and flowers.

Position half-shady to shady, warm, in garden soil containing peat.
Height up to 50 cm (20 in).
Flowering according to species, the whole year through.
Propagation by offsets.

The numerous species which grow wild on the branches of trees in South America's primeval forests develop leaf rosettes. The leaves, green or brightly patterned and slightly curved, form a big funnel towards the centre, from which the pretty, flat flower heads emerge on a long scape.

Species

The Brazilian species *Vriesea carinata* is one of the green-leaved vrieseas. The little flowers, flaming red and yellow and coming to a point, grow in a loose cluster on a red stalk.

The light green leaves of *Vriesea fenestralis,* up to 40 cm (16 in) long, have a sort of lattice pattern in dark green, and red spots. The underside

Left: *Vinca minor*
Below: *Vriesea splendens*

of the leaves is scaly. The yellow flowers, up to 7 cm (3 in) wide, with greenish bracts dotted with browny red, stand on a scape 50 cm (20 in) high.

Vriesea splendens is another popular species. Its leaves of up to 50 cm (20 in) long and 5 cm (2 in) broad, have rusty red transverse stripes and form pretty rosettes. The long, lance-shaped inflorescence grows on a green scape; slender yellow flowers peep out from crowded, bright red bracts.

There are also a number of hybrids with yellow, orange or greenish-white inflorescences.

Cultivation
Vrieseas can be grown either as pot plants or as epiphytes on a frame. They need plenty of light and warmth, but no full sun. Overwintering temperatures are: for *Vriesea carinata* 15-18°C (59-64°F); for *Vriesea fenestralis* 18-20°C (64-68°F); and for *Vriesea splendens* also 18-20°C (64-68°F), with night temperatures of not below 12°C (54°F). Water the plants only moderately, but always leave some lukewarm water in the leaf funnel.

Propagation
Like most bromeliads, vrieseas form new little rosettes at the foot of the mother plant. Carefully detach these and let them root in conditions of high humidity and at temperatures of at least 25°C (77°F).

Vriesea carinata

YUCCA

Adam's Needle, Spanish Bayonet

Evergreen stem-forming shrub with abundant leaf formation and scented flowers.

Position sunny and airy, in compost.
Height up to 2 m (6 ft).
Flowering summer.
Propagation by suckers or seeds.

Yucca gets its popular names from the spines on its leaf tips. The species we grow in pots or tubs form scaly stems on which a profusion of long, narrow leaves grow, making them look like palm trees. The big, white, bell-shaped flowers grow in long panicles. They have a powerful scent, especially in the evening.

Species
The dark, hard leaves of the slender *Yucca aloifolia* have a bluish colour and come to a stiff, reddish brown point. The pale borders of the leaves are slightly toothed. This species often produces dark berries after flowering. Best known of the many varieties are the ornamental-leaved 'Tricolor' and 'Quadricolor'.

Yucca gloriosa, or Adam's Needle, has an exceptionally short stem. The grey-green, supple, sword-like leaves are bordered with reddish brown. The flowers have red stripes and in the course of a year their panicles can reach a height of 2 m (6 ft).

The low-growing *Yucca recurvifolia* is an easy plant to grow. Fibrous threads often grow on the drooping leaves.

Cultivation
Since the yuccas thrive and flower best in a sunny, airy position, put them on the balcony or the terrace in summer. Keep them cool in winter at about 6°C (43°F). Give them plenty of water when in flower and feed them every week. After flowering, give them only a little water to prevent rotting. Repot young plants every year in spring, older plants every three or four years at the same time.

Propagation
Suckers grow thickly over the ground at the base of the stem; detach them carefully from the mother plant and plant them in sandy loam. Fresh seeds can be sown in warm, sandy soil, but it will be some time before the seedlings appear.

Yucca aloifolia

ZANTEDESCHIA

Arum Lily

Perennial with magnificent flowers.

Position sunny and airy, in loamy soil.
Height up to 80 cm (32 in).
Flowering winter and spring.
Propagation by division or seeds.

The arum lily is an extremely attractive aquatic plant from tropical Africa. *Zantedeschia aethiopica* has proved particularly successful as a pot plant. It is grown most for its attractive flowers which also do well when cut. A slender yellow spadix grows at the end of a long, straight stem, surrounded by a huge, white spathe, which makes an asymmetrical funnel, opening upwards and turned down at the rim.

The long-stemmed, slightly wavy leaves are generally heart-shaped and deeply grooved. They grow on the ground, in leaf sheaths which spring from fleshy rhizomes.

Cultivation
The arum lily in flower must be frequently watered and sprayed, and fed with liquid fertilizer once a week. At this time the room temperature must be kept at about 15°C (59°F). During the rest period, in late spring and early summer, let the root ball dry out completely, and keep the plant sunny and warm. A place on the balcony suits it very well. Towards the middle of summer plant in loamy soil and slowly begin watering again. In autumn and early winter keep light and cool at a maximum temperature of 10°C (50°F), then move to a warmer place.

Propagation
You can divide well-developed plants with a sharp knife and plant them out again. If you are propagating by seed, let the seeds germinate in warm soil. The first flowers will only appear after about two years.

Zebrina pendula

ZEBRINA

Trailing perennial with prettily patterned leaves. Good basket plant.

Position sunny or half-shady, warm, in ordinary compost.
Height up to 50 cm (20 in).
Propagation by cuttings.

Zebrina is a pretty and versatile foliage plant. In the wild it grows mostly along the ground, but with its creeping, supple stems it can also be kept in a pot or hanging basket. The little violet flowers are not much to look at, but the opposite-growing, symmetrical, oval leaves are extremely attractive.

Species
The most commonly grown species is *Zebrina pendula.* The silver-striped leaves, red underneath, grow closely on red, green-spotted stems. The variety 'Quadricolor' is even more colourful; the alternate leaves bear longitudinal stripes of dark green, white and light pink.

The slightly hairy leaves of *Zebrina purpusii* are reddish blue in colour, often suffused with olive green on the upper side.

Cultivation
Zebrina likes a lot of light and warmth. Keep it in an airy room or on the balcony in summer. Water regularly with lime-free water, spray often and feed every fortnight. In winter zebrina needs a room temperature that does not fall below 14°C (57°F).

Propagation
Propagation by cuttings is possible at any time of the year, but most successful in the spring. Break off stem cuttings 10 cm (4 in) long and plant them in a pot of peaty soil. You can also let the cuttings root in water first and then plant them.

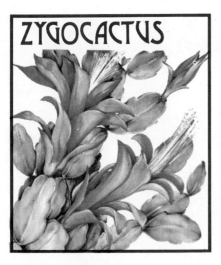

ZYGOCACTUS

Christmas Cactus

Profusely flowering cactus.

Position half-shady, light and warm, in sandy, lime-free humus-rich soil. Do not change the position.

Height up to 40 cm (16 in).
Flowering autumn and winter.
Propagation by cuttings.

Zygocactus used to be called epiphyllum but is better known as the Christmas cactus.

Species
There is only the one species of this leaf-flowering form, *Zygocactus truncatus,* but there are a good many hybrids.

In its home in Brazil the Christmas cactus grows as an epiphyte on trees, but it grows well here in porous, rather sandy soil, which must contain no lime. The plant needs a half-shady position, or else the leaf growths, of up to 5 cm (2 in) long and 2 cm (1 in) wide, will lose their green colour and turn red. New shoots and flowers grow from the ends of these growths. New flowers also grow from areoles in the indentations along the edges of the leaves. They are gener-ally carmine, with drooping tubes and reflexed petals. The Christmas cactus has no thorns or bristles.

Cultivation
The Christmas cactus has its rest period from the end of its flowering period until mid-spring, when its stems (often spoken of as leaves) become a little shrunken. Water generously after this until early autumn, feed once a week and keep in a warm place. Then cut down the water to stimulate the formation of buds, and keep it cooler. From late autumn on, raise the temperature again to 20°C (68°F) and water.

Propagation
You can take cuttings for propagation at any time of year. They root in sandy loam at temperatures of about 22°C (72°F) and must be carefully repotted twice before they shoot.

Zygocactus truncatus

Zygocactus truncatus

PLACES FOR PLANTS

If you want to grow house plants well, you must choose the right plants for your house or apartment. Naturally, the first consideration is your personal preference—for flowering plants or foliage plants, climbing plants or hanging plants.

But then you must consider the conditions where the plants will live. Your choice may be limited to those that can survive dry air or a place on the balcony. And remember that if you put a sun-loving flowering plant in a gloomy hall no amount of care will make it flourish.

To help you make the right choice, here is a guide to popular house plants and where they grow best.

FLOWERING PLANTS

Anthurium scherzerianum (flamingo flower), an evergreen from the tropical regions of America. Needs a warm position shaded from direct sunlight, and high humidity in the summer; keep fairly dry in winter. Produces fine spathes, white to dark red, with a straight or curved spadix. Flowers all the year round.

Calceolaria (slipper flower), from South America. Prefers half-shady to cool positions with high humidity. Cannot tolerate draughts. Flowers in spring, with orange-yellow, brown and red, often dappled blooms.

Cyclamen, a perennial tuberous plant from South and Central Europe and Asia Minor. Likes a bright but not sunny position. Must be kept cool when in flower. Long-lived, freely flowering plant in white and all shades of red.

Cyclamen persicum

Hibiscus (rose mallow), a spreading indoor shrub from the tropics. Needs a sunny position in summer and a slightly heated room in winter. Produces large, red flowers amid bright green foliage from spring to autumn. Hybrids also flower white, yellow and orange.

Nertera (bead plant), a perennial creeping plant from the Southern Hemisphere. Needs a cool, half-shady position, not less than 10°C (50°F) in winter. The low cushions of the plant are covered from summer onwards with a profusion of decorative berries.

Rhododendron indicum (indoor azalea), a small evergreen shrub from the Northern Hemisphere. Flourishes only in lime-free soil in half-shady and cool positions. Perennial flowering plant with many different flowers, white and shades of red, according to variety.

Saintpaulia (African violet), a perennial from East Africa. Prefers a light, warm, but not sunny position. Cannot tolerate draughts. Flowers all the year round, violet, pink and white according to variety. Very sensitive to water on the fine hairy leaves, but compost must be kept moist and it needs humidity. Good plant for a bottle garden or terrarium where it will be free from draughts.

BRIGHT FOLIAGE PLANTS

Aucuba, an evergreen house shrub from Asia. In summer needs a light and airy but not sunny position. Overwinters in a cool room. Foliage has gold spots.

Caladium, a tuberous perennial from tropical America. Needs a light, shady and humid position with plenty of warmth. This decorative plant with brilliantly coloured leaves is sensitive to dry air.

Codiaeum (croton), from the Pacific. Needs half-shady, warm position with high humidity. Even in winter the brightly coloured leaves need plenty of light and warmth, or the patterns on them will fade.

Cordyline (sometimes called the flaming dragon tree or scarlet aspidistra), an evergreen from Asia, Africa and Australia. Prefers half-shade, but green-leaved species will also do well in the sun. Spear-shaped leaves. Older specimens flower.

Dieffenbachia, a subshrub from tropical America. Needs plenty of warmth and humidity, brightness but no sun. Leaves are attractively patterned. All parts are poisonous. Wash hands after handling.

Dieffenbachia seguine

Dracaena draco (dragon tree), an indoor shrub from the tropical regions. Needs light, warm position. Leaves have a white pattern. Roots have an aromatic scent.

Gynura, a subshrub from Africa and Asia with bluish red leaves and orange flowers in the autumn. Needs a light, warm but airy position. Keep warm in winter, in artificial light.

Maranta (arrowroot), a perennial evergreen with ornamental foliage, from the primeval forests of Brazil. Needs a light but not sunny position with daytime temperatures about 22°C (72°F), and at nights not cooler than 16°C (61°F). The leaves have coloured veins.

GREEN FOLIAGE PLANTS

Cocos (cocos palm), an indoor shrub from South America. Needs a position with plenty of warmth and high humidity but no direct sunlight. Older specimens of these attractive, feathery palms are less trouble to look after.

Coffea (coffee plant), an evergreen shrub from tropical Asia, Africa and America. Prefers sunny and airy positions. Undemanding. Turn the plant as little as possible.

Fatsia (fig leaf palm, sometimes called castor oil plant), an evergreen indoor shrub from Japan. Needs a light, shady, cool position. May be put out on the balcony, but will not tolerate draughts. Overwinters in cool conditions.

Fatsia japonica

Ficus elastica (rubber tree), an evergreen indoor tree or shrub. Position should be light. Keep in an unheated room in winter, no lower than 10°C (50°F). Drooping leaves are a sign of too much warmth.
Grevillea robusta (silk bark oak), an evergreen tree from South Asia and Australasia. Needs lime-free soil. Likes a light, airy, but not sunny position. Can be put on the balcony. Overwinters in a cool room, 8-10°C (46-50°F).
Howea (often called kentia palm), a tree with narrow fronds, occurring naturally only in the Australian-administered Lord Howe Islands in the Pacific. Needs light in winter but a little shade in summer. Overwinters in slightly heated rooms, 10-12°C (50-54°F). Do not let soil dry out.
Phoenix dactylifera (date palm), from the tropics of Africa and Asia. Needs a sunny position and moist air. Overwinters in the cool. Water sparingly in winter but do not allow soil to dry out.

CLIMBING PLANTS

Cissus antarctica (kangaroo vine), a climbing, trailing plant from Australia. Likes a light, warm position with no direct sun. Can overwinter in a cool room at 8°C (46°F). Some varieties have leaves with coloured patterns.
Ficus pumila (creeping fig), a climbing plant from eastern Asia, considerably less delicate than all the other rubber and fig trees of the same family. Very hardy. Needs a light,

half-shady position. Never let it dry out or it will quickly die.
Hedera (pot ivy), an evergreen climbing plant. Needs brightness and plenty of air, but cannot stand the full glare of the sun. Bright-leaved varieties must be kept over winter in moderately heated rooms. Green species are less delicate and will tolerate shade.

Hedera colchica 'Variegata'

Passiflora (passion flower), a climbing plant from tropical America. Likes direct sunlight and airy positions. Will overwinter in the warm. Can be put on the balcony in summer.
Peperomia (pepper elder), an evergreen plant from the warm regions of America. Needs a light but shady place in a warm room, and in winter needs a warm room with high humidity. There is a fine, grey sheen on its corrugated leaves. If healthy it will produce white flower spikes.
Philodendron scandens (sweetheart vine), an evergreen climber from the warm regions of America. Position should be light, shady and warm, with high humidity. Keep fairly warm during the winter.

Philodendron scandens

Scindapsus (ivy arum), a climbing herbaceous plant. Wants a warm, shady place with moist air. Must overwinter in light, warm conditions. Makes a good hanging plant.
Stephanotis floribunda (Madagascar jasmine), an evergreen climber from the Malagasy Republic. Needs a warm, half-shady position, the air not too dry, and a winter temperature of 12°C (54°F). The white flowers have a powerful scent. Grows quite large. Susceptible to draughts.
Syngonium, an evergreen from Central America. Likes a warm, shady position during the summer, bright and fairly warm in winter. The bracts of the flowers are deep red at the base.
Thunbergia alata (black-eyed Susan), a freely flowering, climbing annual from tropical Africa and Asia. Needs to be in light and warmth, but overwinters in cool conditions.

HANGING PLANTS

Aeschynanthus, an Asian perennial with beautiful flowers. Needs a shady position, high humidity and in summer temperatures around 25°C (77°F). Overwinters in a heated room. Does not tolerate draughts.

Aeschynanthus pulcher

Allamanda, an evergreen plant from Brazil. Often grown as a climber. Needs full sun and damp air. Keep in a light, warm room in winter.
Asparagus setaceus (asparagus fern), not a fern but a perennial evergreen plant from the temperate zones of Europe and Asia. Likes a well-lit, airy position. Can overwinter in a heated room but cannot tolerate dry soil. Bears red berries.
Columnea, an evergreen shrub from tropical America. A very prettily flowering hanging plant which needs high humidity with plenty of warmth and shade. Will overwinter in a mod-

erately heated room and cannot tolerate draughts.

Piper (pepper plant), a perennial tropical plant, occasionally shrubby when grown indoors. Needs shade and warmth. Green species overwinter in unheated rooms, but those with brightly coloured leaves are more delicate. The leaves are prettily patterned.

Piper ornatum

Plectanthrus, from the warm parts of Asia, Africa and Australia. In summer likes a light and shady position. May be put out on the balcony.

Tradescantia, from South America. Does well in any position. Keep bright-leaved species in a good light or they will lose their colour. Attractive as hanging plants in baskets.

Zebrina, related to the tradescantia. Prefers light and sunny positions and can be put out on the balcony in summer with no trouble. After a few years the stems become unsightly and should be cut back.

FERNS

Adiantum capillus-veneris (maidenhair fern), from South America. Should stand in warmth and shade all the year round. Keep damp, but never in standing water.

Asplenium nidus (bird's nest fern), from the rain forests of Africa and Asia. An epiphyte, it prefers a cool, shady position.

Nephrolepis (ladder fern), found in tropical regions all over the world. Likes to be kept in half-shady, warm positions with humid air. Can overwinter in unheated rooms at 10°C (50°F). Very good for cutting.

Phlebodium, from the tropical regions of South America. Grows on the ground and is not an epiphyte. Prefers warm, shady places with high humidity and must overwinter in a warm room. Cannot tolerate lime.

Phyllitis (hart's tongue fern), grows all over the world. Content with cool and shady positions so long as the air is not too dry. Should be kept close to the window in an unheated room during the winter. Water only with lime-free water.

Phyllitis scolopendrium

Platycerium (stag's horn fern), from South Asia but closely related to several species in Central America and Central Africa. Needs a shady place with high humidity. The broad leaves of this fern will die if the roots are allowed to dry out.

Platycerium bifurcatum

Polystichum (often called aspidium or shield fern), an evergreen, completely winter-hardy open-air fern which nevertheless makes a good house fern. Indoor species should have a half-shady position. Keep cool in winter—10-12°C (50-54°F)—and do not water too much.

SHADE-LOVING PLANTS

Aspidistra, a perennial, completely trouble-free member of the lily family. Evergreen foliage plant with inconspicuous flowers.

Aspidistra elatior 'Variegata'

Chlorophytum (spider plant), among the least demanding of house plants. It is content with any position but should have some light or the leaves will turn light and thin.

Chlorophytum elatum 'Variegatum'

Cyperus alternifolius (umbrella grass), a reedy grass found in every continent. Suitable for planting in shallow tanks and pools, but good as a house plant if kept moist or pot stood in shallow water.

Monstera (Swiss cheese plant or shingle plant), an evergreen climber. Likes a shady place so long as it is not too warm. In excessive light the leaves develop brown spots.

Philodendron, similar to monstera in that it prefers shady positions with ample warmth and humidity, and overwinters in a heated room. Does well in hydroponics.

Selaginella (creeping moss), an evergreen plant of the tropical rain forest and the temperate zones. Position should be shady, moist and warm. Cannot tolerate lime. Makes fine hanging basket.

Sparmannia (African hemp), likes some sun but needs light shade in summer. Position must be airy and not too warm. Has light green leaves and little scented white flowers.

PLANTS FOR DRY AIR

Chamaedorea (mountain palm), a decorative little tree from South and Central America. Can tolerate dry air but not dry soil. Needs a warm and shady place. Does well in rooms with central heating.

Chamaedorea elegans

Clivia, with rich clusters of flowers. Suits a place by the window very well. In winter put in a room with only moderate heating and keep almost dry.

Echeveria, a leaf succulent with bright flowers. Needs a light position. Well suited to dry air.

Euphorbia milii (crown of thorns), a thorny shrub. Needs a sunny, airy position. Does not like draughts. You can put it out on the balcony in summer. Can stand dry air as long as the roots do not get dry.

Kalanchoë, a leaf succulent. Wants a light place, which might be on the balcony in summer. In winter needs a room temperature of at least 10°C (50°F). Central heating does not hurt it.

Kalanchoë tomentosa

Sansevieria (mother-in-law's tongue or snake plant), makes no demands at all on its environment as long as it is not too dark. No wonder you see its sword-shaped leaves in every office. Do not overwater or its roots will rot.

PLANTS FOR WARM ROOMS

Acalypha, from the tropics. Needs to stand in a light spot with plenty of warmth and humidity all the year round. Has long spiky flowers.

Paphiopedilum, a tropical orchid from South Asia. Prefers a warm place with plenty of light and high humidity. Water only with previously boiled water.

Rhoeo (boat lily), from Central America with long, lanceolate leaves which form open rosettes. Will do well in a conservatory and can be put in the shade of bigger plants as ground decoration.

Spathiphyllum (peace lily), a low, stemless evergreen topped by a white spathe with yellowish spadix. Hungry for warmth and some humidity. Needs a half-shady position.

Tillandsia usneoides (Spanish moss), from the tropical rain forests

of Central America. Accustomed to a warm position and light but not direct sun. Can be grown as an epiphyte on a special trunk.

Vriesea, mainly from Brazil. Needs a lot of warmth and can be kept best in a half-shady position in a conservatory. Green-leaved and coloured-leaved species.

Vriesea splendens

PLANTS FOR THE BALCONY

Begonia, a very good, hardy plant for the balcony, but should not be placed facing south.

Bougainvillea, a deciduous shrubby climber from the tropics and sub-tropics of America. Blooms freely in summer on a sheltered balcony.

Browallia, an attractive shrub. Mostly kept as a house plant, it does very well in a box on the balcony if kept out of direct sunlight and watered more than usual.

Coleus (flame nettle), a plant that can display the full glory of its brightly coloured leaves only if kept in a light and fairly sunny position. Does well in a box on the balcony if freely watered, but must be sheltered from the wind.

Fuchsia, another popular balcony plant. Should be lightly shaded. Boxes must be kept light and cool during the winter.

Pelargonium (geranium), next to begonia the most common of all balcony plants. Can tolerate sun as well as shady positions and has long flowering season. Put in a light and airy place in a frost-free room during the winter and keep almost dry.

Vinca (periwinkle), a freely flowering subshrub with bright leaves and light blue, long-stemmed flowers. Needs plenty of water.

GLOSSARY

acid—applied to soils with a pH content below 7.0.

acid soil—*see pH value.*

adventitious root—a root that develops from some other part of a plant than a pre-existing root.

aerial root—a root arising on a stem above ground.

aggregate—artificial, chemically inert soil with no organic content. It is often used in hydroponics.

air layering—a method of *vegetative propagation (q.v.)* by separating a part of the stem with the shoots and leaves. Particularly suitable for indoor shrubs. Cut a slit all round the stem and hold the cut open with a sliver of wood or tuft of moss. The *callus (q.v.),* wrapped in damp moss or peat, forms roots. When the roots are fully developed the cut piece of the stem is removed completely.

alkaline—applied to soils with a pH content above 7.0.

alkaline soil—*see pH value.*

anther—the functional part of a stamen which contains the pollen grains. It comprises two pollen sacs or anther lobes joined on a stalk.

apex—the tip of a shoot or root from where growth is extended.

areole—the area occupied by a group of spines or hairs on a cactus.

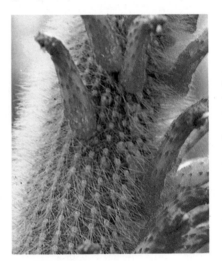

The sharp spines of the cleisto-cactus spring from areoles.

assimilation—conversion by a plant of inorganic substances into organic, producing carbohydrates, oils and protein. *See photosynthesis.*

axil—the solid angle between a stem and the upper surface of a leaf base growing from it.

bipinnate—a leaf that is divided into several segments which are again subdivided.

biternate—a leaf that is divided and sudivided into units of three.

bract—a modified leaf on stalks developed by plants that have inconspicuous flowers, for the protection of the flowers and sometimes also to attract insects. On many plants, like anthuriums, billbergias and *Euphorbia pulcherrima* (poinsettia), they are wrongly taken to be the flowers.

Billbergias display beautiful bracts instead of flowers.

callus—wound tissue of plants, from which a corky layer grows outwards and a *cambium (q.v.)* later inwards.

calyx—the outer whorl of the flower, consisting of sepals. It is usually green and protects the upended bud.

cambium—layer of actively splitting cells in a plant. Cambium, activated when the plant is cut, makes *vegetative propagation (q.v.)* possible.

chlorophyll—the green colouring matter of leaves, from the Greek words *chloros* ('green') and *phyllon* ('leaf'). Chlorophyll plays an essential part as a catalyst in the process of assimilation, with the aid of sunlight. *See assimilation, photosynthesis.*

chlorosis—the loss or poor production of chlorophyll (the green colouring matter in plants), giving a bleached yellow or white appearance to leaves. In extreme cases, browning and death of tissues may follow. The usual cause of chlorosis is lack of essential minerals, although certain viruses may also be responsible.

cladode—a flattened, leaf-like stalk, performing the functions of a leaf.

cordate—a heart-shaped leaf or one or two lobes at the base.

corm—a rounded, swollen underground stem, with scale leaves, adventitious roots, and buds.

corolla—the general name for the whole of the petals of the flower.

corona—a trumpet-like outgrowth from the perianth.

corymb—a flat-topped cluster of flowers, the stalks of which arise one above the other from a vertical stem or axis.

crenate—with rounded teeth. The term usually applies to a leaf margin.

crocks—broken pieces of clay pots used as drainage material in flowerpots, seed trays, and so on.

cutting—*see vegetative propagation.*

cyme—a domed, flattened or rounded cluster of flowers, usually with several arching branches radiating outwards.

dead-heading—the removal of faded flowers to prevent seeding or to tidy the appearance of a plant.

dentate—applied to a leaf that has tooth-like notches to the margins.

digitate—a term used to describe a leaf that is composed of several radiating leaflets.

distichous—usually applied to leaves that are arranged in two flattened opposite ranks on the stem, creating a fan-like effect.

epiphyte—a plant that grows above the soil, usually clinging to another plant or a rock, especially in the tropical rain forests, where epiphytes climb to the tops of trees in their search for light. Epiphytes are not parasites; they have their own independent feeding system. Well-known epiphytes are orchids and ferns.

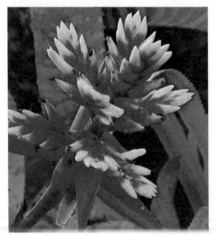

Aechmea is an epiphyte from the tropical forests.

etiolation—disturbed growth of plants caused by lack of light. Leaf stalks and stems grow too long, while the leaves remain small. The plants lack chlorophyll and turn a poor yellowish white colour.

filament—the stalk of a stamen (the

pollen producing part of a plant).

friable—referring to a crumbly soil that is easily worked and raked to a tilth.

glochids—bristles or hairs on the surface of a plant that have hooks on them, so that when touched they break off and cling to the skin. These are a troublesome feature of many cacti.

hard water—*see pH value.*

hybrid—a product of accidental or deliberate crossbreeding, generally between two species of a genus, less often between genera. Hybrids are generally indicated by an X in front of the botanical name.

inflorescence—that part of a plant which bears flowers.

lacinate—fringed. Used to describe leaves, bracts, stipules or petals with margins cut into numerous narrow segments.

lanceolate—shaped like the head of a lance. Applied to a base, tapering to a point and at least three times longer than it is broad.

lateral—a side shoot of plants which, when cut off, very quickly forms roots and develops a new plant. It is used in vegetative propagation in many tropical plants.

layer—a horizontally growing shoot of a new plant which is fixed to the ground and so made to form roots. Layering is a method of vegetative propagation. Roots will form only if the shoot has been wounded, possibly where it has been fastened to the ground.

leaf cutting—*see vegetative propagation.*

light mark—a mark made on the containers of house plants, to ensure that the plants can always present the same side to the source of light.

loam—soil consisting of a friable mixture of varying proportions of clay, silt and sand.

mildew—powdery and downy mildew are plant diseases caused by fungi.

mutation—a transmissible, spontaneously developed alteration of the outward appearance of a plant. This is how varieties are bred.

node—a leaf knot or thickened zone on the shoot of a plant from which the leaves develop. Nodes are important in *vegetative propagation (q.v.),* since it is from these points that roots are formed in propagation by cuttings.

offset—a short prostrate lateral shoot arising from the base of the plant.

pH value—the index of acid-alkaline balance of soil. The scale goes from 1 to 14; the neutral point is pH 7, which indicates complete chemical neutrality and in practice is found only in distilled water. Values between 1 and 7 indicate acidity, between 7 and 14 alkalinity. The pH value of the soil is critical to the survival of a plant, though most plants can normally adapt to tolerate a divergence of two points on the scale.

photosynthesis—conversion of atmospheric carbon dioxide and water by means of sunlight into starch and oxygen, using chlorophyll as a catalyst.

phototropism—the tendency of virtually all plants to grow towards the source of light.

pinnule—one of the lobes or segments when a leaflet of a pinnate leaf is itself more or less divided into parts in a pinnate manner.

pistil—the complete female organ of a flower, comprising an ovary, stigma and style. The style may be short or nonexistant.

raceme—a simple inflorescence in which the elongated axis bears flowers on short stems in succession towards the apex.

rhizome—an underground stem or rootstock used as an organ of storage for the winter. Plants grow new, young plants from horizontally growing rhizomes.

runner—a shoot spreading from the plant over or under the ground, which forms new plants.

scape—a stalk, quite or nearly leafless, arising from the middle of a rosette of leaves and bearing flowers.

short-day plant—a plant that begins its growth or flowering in the days when the light does not last long—that is, in winter; thus, a winter-

A **short-day plant,** *Euphorbia pulcherrima* **blooms in winter.**

flowering plant.

spadex—a spike with a swollen fleshy axis enclosed in a spathe.

spathe—*see bract.* Spathes are large bracts enclosing one or more flowers.

The **brilliant red spathes of the anthurium are very exotic.**

sphagnum moss—a leafy moss growing wild and used as a planting medium for epiphytes. It is completely free from lime and is extremely absorbent and water-retentive. Moss peat is based on sphagnum moss.

spores—reproductive organs of ferns, growing in clusters on the underside of the leaves.

succulent—a plant that stores sometimes remarkable amounts of water in its growth above ground. A distinction is made between leaf succulents and stem succulents.

sucker—a strongly growing shoot arising from the base of the stem or from a root.

tubercle—a general term for a small swelling.

umbel—an inflorescence consisting of numerous small flowers in flat-topped groups borne on stalks all arising from about the same point on the main stem.

variety—a deviation in a species of plant in its outward appearance obtained by breeding and given a botanical name. The botanical term for this is a 'cultivar'. Variety names are written in single quotation marks.

vegetative propagation—asexual propagation by division of plants —either of the natural reproductive organs of the plant such as layers, buds, bulbs, or shoots, or of parts of the plant that can produce shoots, which can include roots, leaves, top cuttings or parts of the stem.

DICTIONARY OF POPULAR NAMES

Adam's needle— *Yucca gloriosa*
African hemp— *Sparmannia*
African violet— *Saintpaulia*
aluminium plant— *Pilea cadierei*
amaryllis (incorrectly)— *Hippeastrum*
angel's tears— *Billbergia nutans*
arrowroot— *Maranta*
artillery plant— *Pilea*
arum lily— *Zantedeschia*
asparagus fern— *Asparagus setaceus*
azalea indica— *Rhododendron indicum*
band plant— *Vinca major*
Barbados lily— *Hippeastrum*
bay laurel— *Laurus*
bead plant— *Nertera*
begonia— *Begonia*
bellflower— *Campanula*
bird of paradise flower— *Strelitzia reginae*
bird's nest bromeliad— *Nidularium*
bird's nest fern— *Asplenium nidus*
bird's tongue flower— *Strelitzia*
black-eyed Susan— *Thunbergia alata*
black pepper— *Piper nigrum*
boat lily— *Rhoeo*
bottle brush— *Callistemon*
bow string hemp— *Sansevieria*
busy lizzie— *Impatiens walleriana*
cabbage palm— *Cordilyne*
calla lily— *Zantedeschia*
Cape leadwort— *Plumbago*
Cape primrose— *Streptocarpus*
cast iron plant— *Aspidistra*
castor oil plant (incorrectly)— *Fatsia*
chillies— *Capsicum*
Chinese primrose— *Primula praenitens*
Christmas cactus— *Zygocactus*
Chusan palm— *Trachycarpus*
cineraria— *Senecio*
club moss— *Selaginella*
clustered waxflower— *Stephanotis*
coffee plant— *Coffea*
common ivy— *Hedera helix*
common myrtle— *Myrtus communis*
copper leaf— *Acalypha*
creeping fig— *Ficus pumila, Ficus repens, Ficus stipulata*
creeping moss— *Selaginella*
creeping sailor— *Tradescantia albiflora*
croton— *Codiaeum*
crown of thorns— *Euphorbia milii*
curly palm— *Howea forsteriana*
cut finger— *Vinca major*
date palm— *Phoenix dactylifera*
dragon tree— *Dracaena draco*
dumb cane— *Dieffenbachia seguine*
dusty miller— *Senecio cineraria*
dwarf date palm— *Phoenix roebelinii*
dwarf gloxinia— *Sinningia pusilla*
dwarf orange— *Citrus mitis*
dwarf umbrella grass— *Cyperus gracilis*
Easter cactus— *Rhipsalidopsis*
elk horn fern— *Platycerium*

fairy primrose— *Primula malacoides*
fan palm— *Trachycarpus*
fern begonia— *Begonia foliosa*
fiddle back fig— *Ficus lyrata, Ficus pandurata*
fig leaf palm— *Fatsia*
flame nettle— *Coleus*
flaming dragon tree— *Cordyline*
flamingo flower— *Anthurium*
flowering maple— *Abutilon*
fruiting duckweed— *Nertera*
fuchsia begonia— *Begonia fuchsioides*
fuchsia tree— *Fuchsia arborescens*
galingale— *Cyperus*
geranium (incorrectly)— *Pelargonium*
gloxinia— *Sinningia*
gold fern— *Pityrogramma*
grape ivy— *Rhoicissus*
greater periwinkle— *Vinca major*
great flamingo flower— *Anthurium andreanum*
gunpowder plant— *Pilea*
hairy bougainvillea— *Bougainvillea spectabilis*
hard shield fern— *Polystichum aculeatum*
hart's tongue fern— *Phyllitis*
humble plant— *Mimosa pudica*
Indian azalea— *Rhododendron*
Indian mallow— *Abutilon*
Indian rubber plant— *Ficus elastica*
indoor azalea— *Rhododendron*
indoor cyclamen— *Cyclamen latifolium, Cyclamen persicum, Cyclamen puniceum*
ivy— *Hedera*
ivy arum— *Scindapsus*
ivy-leafed begonia— *Pelargonium peltatum*
Jerusalem cherry— *Solanum pseudocapsicum*
kangaroo vine— *Cissus antarctica*
kentia palm— *Howea*
ladder fern— *Nephrolepis*
leaf begonia— *Begonia rex*
lemon— *Citrus limon*
lemon geranium— *Pelargonium odoratissimum*
leopard lily— *Sansevieria*
lesser periwinkle— *Vinca minor*
lilac fuchsia— *Fuchsia arborescens*
linden tree— *Sparmannia*
little flamingo flower— *Anthurium scherzerianum*
little ship— *Tradescantia navicularis*
Madagascar jasmin— *Stephanotis floribunda*
maidenhair fern— *Adiantum capillus —veneris*
mistletoe fig— *Ficus deltoidea*
moth king— *Plectranthus fructicosus*
mother-in-law's tongue— *Sansevieria*
mother of thousands— *Saxifraga stolonifera*
mountain palm— *Chamaedorea*
myrtle— *Myrtus*
Norfolk Island pine— *Araucaria*
old man cactus— *Cephalocereus senilis*
oleander— *Nerium*
orange— *Citrus sinensis*

orchid cactus— *Epiphyllum*
ornamental pepper— *Piper ornatum*
painter's palette— *Anthurium scherzerianum*
passion flower— *Passiflora*
peace lily— *Spathiphyllum*
pepper— *Piper*
pepper elder— *Peperomia*
periwinkle— *Vinca*
Persian ivy— *Hedera colchica*
piggy-back plant— *Tolmiea menziesii*
pistol plant— *Pilea*
poinsettia— *Euphorbia pulcherrima*
pot ivy— *Hedera*
prayer plant— *Maranta*
prickly pear— *Opuntia*
queen's tears— *Billbergia nutans*
red pepper— *Capsicum*
red-hot cat's tail— *Acalypha hispida*
rose bay— *Nerium*
rose geranium— *Pelargonium graveolens, Pelargonium radens*
rose mallow— *Hibiscus*
roving sailor— *Saxifraga*
rubber tree— *Ficus elastica*
saxifrage— *Saxifraga*
Scarborough Lily— *Vallota speciosa*
scarlet aspidistra— *Cordyline*
screw pine— *Pandanus*
sensitive plant— *Mimosa pudica*
shield fern— *Polystichum*
shingle plant— *Monstera*
shrimp plant— *Beloperone*
silk bark oak— *Grevillea*
silver fern— *Pityrogramma argentea*
slipper flower— *Calceolaria*
slipper orchid— *Paphiopedilum*
snake plant— *Sansevieria*
South sea laurel— *Codiaeum*
sowbread— *Cyclamen*
Spanish bayonet— *Yucca*
Spanish moss— *Tillandsia usneoides*
spider plant— *Chlorophytum*
spiderwort— *Tradescantia*
spleenwort— *Asplenium*
squill— *Scilla*
stag's horn fern— *Platycerium*
sweet bay— *Laurus*
sweetheart vine— *Philodendron scandens*
Swiss cheese plant— *Monstera*
sword fern— *Nephrolepis*
tail flower— *Anthurium*
thatch leaf palm— *Howea forsteriana*
touch-me-not— *Impatiens*
tree fuchsia— *Fuchsia arborescens*
Trinity flower— *Tradescantia*
umbrella grass— *Cyperus alternifolius*
urn plant— *Aechmea*
violin case rubber tree— *Ficus lyrata, Ficus pandurata*
wall rue— *Asplenium ruta muraria*
wandering Jew— *Tradescantia albiflora, Tradescantia fluminensis*
weeping fig— *Ficus benjamina*
widow's tears— *Tradescantia albiflora*
wild hyacinth— *Scilla*
winter cherry— *Solanum capsicastrum*
youth-on-age— *Tolmiea menziesii*
Zebra plant— *Aphelandra*